# Troubleshooting Ubuntu Server

Make life at the office easier by building resilient
Ubuntu Server systems

**Skanda Bhargav**

BIRMINGHAM - MUMBAI

# Troubleshooting Ubuntu Server

First published: September 2015

Production reference: 1180915

Published by Packt Publishing Ltd.
Livery Place
35 Livery Street
Birmingham B3 2PB, UK.

ISBN 978-1-78528-414-4

www.packtpub.com

# Credits

**Author**
Skanda Bhargav

**Reviewer**
Keenan Payne

**Commissioning Editor**
Priya Singh

**Acquisition Editors**
Shaon Basu

Sonali Vernekar

**Content Development Editor**
Gaurav Sharma

**Technical Editor**
Taabish Khan

**Copy Editor**
Roshni Banerjee

**Project Coordinator**
Bijal Patel

**Proofreader**
Safis Editing

**Indexer**
Hemangini Bari

**Graphics**
Sheetal Aute

**Production Coordinator**
Nitesh Thakur

**Cover Work**
Nitesh Thakur

# About the Author

**Skanda Bhargav** is an engineering graduate from Visvesvaraya Technological University (VTU), Belgaum, Karnataka, India. He did his majors in Computer Science Engineering. He is a Cloudera-certified developer in Apache Hadoop. His interests are Big Data and Hadoop. He is currently pursuing his Master's in Computer Software Engineering from San Jose State University, Silicon Valley, California.

He has been a reviewer for the following books and videos:

- *Building Hadoop Clusters, Sean Mikha, Packt Publishing*
- *Hadoop Cluster Deployment, Danil Zburivsky, Packt Publishing*
- *Instant MapReduce Patterns – Hadoop Essentials How-to, Srinath Perera, Packt Publishing*
- *Cloudera Administration Handbook, Rohit Menon, Packt Publishing*
- *Hadoop Map Reduce v2 Cookbook – Second Edition, Thilina Gunarathne, Packt Publishing*
- *Data Analysis and Business Modeling with Excel 2013, David Rojas, Packt Publishing*

I would like to thank my family for their immense support and faith in me throughout my learning stage. My friends have brought the confidence in me to a level that makes me bring out the best in me. I am happy that god has blessed me with such wonderful people around me, without whom this success would not have been possible.

# About the Reviewer

**Keenan Payne** is a frontend developer for a company called Asana in San Francisco, CA. He has written for many online publications and built a CSS framework called Concise, and in his spare time, he loves to surf and make music.

# www.PacktPub.com

## Support files, eBooks, discount offers, and more

For support files and downloads related to your book, please visit
www.PacktPub.com.

Did you know that Packt offers eBook versions of every book published, with PDF
and ePub files available? You can upgrade to the eBook version at www.PacktPub.
com and as a print book customer, you are entitled to a discount on the eBook copy.
Get in touch with us at service@packtpub.com for more details.

At www.PacktPub.com, you can also read a collection of free technical articles,
sign up for a range of free newsletters and receive exclusive discounts and offers
on Packt books and eBooks.

https://www2.packtpub.com/books/subscription/packtlib

Do you need instant solutions to your IT questions? PacktLib is Packt's online digital
book library. Here, you can search, access, and read Packt's entire library of books.

## Why subscribe?

- Fully searchable across every book published by Packt
- Copy and paste, print, and bookmark content
- On demand and accessible via a web browser

## Free access for Packt account holders

If you have an account with Packt at www.PacktPub.com, you can use this to access
PacktLib today and view 9 entirely free books. Simply use your login credentials for
immediate access.

# Table of Contents

**Preface**                                                                                         **ix**

**Chapter 1: Package Management**                                                                    **1**

**Getting started with packages**                                                                    **1**
    Package                                                                       2
    Repository                                                                    2
    The .deb packages                                                             2
    Dependency                                                                    2
    Open source                                                                   2

**Using dpkg for package management**                                                                **3**

**Understanding the apt-get package management tool**                                                **9**
    Updating the repository list with the apt-get update command                  9
    Installing a package with the apt-get install command                         10
    Upgrading a package with the apt-get upgrade command                          13
    Cleaning with the apt-get clean command                                       14
    Purging a package with the apt-get purge command                              15
    Fixing unsuccessful installations with the apt-get –f command                 16
    Checking for broken dependencies with the apt-get check command               17

**The apt-cache tool**                                                                               **17**
    Searching for a package with the apt-cache search command                     18

**Package management with aptitude**                                                                 **19**

**Configuration and extra repositories**                                                             **22**
    Resolving the "failed to get" error                                           24
    Downloading software from an outside repository                               25

**Automatic updates**                                                                                **25**
    Security updates                                                              25
    Kernel updates                                                                26
    Application updates                                                           26
    The unattended-upgrades package                                               26

| | |
|---|---|
| **Creating a repository mirror** | **28** |
| Setting up a mirror machine | 29 |
| Configuring the /etc/apt/mirror.list file | 29 |
| Using the local mirror | 30 |
| **Summary** | **30** |
| **Chapter 2: Networking and DNS** | **31** |
| **Networking concepts** | **31** |
| IP addressing | 32 |
| DHCP client for dynamic addresses | 33 |
| Assigning a static IP address | 34 |
| **DHCP** | **35** |
| Installation | 36 |
| Configuration | 38 |
| **Network sniffing with tcpdump** | **39** |
| Capturing packets from eth0 | 39 |
| Saving the tcpdump results in a file | 40 |
| Reading packets saved in a file by tcpdump | 41 |
| Readable timestamps in packets | 41 |
| Reading packets of a specific protocol | 42 |
| Reading packets on a specific port | 42 |
| Reading TCP packets between two hosts | 42 |
| **Binding and bonding** | **42** |
| Binding | 42 |
| Bonding | 44 |
| **DNS** | **46** |
| Setting up DNS | 46 |
| Setting up primary and secondary DNS servers | 49 |
| The hints file – zone "." | 50 |
| The local host file – zone "0.0.127.in-addr.arpa" | 50 |
| The reverse zone file – zone "24.126.10.in-addr.arpa" | 51 |
| The primary zone file – zone "ubuntuserver.org" | 51 |
| **The primary zone file** | **53** |
| **The reverse zone file** | **54** |
| PTR records | 55 |
| **Summary** | **56** |
| **Chapter 3: Network Authentication** | **57** |
| **OpenLDAP** | **57** |
| Installation | 57 |
| Populating the database | 60 |
| Logging | 61 |
| Access control | 62 |

**Kerberos** **64**
Installation 65
Database setup 69
Setting up the Kerberos client 72
Kerberos SSH and logon 73
**Integrating LDAP with Kerberos** **75**
Installation 75
Database setup 76
**OpenSSH, public, and private keys – passwordless SSH** **77**
The SSH client and the server 77
Setting up passwordless SSH 78
Disabling password authentication 79
**Allowing or denying users to SSH** **79**
Greeting users with a banner 80
**Summary** **80**
**Chapter 4: Monitoring and Optimization** **81**
**Nagios** **81**
The Nagios setup 81
Adding another host in Nagios 87
Nagios templates 88
Nagios hostgroups and services 90
Nagios setup alerts 92
Writing a Nagios plugin 94
The NRPE plugin 97
Enabling external commands 99
**Puppet** **101**
Installing Puppet 102
Setting up the client 105
Setting up the manifest 105
**ClusterSSH** **106**
**Summary** **107**
**Chapter 5: Process Management** **109**
**The basics of process management** **109**
$$ and $PPID 110
pidof 110
Parent and child 110
fork() and exec() 112
exec 112
ps 113
pstree 118

ps fx                                                                118
ps -C and pgrep                                                      119
top                                                                  120
**Signaling processes**                                              **122**
kill                                                                 122
Listing all signals                                                  122
kill -1 or SIGHUP                                                    123
kill -15 or SIGTERM                                                  123
kill -9 or SIGKILL                                                   123
SIGSTOP and SIGCONT                                                  124
pkill                                                                124
killall                                                              125
**Process priorities**                                               **125**
renice                                                               125
nice                                                                 126
**Background processes**                                             **126**
jobs                                                                 126
& (ampersand)                                                        126
jobs -p                                                              127
Suspended state with Ctrl + Z                                       128
bg                                                                   128
fg                                                                   129
**Summary**                                                          **129**
**Chapter 6: Shell Management, Tools, and User Management**          **131**
**The Secure Shell server**                                          **131**
Installing the SSH server                                            131
Configuration                                                        132
Default settings for the SSH server                                  132
The SSH configuration file                                           133
Using passphrases                                                    136
**Scheduling jobs with cron**                                        **139**
Scheduling user cron jobs                                            141
Configuring jobs using at                                            142
Job schedule security                                                143
**Optimizing the shell**                                             **144**
Bash profiles                                                        144
The /etc/bash.bashrc file                                            145
The /etc/profile file                                                146
Variables in bash                                                    146
**User management and file permissions**                             **147**
User management in Ubuntu                                            148
Adding and removing users                                            148

| | |
|---|---|
| Managing file permissions | 148 |
| Understanding file permissions | 148 |
| Changing permissions with chmod | 149 |
| Modifying ownership using chown and chgrp | 151 |
| Setting default permissions with umask | 152 |
| Special file permissions | 152 |
| **Summary** | **154** |
| **Chapter 7: Virtualization** | **155** |
| **What is virtualization?** | **155** |
| **libvirt** | **156** |
| Installation | 156 |
| virt-install | 156 |
| virt-clone | 157 |
| Managing the virtual machine | 158 |
| virsh | 158 |
| The virtual machine manager | 158 |
| The virtual machine viewer | 159 |
| **JeOS and vmbuilder** | **160** |
| JeOS | 160 |
| vmbuilder | 160 |
| Setup | 161 |
| Installing vmbuilder | 163 |
| Defining the virtual machine | 163 |
| JeOS installation | 165 |
| **Summary** | **169** |
| **Chapter 8: OpenStack with Ubuntu** | **171** |
| **The OpenStack architecture** | **171** |
| **The environment** | **174** |
| Security | 176 |
| Networking | 176 |
| OpenStack networking | 177 |
| Network Time Protocol | 180 |
| OpenStack packages | 181 |
| Database | 182 |
| The messaging server | 183 |
| **The Identity service** | **184** |
| Installing and configuring the Identity service | 184 |
| Configuring the prerequisites | 184 |
| Installing and configuring the components | 185 |
| Finalizing the installation | 185 |
| Tenants, users, and roles | 186 |
| The service entity and API endpoint | 188 |
| **The Image service** | **188** |
| Installing and configuring the Image service | 189 |

Configuring the prerequisites     189
Installing and configuring the Image service components     190
Finalizing the installation     192

**The Compute service**     **192**
Installing and configuring the Compute service     192
Configuring the prerequisites     192
Installing and configuring the Compute service components     194
Finalizing the installation     196
Installing and configuring the compute node     196

**OpenStack networking**     **198**
Installing and configuring the controller node     199
Configuring the prerequisites     199
Installing the Networking components     200
Configuring the server components of Networking     200
Configuring the Modular Layer 2 plugin     202
Configuring Networking on the compute node     203
Finalizing the installation     203
Installing and configuring the network node     204
Configuring the prerequisites     204
Installing the Networking components     204
Configuring the Networking components     204
Configuring the Modular Layer 2 plugin     205
Configuring the Layer 3 agent     206
Configuring the DHCP agent     207
Configuring the metadata agent     207
Configuring the OVS service     208
Finalizing the installation     209
Installing and configuring the compute node     209
Configuring the prerequisites     209
Installing the Networking components     209
Configuring the Networking common components     210
Configuring the ML2 plugin     211
Configuring the OVS service     212
Configuring Compute to use Networking     212
Finalizing the installation     213

**Creating initial networks**     **213**
External networks     214
Creating an external network     214
The tenant network     214
Creating a tenant network     214
Creating the router to attach the external and tenant networks     215

**Dashboard**     **215**
Prerequisites     216
Installing and configuring the dashboard     216
Installing the packages     216
Configuring the dashboard     216
Finalizing the installation     217

**The Block Storage service** **217**
Installing and configuring the controller node 217
Configuring the prerequisites 217
Installing and configuring the Block Storage service components 219
Finalizing the installation 220
Installing and configuring the storage node 220
Configuring the prerequisites 220
Installing and configuring the Block Storage volume components 221
Finalizing the installation 223
**The Object Storage service** **223**
Installing and configuring the controller node 223
Configuring the prerequisites 223
Installing and configuring the controller node components 224
Installing and configuring the controller node 226
Configuring the prerequisites 226
Installing and configuring the storage node components 228
**Summary** **231**
**Chapter 9: OpenStack and Ubuntu Best Practices** **233**
**Creating rings for Object Storage** **233**
Creating an account ring 233
Creating a container ring 234
Creating an object ring 235
Copying the configuration files for rings 236
Finalizing the installation 236
**The Orchestration module** **237**
Installing and configuring 237
Configuring the prerequisites 237
Installing and configuring the Orchestration components 239
Finalizing the installation 240
**The Telemetry module** **240**
Installing and configuring the controller node 240
Configuring the prerequisites 241
Installing and configuring the Telemetry components 242
Finalizing the installation 244
Installing and configuring the Compute agent 244
Configuring the prerequisites 245
Configuring the Compute agent for the Telemetry module 245
Finalizing the installation 246
Configuring the Image service 246
Adding the Block Storage agent for Telemetry 247
Configuring Object Storage for Telemetry 247
**The Database service** **248**
Installing the Database service 248
Taking care of the prerequisites 248

Installing the Database module 249
**The Data Processing service** **252**
Installing the Data Processing service 252
**OpenStack flashback** **254**
**Best practices for Ubuntu Server** **254**
**Summary** **255**
**Index** **257**

# Preface

The mission of this book is to simplify the tasks of an administrator and equip them with the tools to win the battle not once, not twice, but each time the server acts in a way that is not in accordance with the usual behavior. This book will help administrators ensure that the servers do not face even a nanosecond of outage as businesses in today's world are entirely dependent on these machines.

After reading and following the guidelines carefully, you will be able to identify the problems in Ubuntu Server, diagnose the causes, and rectify them. The areas this book intends to cover are networks, CPU, memory, and handling cloud computing-related issues using OpenStack.

## What this book covers

*Chapter 1*, *Package Management*, covers the different ways software can be installed, configured, upgraded, and removed using package management tools. There are various ways and tools to do this. Technical topics that are covered in this chapter are dpkg, aptitude, and apt-get, which are the command-line utilities used to automate some of the package management tasks. You will learn the various tools and methodologies to handle software, such as the command-line tools, as well as GUI for the installation, mirroring, upgrade, and removal of software along with their dependencies.

*Chapter 2, Networking and DNS*, deals with networking. This chapter covers how to understand, configure, and troubleshoot network-related issues. This is a very brief introduction to networking and handling wired and wireless networking. This chapter covers DNS setup, networking concepts, interface configuration, DHCP, network sniffing, binding, and bonding. Regarding DNS, the topics covered are forward zone, reverse zone, and configuring the primary master and secondary master. You will learn the networking concepts, which are key to diagnosing and rectifying networking issues in Ubuntu Server. It also covers the configuration of DHCP, DNS, and interfaces.

*Chapter 3, Network Authentication*, deals with network authentication for managing users' access to other systems in a secure way. It covers the different tools and methods for letting users access systems and services with restricted authentication. The technical topics covered are OpenLDAP, Kerberos, Kerberos with LDAP, NIS, Samba (optional), PAM, SSH, public and private keys, the RSA and DSA algorithms, passwordless SSH, X forwarding, and sshd. You will be able to set up and manage the users' access to systems and services as well as install, configure, and troubleshoot the services and tools.

*Chapter 4, Monitoring and Optimization*, deals with monitoring various resources on the server and load balancing with tools. This chapter also covers Nagios, Munin, Puppet, and ClusterSSH. System monitoring, CPU load, storage, networks, memory, resource monitoring, load balancing with IPVS, and ldirectord are also covered in this chapter. You will learn about resource monitoring for CPU, memory, and networks.

*Chapter 5, Process Management*, covers all the processes, their states, and how to manage them by using the command-line tools. The topics that are covered are ps, top, renice, kill, $$ and $PPID, job, fg, queues, process switching, process priority, and background jobs. You will learn how to handle process management using the command-line tools.

*Chapter 6, Shell Management, Tools, and User Management*, discusses shell, shell management tools, and user management. Topics such as the Secure Shell server, scheduling using cron, shell optimization, file management and permissions, bash functions, managing user accounts, user properties, and temporary disabling are covered in this chapter. You will learn how to use shell effectively, secure user management, and set user properties.

*Chapter 7, Virtualization*, explains how virtualization helps administrators separate the services and keep the working environment safe from the development environment. Topics such as KVM, Xen, and Qemu are addressed. You will learn about virtualization, its pros and cons, setting up KVM, and Xen.

*Chapter 8, OpenStack with Ubuntu,* deals with using OpenStack with Ubuntu Server, understanding the environment, architecture, and the host of services. The topics covered are the OpenStack environment, OpenStack architecture, and a host of services, such as Image, Identity, Networking components, Compute, Object Storage, Block Storage, and dashboard. You will learn how to use OpenStack, its environment, and architecture, along with the Ubuntu Server integration.

*Chapter 9, OpenStack and Ubuntu Best Practices,* discusses the various components of OpenStack, such as Data Processing, Database, Telemetry, and Orchestration. Some of the best practices for using Ubuntu Server are also discussed in this chapter.

# What you need for this book

You will need an active Internet connection and a bootable image of Ubuntu Server 14.04. All the required packages will be downloaded from the Internet.

# Who this book is for

This book is aimed at making the life of server administrators easier by helping them solve the various errors and issues encountered in Ubuntu Server and OpenStack. This book is intended for the people who handle the critical tasks of administrating mission critical servers running on Linux. In today's world of free and open source software (FOSS) technology, Ubuntu has emerged as one of the favorite Linux flavors of both desktop users and administrators alike. The easy-to-use GUI and the powerful built-in security features of Ubuntu are enough to convince tech enthusiasts to adopt it. A large scale use and implementation of Ubuntu on servers has given rise to a vast army of Linux administrators who battle day in and day out to make sure that the systems are in the right frame of operation and preempt any untoward incidents that may result in catastrophes for the businesses using them.

# Conventions

In this book, you will find a number of text styles that distinguish between different kinds of information. Here are some examples of these styles and an explanation of their meaning.

Code words in text, database table names, folder names, filenames, file extensions, pathnames, dummy URLs, user input, and Twitter handles are shown as follows: "The apt-get check command is a diagnostic tool for package management."

A block of code is set as follows:

```
zone "ubuntuserver.org" {
  type slave;
  file "sec.ubuntuserver.org";
  masters {10.200.12.68;};
};
```

Any command-line input or output is written as follows:

```
sudo apt-cache rdepends ssl-cert
```

**New terms** and **important words** are shown in bold. Words that you see on the screen, for example, in menus or dialog boxes, appear in the text like this: "The second line, **New Packages**, shows the number of packages that are new and can be installed on your Ubuntu Server."

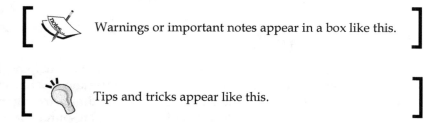

Warnings or important notes appear in a box like this.

Tips and tricks appear like this.

# Reader feedback

Feedback from our readers is always welcome. Let us know what you think about this book—what you liked or disliked. Reader feedback is important for us as it helps us develop titles that you will really get the most out of.

To send us general feedback, simply e-mail feedback@packtpub.com, and mention the book's title in the subject of your message.

If there is a topic that you have expertise in and you are interested in either writing or contributing to a book, see our author guide at www.packtpub.com/authors.

# Customer support

Now that you are the proud owner of a Packt book, we have a number of things to help you to get the most from your purchase.

# Errata

Although we have taken every care to ensure the accuracy of our content, mistakes do happen. If you find a mistake in one of our books—maybe a mistake in the text or the code—we would be grateful if you could report this to us. By doing so, you can save other readers from frustration and help us improve subsequent versions of this book. If you find any errata, please report them by visiting http://www.packtpub.com/submit-errata, selecting your book, clicking on the **Errata Submission Form** link, and entering the details of your errata. Once your errata are verified, your submission will be accepted and the errata will be uploaded to our website or added to any list of existing errata under the Errata section of that title.

To view the previously submitted errata, go to https://www.packtpub.com/books/content/support and enter the name of the book in the search field. The required information will appear under the **Errata** section.

# Piracy

Piracy of copyrighted material on the Internet is an ongoing problem across all media. At Packt, we take the protection of our copyright and licenses very seriously. If you come across any illegal copies of our works in any form on the Internet, please provide us with the location address or website name immediately so that we can pursue a remedy.

Please contact us at copyright@packtpub.com with a link to the suspected pirated material.

We appreciate your help in protecting our authors and our ability to bring you valuable content.

# Questions

If you have a problem with any aspect of this book, you can contact us at questions@packtpub.com, and we will do our best to address the problem.

# 1
# Package Management

This chapter deals with the various tools that will aid the user to install, configure, update, and delete software, documentation, and system functionalities from the server machine. Software in Ubuntu is organized in packages. Almost all of these are available online and also on CDs and other media. In this chapter, we will look at the various command-line tools to handle software and package management. GUI tools are also present, but they are seldom used by server administrators. Command-line tools are faster and more secure, and we will be using only a command-line-based terminal throughout the book.

The following topics will be covered in the chapter:

- Using dpkg for package management
- The apt-get package management tool
- Package management with aptitude
- Configuration of repositories and extra repositories
- Automatic updates of software
- Creating a repository mirror

## Getting started with packages

Ubuntu gets its package management from the Debian Linux distribution under the GNU license. A package usually has the following contents: the actual software files, its metadata, and instructions for the user to install it on the Ubuntu machine. The file extension for Debian packages is `.deb`. A collection of packages is called a repository and the repository list is stored in the local system. Packages are in binary format and are usually precompiled so as to enable faster installation and free the user from having to compile it.

Large and complex packages are built on the concept of dependencies. Dependencies are additional packages that are required for the proper functioning of primary packages. The package management tools in Ubuntu also handle the downloading and installing of these dependencies.

Let's look at some terminologies that are used in package management.

# Package

The software and documentation in Linux is organized in packages. These can be considered to be a collection of components for a software or functionality.

# Repository

A collection of packages is called a repository. Repositories are usually available in one or more centrally distributed servers online. These are tested extensively and are easy to install to or remove from your server machines.

# The .deb packages

Derivatives of Debian such as Ubuntu, Linux Mint, and others use the .deb packages. To install these .deb packages, the package management tools usually used are apt-get and aptitude. Both of these are a frontend for the dpkg tool.

# Dependency

A software or package that requires other software to function properly is said to be dependent on the latter. Package management tools such as apt-get and aptitude in Ubuntu handle the dependencies during installation and/or removal of packages. However, when using dpkg, the user has to manage the dependencies as dpkg does not handle dependencies.

# Open source

Many of the packages or software in the repositories are independent, open source software, which means the software is freely available to use, modify, and distribute. These are often compiled and fine-tuned for specific distributions. It is also possible that the source repositories in your machine have the modified source code as packages.

# Using dpkg for package management

Debian systems have dpkg as their underlying fundamental package management tool. **dpkg** can be used to install, uninstall, and build packages. One of the important points we need to remember is dpkg cannot download packages and its dependencies. The user has to take care of the dependencies and install them manually. dpkg can install the locally available packages. Let's now see some of the operations that dpkg can perform on an Ubuntu Server machine.

Use the following command to list the software already installed on your server machine:

```
dpkg -l
```

This command can generate a large output on your command line, depending upon the installed packages in the server machine, as shown in the following screenshot:

```
Desired=Unknown/Install/Remove/Purge/Hold
| Status=Not/Inst/Conf-files/Unpacked/halF-conf/Half-inst/trig-aWait/Trig-pend
|/ Err?=(none)/Reinst-required (Status,Err: uppercase=bad)
||/ Name                          Version                     Architectu
re Description
+++-=============================-===========================-==========
==-=======================================================================
==
ii  accountsservice               0.6.35-0ubuntu7             amd64
    query and manipulate user account information
ii  acpid                         1:2.0.21-1ubuntu2           amd64
    Advanced Configuration and Power Interface event daemon
ii  adduser                       3.113+nmu3ubuntu3           all
    add and remove users and groups
ii  apparmor                      2.8.95~2430-0ubuntu5        amd64
    User-space parser utility for AppArmor
ii  apport                        2.14.1-0ubuntu3.2           all
    automatically generate crash reports for debugging
ii  apport-symptoms               0.20                        all
    symptom scripts for apport
ii  apt                           1.0.1ubuntu2.1              amd64
    commandline package manager
ii  apt-transport-https           1.0.1ubuntu2.1              amd64
    https download transport for APT
ii  apt-utils                     1.0.1ubuntu2.1              amd64
    package management related utility programs
ii  apt-xapian-index              0.45ubuntu4                 all
    maintenance and search tools for a Xapian index of Debian packages
ii  aptitude                      0.6.8.2-1ubuntu4            amd64
:
```

To list out a specific package, use the following command:

```
dpkg -l | grep apt
```

This will list out the packages with the name apt occurring in any of the installed packages. A sample output is shown here:

```
skanda@server-ubuntu:~$ dpkg -l | grep apt
ii  apt                      1.0.1ubuntu2.1          amd64
    commandline package manager
ii  apt-transport-https      1.0.1ubuntu2.1          amd64
    https download transport for APT
ii  apt-utils                1.0.1ubuntu2.1          amd64
    package management related utility programs
ii  apt-xapian-index         0.45ubuntu4             all
    maintenance and search tools for a Xapian index of Debian packages
ii  aptitude                 0.6.8.2-1ubuntu4        amd64
    terminal-based package manager
ii  aptitude-common          0.6.8.2-1ubuntu4        all
    architecture indepedent files for the aptitude package manager
ii  laptop-detect            0.13.7ubuntu2           amd64
    attempt to detect a laptop
ii  libapt-inst1.5:amd64     1.0.1ubuntu2.1          amd64
    deb package format runtime library
ii  libapt-pkg4.12:amd64     1.0.1ubuntu2.1          amd64
    package management runtime library
ii  libpcap0.8:amd64         1.5.3-2                 amd64
    system interface for user-level packet capture
ii  python-apt               0.9.3.5                 amd64
    Python interface to libapt-pkg
ii  python-apt-common        0.9.3.5                 all
    Python interface to libapt-pkg (locales)
ii  python3-apt              0.9.3.5                 amd64
    Python 3 interface to libapt-pkg
skanda@server-ubuntu:~$ _
```

Here, we can see all of the installed packages in the server containing the word apt as whole or part of it in name of the packages that are installed in this server machine.

Another alternative to check whether a specific package is installed or not is to use the dpkg command with the -l option along with the package name. Let's check for the apt package:

```
dpkg -l apt
```

The output of this command is shown in the following screenshot. The letters `ii` at the start indicate the package is installed. The first letter that you see in the output before the name of the package is the desired status: `i` stands for installed and `p` stands for purged. The actual status is shown in the second letter. `n` stands for not installed and `i` in second place tells us the package is installed. This command also displays the version, architecture, and description, along with the name of the package.

```
skanda@server-ubuntu:/var/cache/apt/archives$ dpkg -l apt
Desired=Unknown/Install/Remove/Purge/Hold
| Status=Not/Inst/Conf-files/Unpacked/halF-conf/Half-inst/trig-aWait/Trig-pend
|/ Err?=(none)/Reinst-required (Status,Err: uppercase=bad)
||/ Name              Version        Architecture Description
+++-===============-=============-============-================================
ii  apt              1.0.1ubuntu2  amd64         commandline package manager
skanda@server-ubuntu:/var/cache/apt/archives$ _
```

Running `dpkg` without any arguments or parameters will show the error in the following screenshot. It requests the user to enter any of the options as arguments with `dpkg`:

```
dpkg
```

```
skanda@server-ubuntu:~$ dpkg
dpkg: error: need an action option

Type dpkg --help for help about installing and deinstalling packages [*];
Use 'apt' or 'aptitude' for user-friendly package management;
Type dpkg -Dhelp for a list of dpkg debug flag values;
Type dpkg --force-help for a list of forcing options;
Type dpkg-deb --help for help about manipulating *.deb files;

Options marked [*] produce a lot of output - pipe it through 'less' or 'more' !
skanda@server-ubuntu:~$
```

If you want to check which files a particular package has installed, use the following command with parameter `-L` and then the package name (here, `apt-utils`):

```
dpkg -L apt-utils
```

The output is shown in the following screenshot:

```
skanda@server-ubuntu:~$ dpkg -L apt-utils
/.
/usr
/usr/share
/usr/share/doc
/usr/share/doc/apt-utils
/usr/share/doc/apt-utils/examples
/usr/share/doc/apt-utils/examples/apt-ftparchive.conf
/usr/share/doc/apt-utils/copyright
/usr/share/man
/usr/share/man/fr
/usr/share/man/fr/man1
/usr/share/man/fr/man1/apt-extracttemplates.1.gz
/usr/share/man/fr/man1/apt-sortpkgs.1.gz
/usr/share/man/fr/man1/apt-ftparchive.1.gz
/usr/share/man/it
/usr/share/man/it/man1
/usr/share/man/it/man1/apt-extracttemplates.1.gz
/usr/share/man/it/man1/apt-sortpkgs.1.gz
/usr/share/man/it/man1/apt-ftparchive.1.gz
/usr/share/man/ja
/usr/share/man/ja/man1
/usr/share/man/ja/man1/apt-extracttemplates.1.gz
/usr/share/man/ja/man1/apt-sortpkgs.1.gz
/usr/share/man/ja/man1/apt-ftparchive.1.gz
/usr/share/man/es
/usr/share/man/es/man1
/usr/share/man/es/man1/apt-extracttemplates.1.gz
/usr/share/man/es/man1/apt-sortpkgs.1.gz
/usr/share/man/es/man1/apt-ftparchive.1.gz
```

We listed all the files that the package apt-utils has installed in the machine. As you may see, it gives the absolute path of each file associated with the apt-utils package.

If you are unsure which package a particular file belongs to, you can use the dpkg command along with the optional -S parameter. The following command lists out the packages that are using this particular file:

```
dpkg -S /etc/logrotate.d
```

The output is as follows:

```
skanda@server-ubuntu:/var/cache/apt/archives$ dpkg -S /etc/logrotate.d
unattended-upgrades, apport, ppp, aptitude, ufw, upstart, rsyslog, logrotate, dp
kg, apt: /etc/logrotate.d
skanda@server-ubuntu:/var/cache/apt/archives$ _
```

We see all the packages that are using /etc/logrotate.d in the preceding output. Let's crosscheck for one of the packages:

```
dpkg -L apport
```

The output is as follows:

```
skanda@server-ubuntu:~$ dpkg -L apport
/.
/etc
/etc/apport
/etc/apport/crashdb.conf
/etc/apport/blacklist.d
/etc/apport/blacklist.d/apport
/etc/apport/blacklist.d/README.blacklist
/etc/default
/etc/default/apport
/etc/bash_completion.d
/etc/bash_completion.d/apport_completion
/etc/cron.daily
/etc/cron.daily/apport
/etc/init
/etc/init/apport.conf
/etc/init.d
/etc/init.d/apport
/etc/logrotate.d
/etc/logrotate.d/apport
/usr
/usr/share
/usr/share/mime
/usr/share/mime/packages
/usr/share/mime/packages/apport.xml
/usr/share/apport
/usr/share/apport/dump_acpi_tables.py
/usr/share/apport/apport
/usr/share/apport/unkillable_shutdown
/usr/share/apport/apport-checkreports
```

In some cases, running dpkg -S may not be able to get the package name that uses a particular file. This is because many files are automatically generated during a package installation that dpkg may not be aware of.

To install a .deb package using dpkg, use the following command:

```
dpkg -i $package_name
```

Replace $package_name with the actual package you want to install. This will start the installation of the package. Please note that installation of software requires administrative access. So, use the dpkg command with the prefix sudo when installing or removing a package. Hence, this command will now become:

```
sudo dpkg -i $package_name
```

Let's now try to remove a package using the dpkg command. Use the option -r with the package name to remove a package. Here, we are removing the byobu package. However, it is recommended you do not use the dpkg tool to remove packages. It generally does not go well as dpkg does not handle dependencies, so it is possible that you may remove a package that is a dependency for some other package and the latter will become unstable or unusable. There are better alternative package management tools such as apt-get and aptitude that can be used for removal of packages, as they handle the dependencies well. We will cover the apt-get and aptitude tools next. The command to remove a package is as follows:

```
sudo dpkg -r byobu
```

As we can see in the following screenshot, when trying to remove a package without the sudo prefix, the system did not allow. After prefacing the command with sudo, we were successfully able to remove the byobu package from the server:

```
skanda@server-ubuntu:/var/cache/apt/archives$ dpkg -r byobu
dpkg: error: requested operation requires superuser privilege
skanda@server-ubuntu:/var/cache/apt/archives$ sudo dpkg -r byobu
[sudo] password for skanda:
(Reading database ... 52371 files and directories currently installed.)
Removing byobu (5.77-0ubuntu1) ...
Processing triggers for man-db (2.6.7.1-1) ...
Processing triggers for mime-support (3.54ubuntu1) ...
skanda@server-ubuntu:/var/cache/apt/archives$
```

The command dpkg -P stands for purge. Configuration files are also removed along with the package when you run this command.

To view all the options dpkg supports, use the following command:

```
man dpkg
```

# Understanding the apt-get package management tool

Ubuntu supports an **Advanced Packaging Tool (APT)** for package management: apt-get is one of the command-line tools to aid the user in installing, removing, upgrading packages, updating package index, and also upgrading the entire Ubuntu OS. Its simplicity is the reason behind its powerful features and why it is better than other GUI package management tools. Server administrators can use it over SSH connections and also they can use it in scripts for administrative purposes. Automation of scripts using cron scheduling is also an added advantage for server administrators when it comes to dealing with package management using apt-get.

Let's first discuss about the apt-get package and its various uses. Later, we will look at other utilities under APT, such as apt-cache, apt-file, apt-ftparchive, and so on.

# Updating the repository list with the apt-get update command

It is recommended to always update the repository list in the local Ubuntu system before installing and/or removing the packages. It is possible that the package could have been upgraded along with changes in the dependencies. To be on the safe side, update the repository list with the following command:

```
sudo apt-get update
```

The preceding command will update the repository list and you will see an output similar to the following screenshot. The repositories are defined in the /etc/apt/sources.list file and the /etc/apt/sources.list.d directory. It is a database of all the packages available in the repositories. When you run the update command from the apt-get tool, it updates the list in the files and directories discussed earlier.

The local package index is updated to the latest list available in the remote repository.

```
skanda@server-ubuntu:~$ sudo apt-get update
[sudo] password for skanda:
Ign http://security.ubuntu.com trusty-security InRelease
Get:1 http://security.ubuntu.com trusty-security Release.gpg [933 B]
Ign http://us.archive.ubuntu.com trusty InRelease
Get:2 http://security.ubuntu.com trusty-security Release [62.0 kB]
Ign http://us.archive.ubuntu.com trusty-updates InRelease
Ign http://us.archive.ubuntu.com trusty-backports InRelease
Get:3 http://us.archive.ubuntu.com trusty Release.gpg [933 B]
Get:4 http://us.archive.ubuntu.com trusty-updates Release.gpg [933 B]
Get:5 http://security.ubuntu.com trusty-security/main Sources [70.3 kB]
Get:6 http://us.archive.ubuntu.com trusty-backports Release.gpg [933 B]
Get:7 http://us.archive.ubuntu.com trusty Release [58.5 kB]
Get:8 http://security.ubuntu.com trusty-security/restricted Sources [2,061 B]
Get:9 http://security.ubuntu.com trusty-security/universe Sources [17.9 kB]
Get:10 http://us.archive.ubuntu.com trusty-updates Release [62.0 kB]
Get:11 http://security.ubuntu.com trusty-security/multiverse Sources [1,896 B]
Get:12 http://security.ubuntu.com trusty-security/main amd64 Packages [214 kB]
Get:13 http://us.archive.ubuntu.com trusty-backports Release [62.0 kB]
Get:14 http://us.archive.ubuntu.com trusty/main Sources [1,064 kB]
Get:15 http://security.ubuntu.com trusty-security/restricted amd64 Packages [8,8
75 B]
Get:16 http://security.ubuntu.com trusty-security/universe amd64 Packages [87.3
kB]
Get:17 http://security.ubuntu.com trusty-security/multiverse amd64 Packages [3,4
58 B]
Get:18 http://security.ubuntu.com trusty-security/main i386 Packages [205 kB]
Get:19 http://security.ubuntu.com trusty-security/restricted i386 Packages [8,84
6 B]
Get:20 http://security.ubuntu.com trusty-security/universe i386 Packages [87.3 k
```

# Installing a package with the apt-get install command

It is quite easy to install a package with the apt-get tool. To install the apache2 package, type the following command:

```
sudo apt-get install apache2
```

The output is shown in the following screenshot:

```
skanda@server-ubuntu:~$ sudo apt-get install apache2
Reading package lists... Done
Building dependency tree
Reading state information... Done
The following extra packages will be installed:
  apache2-bin apache2-data libapr1 libaprutil1 libaprutil1-dbd-sqlite3
  libaprutil1-ldap ssl-cert
Suggested packages:
  apache2-doc apache2-suexec-pristine apache2-suexec-custom apache2-utils
  openssl-blacklist
The following NEW packages will be installed:
  apache2 apache2-bin apache2-data libapr1 libaprutil1 libaprutil1-dbd-sqlite3
  libaprutil1-ldap ssl-cert
0 upgraded, 8 newly installed, 0 to remove and 101 not upgraded.
Need to get 1,284 kB of archives.
After this operation, 5,342 kB of additional disk space will be used.
Do you want to continue? [Y/n] Y_
```

The `install` command will read the repository list and try downloading the package from the URL listed. Once downloaded, the apt-get install tool will unpack and install the software. If there are additional packages required for the proper functioning of this software, then apt-get will also download the additional dependencies and install them too. This is one of the features that makes apt-get one of the desired package management tools for server administrators working on Debian-based systems.

You will see the preceding output after you install apache2 using the apt-get install tool. The user will be prompted if he approves the downloading of the package. Hit *Y* and *Enter* to proceed with download and install.

After successful installation, you will see an output similar to the following screenshot:

```
Enabling module auth_basic.
Enabling module access_compat.
Enabling module authn_file.
Enabling module authz_user.
Enabling module alias.
Enabling module dir.
Enabling module autoindex.
Enabling module env.
Enabling module mime.
Enabling module negotiation.
Enabling module setenvif.
Enabling module filter.
Enabling module deflate.
Enabling module status.
Enabling conf charset.
Enabling conf localized-error-pages.
Enabling conf other-vhosts-access-log.
Enabling conf security.
Enabling conf serve-cgi-bin.
Enabling site 000-default.
 * Starting web server apache2
AH00558: apache2: Could not reliably determine the server's fully qualified doma
in name, using 127.0.1.1. Set the 'ServerName' directive globally to suppress th
is message
   *
Setting up ssl-cert (1.0.33) ...
Processing triggers for libc-bin (2.19-0ubuntu6) ...
Processing triggers for ureadahead (0.100.0-16) ...
Processing triggers for ufw (0.34~rc-0ubuntu2) ...
skanda@server-ubuntu:~$
```

Now, let's try to remove this package using the apt-get tool. We will use the remove option. You need to specify the package name that you wish to remove from the machine. If you wish to remove or install multiple packages at once, you can mention them one after the other with a space as the separator. The following command will remove multiple packages apache2, apache2-bin, and ssl-cert:

```
sudo apt-get remove apache2 apache2-bin ssl-cert
```

After running the preceding command, apt-get removes the packages. The following screenshot shows those packages were removed. apt-get handles the dependencies, unlike the dpkg package management tool.

```
skanda@server-ubuntu:~$ sudo apt-get remove apache2 apache2-bin ssl-cert
Reading package lists... Done
Building dependency tree
Reading state information... Done
The following packages were automatically installed and are no longer required:
  apache2-data libapr1 libaprutil1 libaprutil1-dbd-sqlite3 libaprutil1-ldap
Use 'apt-get autoremove' to remove them.
The following packages will be REMOVED:
  apache2 apache2-bin ssl-cert
0 upgraded, 0 newly installed, 3 to remove and 101 not upgraded.
After this operation, 3,958 kB disk space will be freed.
Do you want to continue? [Y/n] Y
(Reading database ... 52855 files and directories currently installed.)
Removing apache2 (2.4.7-1ubuntu4.1) ...
 * Stopping web server apache2
 *
Removing apache2-bin (2.4.7-1ubuntu4.1) ...
Removing ssl-cert (1.0.33) ...
Processing triggers for man-db (2.6.7.1-1) ...
Processing triggers for ufw (0.34~rc-0ubuntu2) ...
skanda@server-ubuntu:~$
```

# Upgrading a package with the apt-get upgrade command

Before we upgrade, we need to run the update command. The update command will update all packages to the latest version, and the upgrade command actually downloads and installs the updated packages. The command for updating a package is as follows:

```
sudo apt-get update
```

apt-get allows the software packages to be upgraded to newer versions with the upgrade option. Newer versions of software become available with bug fixes or with additional functionalities on the remote repositories. Running the following command will upgrade the installed packages already installed on your machine with newer versions. Be sure to run the update command before you do an upgrade:

```
sudo apt-get upgrade
```

You will see an output similar to the following screenshot:

```
Reading state information... Done
Calculating upgrade... Done
The following packages were automatically installed and are no longer required:
  apache2-data libapr1 libaprutil1 libaprutil1-dbd-sqlite3 libaprutil1-ldap
Use 'apt-get autoremove' to remove them.
The following packages have been kept back:
  linux-generic linux-headers-generic linux-image-generic
The following packages will be upgraded:
  accountsservice apparmor apport apt apt-transport-https apt-utils base-files
  bash bind9-host bsdutils coreutils cpio curl dbus dnsutils file gcc-4.9-base
  gir1.2-glib-2.0 irqbalance krb5-locales landscape-common
  language-selector-common libaccountsservice0 libapparmor-perl libapparmor1
  libapt-inst1.5 libapt-pkg4.12 libbind9-90 libblkid1 libc-bin libc6
  libcgmanager0 libcurl3 libcurl3-gnutls libdbus-1-3 libdns100 libdrm2 libelf1
  libevent-2.0-5 libfreetype6 libgcc1 libgcrypt11 libgirepository-1.0-1
  libglib2.0-0 libglib2.0-data libgssapi-krb5-2 libisc95 libisccc90
  libisccfg90 libk5crypto3 libkrb5-3 libkrb5support0 liblwres90 libmagic1
  libmount1 libpam-systemd libplymouth2 libprocps3 libsepol1 libssl1.0.0
  libsystemd-daemon0 libsystemd-login0 libudev1 libuuid1 libxml2
  linux-firmware lshw man-db mime-support mount multiarch-support net-tools
  ntpdate openssl plymouth plymouth-theme-ubuntu-text ppp procps python-apt
  python-apt-common python3-apport python3-apt python3-distupgrade python3-gi
  python3-problem-report python3-software-properties rsyslog
  software-properties-common systemd-services tcpdump tzdata
  ubuntu-release-upgrader-core udev update-notifier-common util-linux
  uuid-runtime wget wpasupplicant
98 upgraded, 0 newly installed, 0 to remove and 3 not upgraded.
Need to get 43.9 MB of archives.
After this operation, 73.7 kB of additional disk space will be used.
Do you want to continue? [Y/n] _
```

Here, we see that around 98 packages are ready to be upgraded. The server will get 49 MB of data downloaded from the repositories and install them.

# Cleaning with the apt-get clean command

Over a period of time, your system will accumulate loads of downloaded packages, copies of which are stored in /var/cache/apt/archives. If you want to remove only the packages that are obsolete, then use the autoclean option instead of clean with the apt-get tool. If you want to remove the .deb packages from the directory, run the following command:

```
sudo apt-get clean
```

The content of the folder is shown in the following screenshot:

```
skanda@server-ubuntu:~$ ls -ltr /var/cache/apt/archives/
total 44356
-rw-r--r-- 1 root root    16650 Aug 27  2013 ssl-cert_1.0.33_all.deb
-rw-r--r-- 1 root root    10538 Dec 10  2013 libaprutil1-dbd-sqlite3_1.5.3-1_amd
64.deb
-rw-r--r-- 1 root root    76376 Dec 10  2013 libaprutil1_1.5.3-1_amd64.deb
-rw-r--r-- 1 root root     8634 Dec 10  2013 libaprutil1-ldap_1.5.3-1_amd64.deb
-rw-r--r-- 1 root root    85056 Dec 31  2013 libapr1_1.5.0-1_amd64.deb
-rw-r--r-- 1 root root   154310 Jul  9  2014 python3-gi_3.12.0-1ubuntu1_amd64.de
b
-rw-r--r-- 1 root root    60372 Jul 23  2014 accountsservice_0.6.35-0ubuntu7.1_a
md64.deb
-rw-r--r-- 1 root root    69600 Jul 23  2014 libaccountsservice0_0.6.35-0ubuntu7
.1_amd64.deb
-rw-r------ 1 root root        0 Jul 23  2014 lock
-rw-r--r-- 1 root root   838846 Jul 24  2014 apache2-bin_2.4.7-1ubuntu4.1_amd64.
deb
-rw-r--r-- 1 root root   159942 Jul 24  2014 apache2-data_2.4.7-1ubuntu4.1_all.d
eb
-rw-r--r-- 1 root root    87534 Jul 24  2014 apache2_2.4.7-1ubuntu4.1_amd64.deb
-rw-r--r-- 1 root root    39184 Jul 25  2014 libgcc1_1%3a4.9.1-0ubuntu1_amd64.de
b
-rw-r--r-- 1 root root    14764 Jul 25  2014 gcc-4.9-base_4.9.1-0ubuntu1_amd64.d
eb
-rw-r--r-- 1 root root   175108 Aug  5  2014 net-tools_1.60-25ubuntu2.1_amd64.de
b
-rw-r--r-- 1 root root    85628 Aug  9  2014 libgirepository-1.0-1_1.40.0-1ubunt
u0.2_amd64.deb
-rw-r--r-- 1 root root   123680 Aug  9  2014 gir1.2-glib-2.0_1.40.0-1ubuntu0.2_a
md64.deb
```

# Purging a package with the apt-get purge command

If you wish to remove a package along with all its configuration files, use the following command:

```
sudo apt-get purge ssl-cert
```

You can remove and purge multiple packages too, as we did for the remove package command. Once you execute the preceding command, you will be able to see the output similar to the following screenshot. Once you purge a package, the dkpg tool will have no information about the package. All it will know is that the package was removed.

```
skanda@server-ubuntu:~$ sudo apt-get purge ssl-cert
[sudo] password for skanda:
Reading package lists... Done
Building dependency tree
Reading state information... Done
The following packages were automatically installed and are no longer required:
  apache2-data libapr1 libaprutil1 libaprutil1-dbd-sqlite3 libaprutil1-ldap
Use 'apt-get autoremove' to remove them.
The following packages will be REMOVED:
  ssl-cert*
0 upgraded, 0 newly installed, 1 to remove and 3 not upgraded.
After this operation, 0 B of additional disk space will be used.
Do you want to continue? [Y/n] Y
(Reading database ... 52701 files and directories currently installed.)
Removing ssl-cert (1.0.33) ...
Purging configuration files for ssl-cert (1.0.33) ...
skanda@server-ubuntu:~$
```

# Fixing unsuccessful installations with the apt-get –f command

There are times when your package is not getting installed in spite of multiple tries. Sometimes, you might face a dependency issue whilst you are installing a package using the apt-get install command. Even though the apt-get package management tool is built to handle dependencies, this issue can pop up. To solve this issue, use the following command:

```
sudo apt-get -f install
```

This command will try and repair the broken dependencies in your system and the installation of the package will be successful. You might need to run this command when you are using the apt-get install command to install anything for the first time on a new server.

The output is shown in the following screenshot:

```
skanda@server-ubuntu:/var/lib$ sudo apt-get -f install apache2
Reading package lists... Done
Building dependency tree
Reading state information... Done
The following extra packages will be installed:
  ssl-cert
Suggested packages:
  apache2-doc apache2-suexec-pristine apache2-suexec-custom apache2-utils
  openssl-blacklist
The following NEW packages will be installed:
  apache2 ssl-cert
0 upgraded, 2 newly installed, 0 to remove and 0 not upgraded.
Need to get 0 B/104 kB of archives.
After this operation, 578 kB of additional disk space will be used.
Do you want to continue? [Y/n] 262722
```

# Checking for broken dependencies with the apt-get check command

The apt-get check command is a diagnostic tool for package management. There can be instances where your system has broken dependencies. To verify the broken dependency issues, you can use the following command:

```
sudo apt-get check
```

This will update the package lists and check for the broken dependencies. It also updates the package cache.

This brings us to the end of the apt-get tool. However, there are additional tools from the apt-* family. We will look at apt-ftparchive in the *Creating a repository mirror* section where we will set up a repository mirror. Let's first look at the apt-cache tool.

# The apt-cache tool

The apt-cache tool is used to check for packages that are available in the local system. Search, dependency, and reverse dependency can be checked with the help of the apt-cache tool.

# Searching for a package with the apt-cache search command

Use the following command to search for a package. Here, we are searching for the apache2-bin package using the `apt-cache` command with the `search` option:

```
sudo apt-cache search apache2-bin
```

As we can see in the following screenshot, the preceding command lists out the package and a short description:

```
skanda@server-ubuntu:~$ sudo apt-cache search apache2-bin
apache2-bin - Apache HTTP Server (binary files and modules)
apache2.2-bin - Transitional package for apache2-bin
libapache2-mod-macro - Transitional package for apache2-bin
libapache2-mod-proxy-html - Transitional package for apache2-bin
skanda@server-ubuntu:~$
```

If you want to check the dependencies for a particular package, then use the `depends` option with the apt-cache tool. The command is as follows:

```
sudo apt-cache depends apache2
```

The output is shown in the following screenshot:

```
skanda@server-ubuntu:~$ sudo apt-cache depends apache2
apache2
  Depends: lsb-base
  Depends: procps
    procps:i386
  Depends: perl
  Depends: mime-support
  Depends: apache2-bin
  Depends: apache2-data
  Suggests: <www-browser>
    arora
    dillo
    dwb
    lynx-cur:i386
    lynx-cur
    netsurf
    netsurf-fb
    netsurf-gtk
    uzbl
    chimera2
    chromium-browser
    elinks
    epiphany-browser
    firefox
    konqueror
    links
    links2
    midori
    netrik
    rekonq
```

The other way is also supported. If you need to check what packages are dependent on a particular package, then use the following command:

```
sudo apt-cache rdepends ssl-cert
```

The output is shown in the following screenshot:

```
skanda@server-ubuntu:~$ sudo apt-cache rdepends ssl-cert
ssl-cert
Reverse Depends:
  prosody
  squid3
  postgresql-9.3
  postfix
  keystone
  dovecot-core
  cups-daemon
  apache2
  yaws
  tryton-server
  prosody
  prayer
  postgres-xc
  nufw
  nuauth
  flumotion
  filetea
  dkimproxy
  cipux-rpcd
  calendarserver
  squid3
  postgresql-common
  postgresql-9.3
  postfix
  keystone
  freeradius
  dovecot-core
```

An important point to remember is to run the `apt-get update` command before doing any of the dependency checks. It's time we learn about another package management tool, aptitude.

# Package management with aptitude

Type `aptitude` as shown here:

```
aptitude
```

The resulting screen is shown in the next screenshot. It is an interactive menu-driven frontend window for the APT to perform numerous tasks related to package management on your Ubuntu Server. You can install, remove, and upgrade packages with minimal operations from this window.

```
Actions  Undo  Package  Resolver  Search  Options  Views  Help
C-T: Menu  ?: Help  q: Quit  u: Update  g: Download/Install/Remove Pkgs
aptitude 0.6.8.2                  Will free 739 kB of disk space DL Size: 103 kB
--- Upgradable Packages (3)
--- New Packages (70971)
--- Installed Packages (420)
--- Not Installed Packages (1)
--- Virtual Packages (9861)
--- Tasks (42149)




A newer version of these packages is available.

This group contains 3 packages.
```

**aptitude** is best suited for a nongraphical environment, as it makes sure the command key operations are performed properly. Some of the experts believe that aptitude is a better suited package management tool compared to apt-get for dealing with packages that have dependencies. aptitude is the newer version and easier to use. Both aptitude and apt are abstractions over dpkg. Press *F10* to enable the menu at the top. apt and aptitude use the same configuration, hence these are both interchangeable. aptitude has a menu-driven approach and supports all the apt-* commands.

aptitude presents the packages in categories as seen in the preceding screenshot. Use the navigation keys (Up and Down arrows) to jump to the categories. Each category's brief description is given in the second half of the window. The first category we see is **Upgradable Packages**, which shows the number of packages that are ready to be upgraded. The second line, **New Packages**, shows the number of packages that are new and can be installed on your Ubuntu Server. The next two are fairly simple to guess and understand. **Virtual Packages** gives an option to the administrators to organize the packages as they feel appropriate. **Tasks** are the packages that aren't categorized into any of these categories.

Some of the command keys to work with aptitude are as follows:

- +: This adds a package to install
- -: This removes a package
- _: This purges a package
- *u*: This updates a package
- *g*: This performs the operation for which the packages are marked
- *?*: This opens a help box and shows all the command keys and their operations
- *Ctrl* + *T*: This is same as *F10*, and it accesses the top menu
- *q*: This enables you to go one screen back
- *Q*: This quits aptitude

Take a look at the following screenshot:

```
Actions  Undo  Package  Resolver  Search  Options  Views  Help
C-T: Menu  ?: Help  q: Quit  u: Update  g: Download/Install/Remove Pkgs
aptitude 0.6.8.2              Will free 739 kB of disk space DL Size: 103 kB
--\ Upgradable Packages (3)
  --- devel - Utilities and programs for software development (1)
  --\ kernel - Kernel and kernel modules (2)
    --\ main - Fully supported Free Software. (2)
i     linux-generic                   3.13.0.32.38   3.13.0.45.52
i A   linux-image-generic             3.13.0.32.38   3.13.0.45.52
--- New Packages (70971)
--- Installed Packages (420)
--- Not Installed Packages (1)
--- Virtual Packages (9061)
--- Tasks (42149)




View available packages and choose actions to perform
```

When you highlight a package, as shown in this screenshot, aptitude displays a character on the first column. These are the descriptions of the state of the package in your local machine. The following are the letters you may encounter:

- i: This means the package is installed
- p: This means the package is purged
- c: This means the configuration file is present but package is not installed
- v: This means it is a virtual package
- u: This means the package is not configured but the files are unpacked
- B: This means the package is broken
- C: This means the package is half-configured
- H: This means the package is half-installed (may be due to removal failure)

# Configuration and extra repositories

The APT configurations are stored in the /etc/apt/sources.list.d directory and the /etc/apt/sources.list file in the server. An example of the file can be seen in the following screenshot. This will vary from system to system based on the remote repositories configured. You can enable or disable repositories by commenting the lines in the /etc/apt/sources.list file. To edit this file, you may require root permissions.

```
skanda@server-ubuntu:~$ cat /etc/apt/sources.list
#
# deb cdrom:[Ubuntu-Server 14.04.1 LTS _Trusty Tahr_ - Release amd64 (20140722.3
)]/ trusty main restricted

#deb cdrom:[Ubuntu-Server 14.04.1 LTS _Trusty Tahr_ - Release amd64 (20140722.3)
]/ trusty main restricted

# See http://help.ubuntu.com/community/UpgradeNotes for how to upgrade to
# newer versions of the distribution.
deb http://us.archive.ubuntu.com/ubuntu/ trusty main restricted
deb-src http://us.archive.ubuntu.com/ubuntu/ trusty main restricted

## Major bug fix updates produced after the final release of the
## distribution.
deb http://us.archive.ubuntu.com/ubuntu/ trusty-updates main restricted
deb-src http://us.archive.ubuntu.com/ubuntu/ trusty-updates main restricted

## N.B. software from this repository is ENTIRELY UNSUPPORTED by the Ubuntu
## team. Also, please note that software in universe WILL NOT receive any
## review or updates from the Ubuntu security team.
deb http://us.archive.ubuntu.com/ubuntu/ trusty universe
deb-src http://us.archive.ubuntu.com/ubuntu/ trusty universe
deb http://us.archive.ubuntu.com/ubuntu/ trusty-updates universe
deb-src http://us.archive.ubuntu.com/ubuntu/ trusty-updates universe

## N.B. software from this repository is ENTIRELY UNSUPPORTED by the Ubuntu
## team, and may not be under a free licence. Please satisfy yourself as to
## your rights to use the software. Also, please note that software in
```

There are numerous repositories available other than the official Ubuntu one for installing packages on your server. Two of the popular ones are Universe and Multiverse. Both are open source and are supported widely by the community, and thus make it safe to use with your server. There are no security updates to these packages, but in some countries there might be some issues with the Multiverse package. This is also one of the reasons why Ubuntu does not have the Multiverse package support out of the box. If you take a look at the configuration files, you will observe that these repositories are enabled by default. You can disable them by commenting it out. Comment these lines to disable both the repositories:

```
deb http://archive.ubuntu.com/ubuntu precise universe multiverse deb-
src http://archive.ubuntu.com/ubuntu precise universe multiverse  deb
http://us.archive.ubuntu.com/ubuntu/ precise universe deb-src http://
us.archive.ubuntu.com/ubuntu/ precise universe deb http://us.archive.
ubuntu.com/ubuntu/ precise-updates universe deb-src http://us.archive.
ubuntu.com/ubuntu/ precise-updates universe  deb http://us.archive.
ubuntu.com/ubuntu/ precise multiverse deb-src http://us.archive.
ubuntu.com/ubuntu/ precise multiverse deb http://us.archive.ubuntu.
com/ubuntu/ precise-updates multiverse deb-src http://us.archive.
ubuntu.com/ubuntu/ precise-updates multiverse  deb http://security.
ubuntu.com/ubuntu precise-security universe deb-src http://security.
ubuntu.com/ubuntu precise-security universe deb http://security.
ubuntu.com/ubuntu precise-security multiverse deb-src http://security.
ubuntu.com/ubuntu precise-security multiverse
```

To view the support status of your Ubuntu machine, run the following command:

`ubuntu-support-status`

To view all the packages that are supported or not supported run the same command with the `--show-all` option.

You will be able to see a summary of the package support and its expiry time. It will be something similar to the following screenshot:

```
skanda@server-ubuntu:~$ ubuntu-support-status
Support status summary of 'server-ubuntu':

You have 8 packages (1.8%) supported until November 2015 (9m)
You have 425 packages (98.2%) supported until May 2019 (5y)

You have 0 packages (0.0%) that can not/no-longer be downloaded
You have 0 packages (0.0%) that are unsupported

Run with --show-unsupported, --show-supported or --show-all to see more details
skanda@server-ubuntu:~$
```

One of the cons of using third-party repositories is the chance of dependencies not being available or any package conflicting with any Ubuntu package. This can be a cycle and is termed as dependency hell. Make sure you go through other users' feedback on any issues with a particular package before installing it.

Finding the right mirror is crucial if you want to ensure a clean and fast installation. A mirror is a replica of the repository at a different physical location. You will need to look at the following factors when selecting a mirror and decide on it:

- **Distance**: Try and use a mirror that is physically close to you.
- **Protocol**: Your chosen mirror may not support all of the protocols such as HTTP,FTP, rsync, and so on.
- **Speed**: Less number of people connecting to a mirror means more speed.

Visit `https://launchpad.net/ubuntu/+archivemirrors` for a list of mirrors and choose a mirror that best fits on the factors.

# Resolving the "failed to get" error

It is often observed that when a user tries to install a package using `apt-get install`, they might get an error such as the one shown here:

```
W: Failed to fetch gzip:/var/lib/apt/lists/partial/us.archive.ubuntu.com_
ubuntu_dists_natty_main_source_Sources  Hash Sum mismatch,

E: Some index files failed to download. They have been ignored, or old
ones used instead.
```

Fix your configuration list. Run the following commands to resolve this issue:

```
sudo rm /var/lib/apt/lists/*
sudo apt-get update
```

# Downloading software from an outside repository

There may be some packages that you require that are not available in any of the repositories. Individuals may create a package and make it available online for others to download and install it manually. The package may be in one of the following formats: `.tar.gz` or `.tgz`. These packages always come with README files. Always make a point to read this file before performing any operation related to installation. This file is self-explanatory and has the directions to install the particular package onto your machine.

# Automatic updates

Let's discuss the three main categories of updates that determines how you keep your system up-to-date and working in optimum conditions. The three broad categories we will discuss here are security updates, kernel updates, and application updates.

# Security updates

It is recommended that server administrators install the security patch updates as soon as it becomes available. However, if a particular package isn't being used in the server, then you may skip the security update for that particular package. Depending on your need, you may choose and install the security updates.

Administrators can refer to **Ubuntu Security Notices (USN)** to understand the security updates available and if they should be installing a particular update. USN can be accessed at `http://www.ubuntu.com/usn/`. The admins can also subscribe to RSS feeds for these security updates.

# Kernel updates

It may seem like kernel updates are of the utmost importance and they should be applied as soon as the updates are available. But it is tricky, as updates to kernel can actually cause some programs not to function in a proper way. Kernel updates rectify the security issues but have to be updated only after considering and making sure that other applications' behavior won't be hampered with it.

By default, the package management tools such as apt-get, aptitude, and synaptic enable the kernel updates. For command-line tools, you can disable automatic kernel updates using the following command:

```
sudo aptitude hold linux-image-name
```

# Application updates

Admins need to be careful when installing the application updates. A case may arise wherein some of the functionality of other packages may not work after installing the update. Refer to USN and other Ubuntu related forums to keep yourself updated about the possible application updates and the issues faced by other users.

# The unattended-upgrades package

The unattended-upgrades package can be used to schedule and enforce rules on what packages to be updated and what packages should be restricted from upgrading itself. To use this, install the unattended-upgrades package using the following command:

```
sudo apt-get install unattended-upgrades
```

Once the package is installed, configure the unattended-upgrades package in the following file and make necessary changes as per your needs. I am opening the file in the Nano editor:

```
nano /etc/apt/apt.conf.d/50unattended-upgrades
```

The output of this command is shown in the following screenshot:

```
  GNU nano 2.2.6    File: /etc/apt/apt.conf.d/50unattended-upgrades

// Automatically upgrade packages from these (origin:archive) pairs
Unattended-Upgrade::Allowed-Origins {
        "${distro_id}:${distro_codename}-security";
//      "${distro_id}:${distro_codename}-updates";
//      "${distro_id}:${distro_codename}-proposed";
//      "${distro_id}:${distro_codename}-backports";
};

// List of packages to not update (regexp are supported)
Unattended-Upgrade::Package-Blacklist {
//      "vim";
//      "libc6";
//      "libc6-dev";
//      "libc6-i686";
};

// This option allows you to control if on a unclean dpkg exit
// unattended-upgrades will automatically run
//    dpkg --force-confold --configure -a
// The default is true, to ensure updates keep getting installed
//Unattended-Upgrade::AutoFixInterruptedDpkg "false";

// Split the upgrade into the smallest possible chunks so that
// they can be interrupted with SIGUSR1. This makes the upgrade
// a bit slower but it has the benefit that shutdown while a upgrade
               [ Read 59 lines (Warning: No write permission) ]
^G Get Help   ^O WriteOut   ^R Read File  ^Y Prev Page  ^K Cut Text   ^C Cur Pos
^X Exit       ^J Justify    ^W Where Is   ^V Next Page  ^U UnCut Text ^T To Spell
```

The first section is for the packages where you want to allow automatic upgrades. Here, the first line for security is enabled, so the security updates will be installed by default. The // symbol means the lines are commented and will not be evaluated, as shown here:

```
Unattended-Upgrade::Allowed-Origins {          "Ubuntu precise-
security"; //       "Ubuntu precise-updates"; };
```

The second section is for the blacklisted packages. You put the package names here for which you want to disable automatic updates. Again, // has the same meaning—those lines will not be evaluated. Add the packages in this section to blacklist them and disallow automatic updates:

```
Unattended-Upgrade::Package-Blacklist { //       "vim"; //
"libc6"; //       "libc6-dev"; //       "libc6-i686"; };
```

One last step is to enable the automatic updates by setting the appropriate configuration in the `/etc/apt/apt.conf.d/10periodic` file, as shown in the following screenshot:

```
  GNU nano 2.2.6          File: /etc/apt/apt.conf.d/10periodic

APT::Periodic::Update-Package-Lists "1";
APT::Periodic::Download-Upgradeable-Packages "0";
APT::Periodic::AutocleanInterval "0";

                     [ Read 3 lines (Warning: No write permission) ]
^G Get Help  ^O WriteOut  ^R Read File ^Y Prev Page ^K Cut Text  ^C Cur Pos
^X Exit      ^J Justify   ^W Where Is  ^V Next Page ^U UnCut Text^T To Spell
```

In this example, the interval is set to 1, which means the packages list will be updated, packages will be downloaded, and they will be upgraded every day.

# Creating a repository mirror

When there are multiple machines on your network, it makes sense to have local repository mirrored from the remote repository. The main advantage is the reduced bandwidth usage by limiting the number of machines connecting to the remote repositories and downloading huge files associated with packages. Only one system will connect to the remote repository and mirror the contents to the local system. Another advantage is that when all the machines are pointed to this repository the packages in each one of them will be of the same version.

There are three tasks that we will need to perform in order to get the local mirror repository working. First, set up the mirror on one of the machines, and then configure the machine to mirror only certain repositories. This will limit the amount of data downloaded and also keep the unwanted packages away. The third task is to point the local clients to this newly created repository so that they use only this repository to upgrade the packages.

# Setting up a mirror machine

You can set up the mirroring in two ways: rsync and apt-mirror. Traditionally, rsync was being used to synchronize the local and remote files. Now, admins prefer the `apt-mirror` command, at least for the initial mirroring setup. First, install the apt-mirror package using the following command:

```
sudo apt-get install apt-mirror
```

Now, try running the `apt-mirror` command. Don't be surprised by the sheer size of download data it asks to be downloaded. Now, let's limit the repositories that we want and also set up other configuration for the mirror.

# Configuring the /etc/apt/mirror.list file

You will be required to configure the `/etc/apt/mirror.list` file to set up the desired repositories you wish to mirror. The file looks like this:

```
skanda@server-ubuntu:~$ cat /etc/apt/mirror.list
############# config ##################
#
# set base_path      /var/spool/apt-mirror
#
# set mirror_path    $base_path/mirror
# set skel_path      $base_path/skel
# set var_path       $base_path/var
# set cleanscript    $var_path/clean.sh
# set defaultarch    <running host architecture>
# set postmirror_script $var_path/postmirror.sh
# set run_postmirror 0
set nthreads       20
set _tilde 0
#
############# end config ##############

deb http://archive.ubuntu.com/ubuntu trusty main restricted universe multiverse
deb http://archive.ubuntu.com/ubuntu trusty-security main restricted universe mu
ltiverse
deb http://archive.ubuntu.com/ubuntu trusty-updates main restricted universe mul
tiverse
#deb http://archive.ubuntu.com/ubuntu trusty-proposed main restricted universe m
ultiverse
#deb http://archive.ubuntu.com/ubuntu trusty-backports main restricted universe
multiverse

deb-src http://archive.ubuntu.com/ubuntu trusty main restricted universe multive
rse
deb-src http://archive.ubuntu.com/ubuntu trusty-security main restricted univers
```

The first section has the default configuration related to the storage of downloaded files, base mirror path, cleanscript, concurrent threads to be run when downloading, and others. By default, the files are copied to the /var/spool/apt-mirror path. The admin should ensure there is enough disk space to store the files. If all the systems are on the same architecture, then let defaultarch be same as default, which is set to <running host architecture>. If you are mirroring the repositories for any other architecture, then you need to set it explicitly. Next, comment out the lines related to the repositories in the second section. Have only those repositories active that you need and comment out the others as keeping all active will mean you are downloading a very large amount of data, somewhere close to 50 GB maybe.

After you have made the changes, run the apt-mirror command to mirror the remote repository to the local one. Once completed, you can see the directory listing similar to the one you observe on the remote servers.

## Using the local mirror

This is an important task if you want to make sure the local mirror is completely functional. In each of the client machines on your network, change the repository URL to access the locally set up mirror. You will need to point to the IP of the machine acting as the mirror. Open the /etc/apt/sources.list configuration file and make the following changes:

```
deb http://192.168.1.8/mirror/ubuntu trusty main restricted
```

We are all set to use the mirror as the repository for all our local client machines.

## Summary

In this chapter, we discussed various package management tools such as dpkg, apt-get, and aptitude. You learned about the limitations of dpkg, how apt overcomes these limitations, and the ease of using aptitude. You also learned about auto updates and configuring the repositories as per your requirements. Later, we covered how to create, maintain, and use the local mirrors for your cluster.

In the next chapter you will learn about the network and DNS, as well as how to set up and maintain them.

# 2
# Networking and DNS

This chapter is about networking and DNS. We will discuss understanding, configuring, and troubleshooting DNS and network issues pertaining to the Ubuntu Server. Topics covered in this chapter are networking concepts, interface configuration, DHCP, network sniffing, binding, and bonding. We will discuss DNS topics such as forward zone, reverse zone, and configuring primary and secondary masters.

By the end of this chapter, you will be able to set up your own DNS, diagnose and rectify network issues, and configure DHCP on your server.

The following topics will be covered in this chapter:

- Networking concepts
- DHCP
- Network sniffing
- Binding and bonding
- DNS
- Primary and reverse zone files

## Networking concepts

Let's take a look at some of the important networking concepts relevant to Ubuntu and how to troubleshoot issues that may occur.

# IP addressing

We will need to configure IP addresses and a default gateway for communications on local networks as well as the Internet. If we need to assign IP addresses temporarily, we would use commands such as `ifconfig`, `ip`, and `route`. These commands are found on most of the Linux systems, and change the network settings with immediate effect:

```
sudo ifconfig eth0 192.168.1.100 netmask 255.255.255.0
```

Remember that this setting is temporary and will be lost when we reboot the server machine. This will assign the IP on `eth0` to your server machine, so any other machines can talk to this server using the recently set IP. We can verify the same using the following command:

```
ifconfig eth0
```

You will be able to see the following screen:

```
skanda@server-ubuntu:~$ ifconfig eth0
eth0      Link encap:Ethernet  HWaddr 08:00:27:f2:06:e5
          inet addr:192.168.1.100  Bcast:192.168.1.255  Mask:255.255.255.0
          inet6 addr: fe80::a00:27ff:fef2:6e5/64 Scope:Link
          UP BROADCAST RUNNING MULTICAST  MTU:1500  Metric:1
          RX packets:754 errors:0 dropped:0 overruns:0 frame:0
          TX packets:47 errors:0 dropped:0 overruns:0 carrier:0
          collisions:0 txqueuelen:1000
          RX bytes:69997 (69.9 KB)  TX bytes:9610 (9.6 KB)

skanda@server-ubuntu:~$
```

Use the `route` command to configure the default gateway. This will make sure all the network-related requests will be sent via the default gateway only. The command is as follows:

```
sudo route add default gw 192.168.1.1 eth0
```

Verify the change with the `route` command, as shown here:

```
skanda@server-ubuntu:~$ route -n
Kernel IP routing table
Destination     Gateway         Genmask         Flags Metric Ref    Use Iface
0.0.0.0         192.168.1.1     0.0.0.0         UG    0      0        0 eth0
192.168.1.0     0.0.0.0         255.255.255.0   U     0      0        0 eth0
skanda@server-ubuntu:~$
```

If you no longer require these temporary network configurations, you can remove or purge the settings using the `flush` command:

```
sudo ip addr flush eth0
```

# DHCP client for dynamic addresses

We will use the **DHCP** client for automatic dynamic address assignment. To do this, add the `dhcp` method as follows. Open the `/etc/network/interfaces` file and add the following lines:

```
auto eth0
iface etho inet dhcp
```

The first line is to set the Ethernet connection to auto mode. The next line sets DHCP to `eht0`. This is shown in the following screenshot:

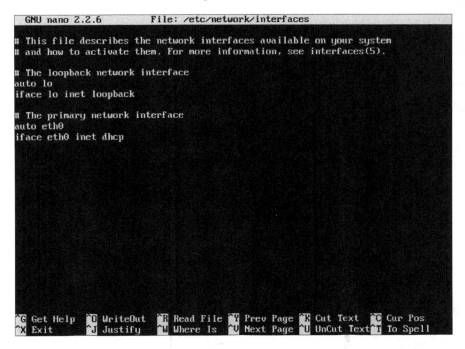

Once done, manually enable it using the `ifup` command:

```
sudo ifup etho0
```

The command to disable the DHCP interface is as follows:

```
sudo ifdown eth0
```

The preceding command will shut down the interface.

# Assigning a static IP address

Many a times, we require the server machines to have a static IP every time they boot up. The reasons for this may be plentiful, but it is always better to have static IPs for servers. We will discuss DNS in the later sections; maybe then you'll be able to understand the importance of static IPs.

You will need to modify the /etc/network/interfaces file to configure the server to use a static IP address assignment. Also, mention the IP that the server should be assigned. Let's set the values for address, netmask, and gateway for eth0 now:

```
auto eth0
iface eth0 inet static     #makes the IP address static
address 192.168.1.100      #set a static IP address
netmask 255.255.255.0      #set a netmask for the IP address above
gateway 192.168.1.1        #set the default gateway
```

This is shown in the following screenshot:

```
  GNU nano 2.2.6          File: /etc/network/interfaces

# This file describes the network interfaces available on your system
# and how to activate them. For more information, see interfaces(5).

# The loopback network interface
auto lo
iface lo inet loopback

# The primary network interface
auto eth0
iface eth0 inet static
address 192.168.1.100
netmask 255.255.255.0
gateway 192.168.1.1




                         [ Wrote 14 lines ]
^G Get Help   ^O WriteOut   ^R Read File  ^Y Prev Page  ^K Cut Text   ^C Cur Pos
^X Exit       ^J Justify    ^W Where Is   ^V Next Page  ^U UnCut Text ^T To Spell
```

Remember to enable the interface manually after setting the values in the interfaces file. You might see the following message:

```
ifup: interface etho0 already configured
```

You should first disable the interface and then enable it again.

# DHCP

**DHCP** stands for **Dynamic Host Configuration Protocol**. It is a service that automatically assigns network settings to the hosts from a server. There are two parts to DHCP, namely the server and the client. Server sends settings to each client and assigns the following configuration properties:

- Host name
- Domain name
- Default gateway
- Time server
- Print server

DHCP is useful in many ways to the server administrators. Firstly, settings need to be changed only at one place. The settings will be updated automatically on other DHCP clients whenever they poll the DHCP server. Conflicts are greatly reduced as the server handles all the IP address assignment. Also, it is easier to add new machines to the network and assign IP addresses to them.

DHCP clients can be provided with configuration settings by the DHCP server in the following two methods:

- **MAC address**: Each network has a unique number on its NIC known as the MAC address. The server has the MAC addresses of each client and also the configuration settings to be supplied to the client. Each time a client polls the DHCP server, it is served with the same configuration corresponding to the client, and the client is identified by its MAC address.

- **Address pool**: The DHCP server maintains a list or range of IP addresses called as the address pool. When a client polls the server, it is served with configuration properties dynamically on a *first come, first serve* basis. Every client is given an expiry time. When the client fails to poll the server within this time, its settings get expired and the same is added back to the list in the pool.

Ubuntu has both the server and client parts of the DHCP. dhcpd is the server process and dhclient is the client. You need to install the client part of DHCP on all the machines for which you want automatic configuration. Let's look at the installation and configuration now.

# Installation

Here's the command to install the DHCP server on your machine:

```
sudo apt-get install dhcp3-server
```

The output is shown in the following screenshot:

```
skanda@server-ubuntu:~$ sudo apt-get install dhcp3-server
[sudo] password for skanda:
Reading package lists... Done
Building dependency tree
Reading state information... Done
Note, selecting 'isc-dhcp-server' instead of 'dhcp3-server'
Suggested packages:
  isc-dhcp-server-ldap
The following NEW packages will be installed:
  isc-dhcp-server
0 upgraded, 1 newly installed, 0 to remove and 0 not upgraded.
Need to get 762 kB of archives.
After this operation, 2,138 kB of additional disk space will be used.
Get:1 http://us.archive.ubuntu.com/ubuntu/ trusty/main isc-dhcp-server amd64 4.2
.4-7ubuntu12 [762 kB]
Fetched 762 kB in 4s (170 kB/s)
Preconfiguring packages ...
Selecting previously unselected package isc-dhcp-server.
(Reading database ... 82667 files and directories currently installed.)
Preparing to unpack .../isc-dhcp-server_4.2.4-7ubuntu12_amd64.deb ...
Unpacking isc-dhcp-server (4.2.4-7ubuntu12) ...
Processing triggers for man-db (2.6.7.1-1ubuntu1) ...
Processing triggers for ureadahead (0.100.0-16) ...
ureadahead will be reprofiled on next reboot
Setting up isc-dhcp-server (4.2.4-7ubuntu12) ...
Generating /etc/default/isc-dhcp-server...
isc-dhcp-server start/running, process 1577
isc-dhcp-server6 stop/pre-start, process 1656
Processing triggers for ureadahead (0.100.0-16) ...
skanda@server-ubuntu:~$
```

Once the DHCP server package is installed, go to `/etc/default/isc-dhcp-server` and specify the interface. The default is `eth0`. The file will look similar to the one shown in the following screenshot:

```
  GNU nano 2.2.6          File: /etc/default/isc-dhcp-server

# Defaults for isc-dhcp-server initscript
# sourced by /etc/init.d/isc-dhcp-server
# installed at /etc/default/isc-dhcp-server by the maintainer scripts

#
# This is a POSIX shell fragment
#

# Path to dhcpd's config file (default: /etc/dhcp/dhcpd.conf).
#DHCPD_CONF=/etc/dhcp/dhcpd.conf

# Path to dhcpd's PID file (default: /var/run/dhcpd.pid).
#DHCPD_PID=/var/run/dhcpd.pid

# Additional options to start dhcpd with.
#        Don't use options -cf or -pf here; use DHCPD_CONF/ DHCPD_PID instead
#OPTIONS=""

# On what interfaces should the DHCP server (dhcpd) serve DHCP requests?
#        Separate multiple interfaces with spaces, e.g. "eth0 eth1".
INTERFACES="eth0"




                          [ Wrote 21 lines ]
^G Get Help   ^O WriteOut   ^R Read File  ^Y Prev Page  ^K Cut Text   ^C Cur Pos
^X Exit       ^J Justify    ^W Where Is   ^V Next Page  ^U UnCut Text ^T To Spell
```

Let's now take a look at the configuration of DHCP.

# Configuration

Open the /etc/dhcp/dhcpd.conf file to configure the settings for the DHCP server that will be used to assign IP addresses and serve other settings to the DHCP clients:

```
GNU nano 2.2.6              File: /etc/dhcp/dhcpd.conf

#
# Sample configuration file for ISC dhcpd for Debian
#
# Attention: If /etc/ltsp/dhcpd.conf exists, that will be used as
# configuration file instead of this file.
#
#

# The ddns-updates-style parameter controls whether or not the server will
# attempt to do a DNS update when a lease is confirmed. We default to the
# behavior of the version 2 packages ('none', since DHCP v2 didn't
# have support for DDNS.)
ddns-update-style none;

# option definitions common to all supported networks...
option domain-name "example.org";
option domain-name-servers ns1.example.org, ns2.example.org;

default-lease-time 600;
max-lease-time 7200;

subnet 192.168.1.0 netmask 255.255.255.0 {
range 192.168.1.10 192.168.1.100;
range 192.168.1.125_192.168.1.225;
}
                          [ Wrote 115 lines ]
^G Get Help   ^O WriteOut  ^R Read File ^Y Prev Page ^K Cut Text  ^C Cur Pos
^X Exit       ^J Justify   ^W Where Is  ^V Next Page ^U UnCut Text^T To Spell
```

The following are the configuration settings:

```
default-lease-time 600;
max-lease-time 7200;
subnet 192.168.1.0 netmask 255.255.255.0 {
range 192.168.1.10 192.168.1.100;
range 192.168.1.125 192.168.1.225;
}
```

Any client that polls the DHCP server for an IP address will be given one of the address from range 192.168.1.10 to 192.168.1.100 or 192.168.1.125 to 192.168.1.225. Also, the lease time will be 600 seconds by default. The client can also mention the lease time while requesting for an IP; however, that cannot be more than the maximum lease time defined in this configuration file, which we have set as 7200 seconds.

# Network sniffing with tcpdump

Network administrators can use sniffers to discover network issues and to monitor the network traffic. This information can be used to identify packets that are having errors, thereby getting to the root of problems and solving it to have an efficient network.

A packet sniffer captures all the data that is being transmitted through a network interface. Let's use **tcpdump**, which is a command-line tool for network sniffing.

## Capturing packets from eth0

The `tcpdump` command can be used to capture packets from a particular interface. The following command will help us capture the packets on the `eth0` interface:

```
sudo tcpdump -i eth0
```

I initiated a ping from this machine (`192.168.1.100`) to another machine (`192.168.1.8`) in the same network. After running the preceding command, you will see a screen similar to the one in the following screenshot:

```
ngth 46
03:24:29.999102 IP 192.168.1.100 > 192.168.1.8: ICMP echo request, id 1859, seq
80, length 64
03:24:30.102343 IP 192.168.1.8 > 192.168.1.100: ICMP echo reply, id 1859, seq 80
, length 64
03:24:31.000499 IP 192.168.1.100 > 192.168.1.8: ICMP echo request, id 1859, seq
81, length 64
03:24:31.024033 IP 192.168.1.8 > 192.168.1.100: ICMP echo reply, id 1859, seq 81
, length 64
03:24:32.002246 IP 192.168.1.100 > 192.168.1.8: ICMP echo request, id 1859, seq
82, length 64
03:24:32.048916 IP 192.168.1.8 > 192.168.1.100: ICMP echo reply, id 1859, seq 82
, length 64
03:24:32.703734 IP 192.168.1.5.3106 > 239.255.255.250.1900: UDP, length 325
03:24:32.809560 IP 192.168.1.5.3106 > 239.255.255.250.1900: UDP, length 325
03:24:32.917774 IP 192.168.1.5.3106 > 239.255.255.250.1900: UDP, length 334
03:24:33.005119 IP 192.168.1.100 > 192.168.1.8: ICMP echo request, id 1859, seq
83, length 64
03:24:33.025878 IP 192.168.1.5.3106 > 239.255.255.250.1900: UDP, length 334
03:24:33.073634 IP 192.168.1.8 > 192.168.1.100: ICMP echo reply, id 1859, seq 83
, length 64
03:24:33.134222 IP 192.168.1.5.3106 > 239.255.255.250.1900: UDP, length 389
03:24:33.242214 IP 192.168.1.5.3106 > 239.255.255.250.1900: UDP, length 389
03:24:33.350151 IP 192.168.1.5.3106 > 239.255.255.250.1900: UDP, length 399
03:24:33.457786 IP 192.168.1.5.3106 > 239.255.255.250.1900: UDP, length 399

38 packets captured
42 packets received by filter
0 packets dropped by kernel
skanda@server-ubuntu:~$
```

Here, we see the ICMP requests and replies. We see the source and destination IPs, ID, sequence, and length of each packet. These results of tcpdump were displayed on the terminal, but what if we wanted to save the results in a file to analyze it later?

# Saving the tcpdump results in a file

tcpdump provides us with an option –w to save the results of packet sniffing to a file. Use the following command to save the results in a file:

```
tcpdump -w results11Mar.pcap -i eth0
```

Remember to save the file with extension .pcap so any network protocol analyzer can read the file. This is shown in the following screenshot:

```
skanda@server-ubuntu:~$ sudo tcpdump -w results11Mar.pcap -i eth0 &
[1] 1975
skanda@server-ubuntu:~$ ping 192.168.1.8
PING 192.168.1.8 (192.168.1.8) 56(84) bytes of data.
64 bytes from 192.168.1.8: icmp_seq=1 ttl=64 time=80.1 ms
64 bytes from 192.168.1.8: icmp_seq=2 ttl=64 time=1.71 ms
64 bytes from 192.168.1.8: icmp_seq=3 ttl=64 time=20.5 ms
64 bytes from 192.168.1.8: icmp_seq=4 ttl=64 time=42.5 ms
64 bytes from 192.168.1.8: icmp_seq=5 ttl=64 time=66.3 ms
64 bytes from 192.168.1.8: icmp_seq=6 ttl=64 time=87.3 ms
64 bytes from 192.168.1.8: icmp_seq=7 ttl=64 time=108 ms
64 bytes from 192.168.1.8: icmp_seq=8 ttl=64 time=28.2 ms
64 bytes from 192.168.1.8: icmp_seq=9 ttl=64 time=49.9 ms
64 bytes from 192.168.1.8: icmp_seq=10 ttl=64 time=72.6 ms
64 bytes from 192.168.1.8: icmp_seq=11 ttl=64 time=1.99 ms
64 bytes from 192.168.1.8: icmp_seq=12 ttl=64 time=2.20 ms
64 bytes from 192.168.1.8: icmp_seq=13 ttl=64 time=35.5 ms
64 bytes from 192.168.1.8: icmp_seq=14 ttl=64 time=1.31 ms
^C
--- 192.168.1.8 ping statistics ---
14 packets transmitted, 14 received, 0% packet loss, time 13027ms
rtt min/avg/max/mdev = 1.311/42.769/108.227/34.477 ms

[1]+  Stopped                 sudo tcpdump -w results11Mar.pcap -i eth0
skanda@server-ubuntu:~$
skanda@server-ubuntu:~$
skanda@server-ubuntu:~$
skanda@server-ubuntu:~$
skanda@server-ubuntu:~$
```

# Reading packets saved in a file by tcpdump

Let's now read the file that we saved in the previous command. The file is not a plain text file but a `.pcap` file. Using the `tcpdump` command with `-r` option will helps us read the file:

```
tcpdump -tttt -r results11Mar.pcap
```

You will see something similar to the following screenshot. It is the same data that we saw in the previous section, but this time in a file.

```
skanda@server-ubuntu:~$ tcpdump -tttt -r results11Mar.pcap
reading from file results11Mar.pcap, link-type EN10MB (Ethernet)
2015-03-11 03:58:07.709978 IP 192.168.1.100 > 192.168.1.8: ICMP echo request, id
 1859, seq 2094, length 64
2015-03-11 03:58:07.785294 IP 192.168.1.8 > 192.168.1.100: ICMP echo reply, id 1
859, seq 2094, length 64
2015-03-11 03:58:08.711462 IP 192.168.1.100 > 192.168.1.8: ICMP echo request, id
 1859, seq 2095, length 64
2015-03-11 03:58:08.807366 IP 192.168.1.8 > 192.168.1.100: ICMP echo reply, id 1
859, seq 2095, length 64
2015-03-11 03:58:09.713580 IP 192.168.1.100 > 192.168.1.8: ICMP echo request, id
 1859, seq 2096, length 64
2015-03-11 03:58:09.831174 IP 192.168.1.8 > 192.168.1.100: ICMP echo reply, id 1
859, seq 2096, length 64
2015-03-11 03:58:10.715295 IP 192.168.1.100 > 192.168.1.8: ICMP echo request, id
 1859, seq 2097, length 64
2015-03-11 03:58:10.754153 IP 192.168.1.8 > 192.168.1.100: ICMP echo reply, id 1
859, seq 2097, length 64
2015-03-11 03:58:11.718333 IP 192.168.1.100 > 192.168.1.8: ICMP echo request, id
 1859, seq 2098, length 64
2015-03-11 03:58:11.719996 IP 192.168.1.8 > 192.168.1.100: ICMP echo reply, id 1
859, seq 2098, length 64
2015-03-11 03:58:12.720355 IP 192.168.1.100 > 192.168.1.8: ICMP echo request, id
 1859, seq 2099, length 64
2015-03-11 03:58:12.796804 IP 192.168.1.5.3106 > 239.255.255.250.1900: UDP, leng
th 325
2015-03-11 03:58:12.889422 IP 192.168.1.8 > 192.168.1.100: ICMP echo reply, id 1
859, seq 2099, length 64
2015-03-11 03:58:12.902735 IP 192.168.1.5.3106 > 239.255.255.250.1900: UDP, leng
th 325
```

# Readable timestamps in packets

Use the parameter option `-tttt` to make the timestamp readable in plain text format for the tcpdump results. Here's the command to do so:

```
sudo tcpdump -tttt -i etho0
```

# Reading packets of a specific protocol

Suppose you are interested in only reading packing of a specific protocol. tcpdump supports the following protocols: `wlan`, `ip`, `ip6`, `tcp`, `udp`, `arp`, `rarp`, `fddi`, `tr`, and `decnet`. To capture packets pertaining to the `udp` protocol, use the following command:

```
sudo tcpdump -i eth0 udp
```

# Reading packets on a specific port

Using the `tcpdump port` command, you can read all the packets that are received on a particular port on your server machine. Here's the command to read packets received on port 22 on the `eth0` interface:

```
sudo tcpdump -i eth0 port 22
```

# Reading TCP packets between two hosts

We can capture all the packets between two hosts that are communicating over the TCP protocol using the following `tcpdump` command:

```
sudo tcpdump -w tcp2hosts.pcap -i eth0 dst 192.168.1.5 and port 22
```

There are many more options for running `tcpdump`. Refer to the output of the `man tcpdump` command for more information.

# Binding and bonding

Let's now look at the concepts of binding and bonding.

# Binding

The process of assigning a server more than one IP address on the same network card is known as **binding**. There may be cases where the same server is hosting services, which are defined on separate IP addresses. Let's see how we can bind multiple IP addresses to our Ubuntu Server.

Go to the `/etc/network/interfaces` file and add the following lines:

```
auto eth0:0
iface eth0:0 inet static
address 192.168.1.104
```

```
netmask 255.255.255.0

auto eth0:1
iface eth0:1 inet static
address 192.168.1.240
netmask 255.255.255.0
```

The first line in the code snippet is for adding a device. We then specify the address to be static and also mention the IP address. Note you have to mention the netmask. It is mandatory. The file will look similar to the following screenshot:

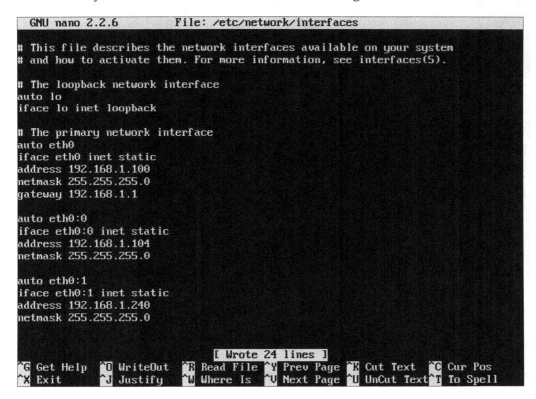

Now, we need to enable these addresses using the `ifup` command:

```
sudo ifup eth0:0
sudo ifuo eth0:1
```

To verify this, ping these IP addresses from external machines on the same network. Alternatively, you may also use the `ifconfig` command, as shown here:

```
skanda@server-ubuntu:~$ ifconfig
eth0      Link encap:Ethernet  HWaddr 08:00:27:f2:06:e5
          inet addr:192.168.1.100  Bcast:192.168.1.255  Mask:255.255.255.0
          inet6 addr: fe80::a00:27ff:fef2:6e5/64 Scope:Link
          UP BROADCAST RUNNING MULTICAST  MTU:1500  Metric:1
          RX packets:33583 errors:0 dropped:0 overruns:0 frame:0
          TX packets:9655 errors:0 dropped:0 overruns:0 carrier:0
          collisions:0 txqueuelen:1000
          RX bytes:3927793 (3.9 MB)  TX bytes:940934 (940.9 KB)

eth0:0    Link encap:Ethernet  HWaddr 08:00:27:f2:06:e5
          inet addr:192.168.1.104  Bcast:192.168.1.255  Mask:255.255.255.0
          UP BROADCAST RUNNING MULTICAST  MTU:1500  Metric:1

eth0:1    Link encap:Ethernet  HWaddr 08:00:27:f2:06:e5
          inet addr:192.168.1.240  Bcast:192.168.1.255  Mask:255.255.255.0
          UP BROADCAST RUNNING MULTICAST  MTU:1500  Metric:1

lo        Link encap:Local Loopback
          inet addr:127.0.0.1  Mask:255.0.0.0
          inet6 addr: ::1/128 Scope:Host
          UP LOOPBACK RUNNING  MTU:65536  Metric:1
          RX packets:134 errors:0 dropped:0 overruns:0 frame:0
          TX packets:134 errors:0 dropped:0 overruns:0 carrier:0
          collisions:0 txqueuelen:0
          RX bytes:9900 (9.9 KB)  TX bytes:9900 (9.9 KB)

skanda@server-ubuntu:~$
```

# Bonding

Bonding can be considered as the reverse of binding. The process of assigning multiple network cards with same IP address is called **bonding**. Let's see the process of bonding in our Ubuntu Server.

First, check for the available network cards on your server using the following command:

```
ifconfig | grep 'Ethernet'
```

An example output is shown in the following screenshot:

```
skanda@server-ubuntu:~$ ifconfig | grep 'Ethernet'
eth0          Link encap:Ethernet  HWaddr 08:00:27:f2:06:e5
eth0:0        Link encap:Ethernet  HWaddr 08:00:27:f2:06:e5
eth0:1        Link encap:Ethernet  HWaddr 08:00:27:f2:06:e5
skanda@server-ubuntu:~$ _
```

We see three Ethernet cards, but with same hardware addresses as these were the ones we performed the binding operation on. However, your results will have different hardware addresses for each Ethernet card. We will bond eth0 and eth1.

First, install the ifenslave package:

```
sudo apt-get install ifenslave
```

The output is shown in the following screenshot:

```
skanda@server-ubuntu:~$ sudo apt-get install ifenslave
Reading package lists... Done
Building dependency tree
Reading state information... Done
The following NEW packages will be installed:
  ifenslave
0 upgraded, 1 newly installed, 0 to remove and 16 not upgraded.
Need to get 12.9 kB of archives.
After this operation, 88.1 kB of additional disk space will be used.
Get:1 http://us.archive.ubuntu.com/ubuntu/ trusty/main ifenslave all 2.4ubuntu1
[12.9 kB]
Fetched 12.9 kB in 1s (12.3 kB/s)
Selecting previously unselected package ifenslave.
(Reading database ... 82686 files and directories currently installed.)
Preparing to unpack .../ifenslave_2.4ubuntu1_all.deb ...
Unpacking ifenslave (2.4ubuntu1) ...
Processing triggers for man-db (2.6.7.1-1ubuntu1) ...
Setting up ifenslave (2.4ubuntu1) ...
skanda@server-ubuntu:~$
```

Once the package is installed, go to the /etc/network/interfaces file and update the following lines:

```
iface bond0 inet static
address 192.168.1.108
netmask 255.255.255.0
gateway 192.168.1.1
slaves eth0 eth1
bond-mode active backup
bond_primary eth1
```

Then, enable the interface using the `ifup` command:

```
sudo ifup bond0
```

Check for the status with the following command:

```
ifconfig bond0
```

The output is shown in the following screenshot:

```
skanda@server-ubuntu:~$ ifconfig bond0
bond0     Link encap:Ethernet  HWaddr 4a:fa:e1:73:d6:91
          inet addr:192.168.1.108  Bcast:192.168.1.255  Mask:255.255.255.0
          UP BROADCAST MASTER MULTICAST  MTU:1500  Metric:1
          RX packets:0 errors:0 dropped:0 overruns:0 frame:0
          TX packets:0 errors:0 dropped:0 overruns:0 carrier:0
          collisions:0 txqueuelen:0
          RX bytes:0 (0.0 B)  TX bytes:0 (0.0 B)
```

# DNS

We will set up the DNS server using **Berkeley Internet Name Daemon (BIND)**. Most of you might be familiar with DNS and its working. DNS is the largest distributed directory used for IP address lookup against domain names. Most administrators use BIND to run the DNS server. The version we will be using is BIND9.

BIND comes with three components: **named, resolver,** and **tools** such as **dig**. The named (pronounced *name-dee*) daemon does the job of answering. Resolver is the daemon that runs the queries to find IP addresses for domain names. It uses the `resolv.conf` directory for this purpose. Network administrators configure the `resolv.conf.d` folder. BIND provides tools such as dig to test DNS. We will look at more tools in a later section of this chapter.

# Setting up DNS

Install BIND on your Ubuntu Server using the following command:

```
sudo apt-get install bind9
```

You will see a message similar to what is shown in the following screenshot:

```
Get:1 http://us.archive.ubuntu.com/ubuntu/ trusty-updates/main bind9utils amd64
1:9.9.5.dfsg-3ubuntu0.2 [145 kB]
Get:2 http://us.archive.ubuntu.com/ubuntu/ trusty-updates/main bind9 amd64 1:9.9
.5.dfsg-3ubuntu0.2 [287 kB]
Fetched 432 kB in 1s (221 kB/s)
Preconfiguring packages ...
Selecting previously unselected package bind9utils.
(Reading database ... 82700 files and directories currently installed.)
Preparing to unpack .../bind9utils_1%3a9.9.5.dfsg-3ubuntu0.2_amd64.deb ...
Unpacking bind9utils (1:9.9.5.dfsg-3ubuntu0.2) ...
Selecting previously unselected package bind9.
Preparing to unpack .../bind9_1%3a9.9.5.dfsg-3ubuntu0.2_amd64.deb ...
Unpacking bind9 (1:9.9.5.dfsg-3ubuntu0.2) ...
Processing triggers for man-db (2.6.7.1-1ubuntu1) ...
Processing triggers for ureadahead (0.100.0-16) ...
ureadahead will be reprofiled on next reboot
Processing triggers for ufw (0.34~rc-0ubuntu2) ...
Setting up bind9utils (1:9.9.5.dfsg-3ubuntu0.2) ...
Setting up bind9 (1:9.9.5.dfsg-3ubuntu0.2) ...
Adding group `bind' (GID 115) ...
Done.
Adding system user `bind' (UID 106) ...
Adding new user `bind' (UID 106) with group `bind' ...
Not creating home directory `/var/cache/bind'.
wrote key file "/etc/bind/rndc.key"
#
 * Starting domain name service... bind9                                [ OK ]
Processing triggers for ureadahead (0.100.0-16) ...
Processing triggers for ufw (0.34~rc-0ubuntu2) ...
skanda@server-ubuntu:~$
```

For security reasons, it is recommended to run BIND as non-root user in isolation. This is called as **chroot environment**. Create a directory to put the files required for BIND that only the root can access. Stop the BIND service before making any changes:

```
sudo /etc/inti.d/bind9 stop
```

Once the service is stopped, go to the /etc/default/bind9 file and edit the following line:

```
OPTS=-u bind"
```

Change the preceding line to this:

```
OPTIONS="-u bind -t /var/lib/named"
```

Next, create the following directories under `/var/lib` for BIND to use:

- `/var/lib/named/etc`
- `/var/lib/named/dev`
- `/var/lib/named/var/cache/bind`
- `/var/lib/named/var/run/bind/run`

Now, execute the following commands:

```
sudo mkdir -p /var/lib/named/etc
sudo mkdir /var/lib/named/dev
sudo mkdir -p /var/lib/named/var/cache/bind
sudo mkdir -p /var/lib/named/var/cache/run
```

Move the config directory of BIND from `/etc` to `/var/lib/named/etc` using the following command:

```
sudo mv /etc/bind /var/lib/named/etc
```

This is shown in the following screenshot:

```
skanda@server-ubuntu:/etc/bind$ sudo mkdir -p /var/lib/named/etc
skanda@server-ubuntu:/etc/bind$ sudo mkdir /var/lib/named/dev
skanda@server-ubuntu:/etc/bind$ sudo mkdir -p /var/lib/named/var/cache/bind
skanda@server-ubuntu:/etc/bind$ sudo mkdir -p /var/lib/named/var/cache/run
skanda@server-ubuntu:/etc/bind$ mv /etc/bind /var/lib/named/etc/
mv: cannot move '/etc/bind' to '/var/lib/named/etc/bind': Permission denied
skanda@server-ubuntu:/etc/bind$ sudo mv /etc/bind /var/lib/named/etc/
skanda@server-ubuntu:/etc/bind$ _
```

Create a symbolic link from the old to the new BIND location:

```
sudo ln -s /var/lib/named/etc/bin/ /etc/bind
```

Create new devices `null` and `random` and edit the permissions:

```
sudo mknod /var/lib/named/dev/null c 1 3
sudo mknod /var/lib/named/dev/random c 1 38
sudo chmod 666 /var/lib/named/dev/null /var/lib/named/dev/random
sudo chown -R bind:bind /var/lib/named/var/*
sudo chown -R bind:bind /var/lib/named/etc/bind
```

Finally, start BIND with the following command:

```
sudo /etc/init.d/bind9 start
```

# Setting up primary and secondary DNS servers

Network administrators provide at least two DNS servers at the time of registration. You can make an exact duplicate of one DNS server and put it on a second server. Ideally, you should make one machine as primary server and the other as secondary server. Then, the secondary server can talk to primary server and update itself; this process is known as **zone transfer**. Whatever changes are done in the primary server will get reflected in the secondary server during the next poll. It is not a push process from primary, but rather a pull from secondary.

The following lines are for a secondary server in its `named.conf` file:

```
zone "ubuntuserver.org" {
    type slave;
    file "sec.ubuntuserver.org";
    masters {10.200.12.68;};
};
```

Pay close attention to the keyword `slave`. Also, a `masters` list is defined for the secondary slave. This has the IP address of the primary server that needs to be polled for updating itself. The IP address should be the same that is mentioned in the `resolv.conf` file of the primary server.

The `resolv.conf` file is used by clients to connect to DNS and `named.conf` is used by secondary servers to find the primary server.

The `named.conf` file on the primary name server will look like the following screenshot. This file is referring to four configuration files.

```
GNU nano 2.2.6       File: /var/lib/named/etc/bind/named.conf

// This is the primary configuration file for the BIND DNS server named.
//
// Please read /usr/share/doc/bind9/README.Debian.gz for information on the
// structure of BIND configuration files in Debian, *BEFORE* you customize
// this configuration file.
//
// If you are just adding zones, please do that in /etc/bind/named.conf.local

include "/etc/bind/named.conf.options";
include "/etc/bind/named.conf.local";
include "/etc/bind/named.conf.default-zones";

options {
pid-file"var/run/bind/run/named.pid";
directory "/etc/bind";
};

zone "." {
type hint;
file "db.root";
};

zone "0.0.127.in-addr.arpa" {
type master;
file "db.local";
                          [ Read 38 lines ]
^G Get Help  ^O WriteOut  ^R Read File  ^Y Prev Page  ^K Cut Text   ^C Cur Pos
^X Exit      ^J Justify   ^W Where Is   ^V Next Page  ^U UnCut Text ^T To Spell
```

## The hints file – zone "."

Hints file will have the names and address of root servers. named should know the address of these root servers as this is the starting point of any query.

## The local host file – zone "0.0.127.in-addr.arpa"

IP `127.0.0.1` is the address of the local system. DNS will get the address of the local system. It helps reduce the traffic and allow software without wanting to know if it is running on local or remote network.

# The reverse zone file – zone "24.126.10.in-addr.arpa"

The reverse zone file is like a mirror to the primary zone file. It has mappings of IP addresses to hostnames. Reverse zone files have extension as in-addr.arpa.

# The primary zone file – zone "ubuntuserver.org"

The primary zone files (primary zone is the same as forward zone) have mapping from hostnames to IP address. The information required to resolve the queries are contained in this file. It also includes the services that a particular server is offering to the Internet.

All these files are shown in the following screenshot:

```
  GNU nano 2.2.6      File: /var/lib/named/etc/bind/named.conf      Modified

pid-file"var/run/bind/run/named.pid";
directory "/etc/bind";
};

zone "." {
type hint;
file "db.root";
};

zone "0.0.127.in-addr.arpa" {
type master;
file "db.local";
};

zone "24.126.10.in-addr.arpa" {
type master;
file "pri.24.126.10.in-addr.arpa";
};

zone "ubuntuserver.org" {
type master;
file "pri.ubuntuserver.org";
};




^G Get Help   ^O WriteOut   ^R Read File  ^Y Prev Page  ^K Cut Text   ^C Cur Pos
^X Exit       ^J Justify    ^W Where Is   ^V Next Page  ^U UnCut Text ^T To Spell
```

The following record types can be seen in zone files:

- **SOA**: This means start of authority
- **NS**: This refers to the name server
- **MX**: This refers to the mail exchanger
- **A**: This refers to the hostname to address mapping
- **CNAME**: This refers to the canonical name or alias
- **PTR**: This is a pointer to map address to names

A typical `named.conf` file for a secondary name server will look like this:

```
GNU nano 2.2.6        File: /var/lib/named/etc/bind/named.conf        Modified

pid-file"var/run/bind/run/named.pid";
directory "/etc/bind";
};

zone "." {
type hint;
file "db.root";
};

zone "0.0.127.in-addr.arpa" {
type master;
file "db.local";
};

zone "ubuntuserver.org" {
type slave;
file "sec.ubuntuserver.org";
masters { 10.126.168.24; };
};




^G Get Help    ^O WriteOut    ^R Read File   ^Y Prev Page   ^K Cut Text    ^C Cur Pos
^X Exit        ^J Justify     ^W Where Is    ^V Next Page   ^U UnCut Text  ^T To Spell
```

Only the last part of the `named.conf` file differs from the one for the primary name server. The secondary name server will zone-transfer the information from the primary name server. Whenever a new serial number is seen on the primary name server, the secondary name server will update itself.

# The primary zone file

Most of the information that the DNS needs is contained in the primary zone file. Let's name our primary zone file as `pri.ubuntuserver.org`. Let's see what each part of the primary zone file signifies.

The first lines have the information required by secondary or slave servers:

```
@ IN SOA server1.ubuntuserver.org. root.localhost. (
        2015031106; serial-no
        28800; refresh, seconds
        7200; retry, seconds
        608440; expiry, seconds
        86400 ); minimum-TTL, seconds
;
```

Let's examine the components of the primary zone file:

- **Name**: This is the current name of the zone in `/etc/named.conf` and is referenced by @. The sign is called origin.

- **Class**: This is the DNS class. **IN** stands for **Internet Class**.

- **Type**: This is the resource record type; here, it is **SOA**.

- **Name server**: This is the fully qualified name for the primary name server. Pay close attention to the dot at the end of the name.

- **E-mail address**: Specify the e-mail address of the person who handles this domain. If you recall, @ is already used for origin. So the e-mail parts are separated with a dot. Also, an e-mail address must end with a dot.

SOA contains the following options which will help the slave server:

- **Serial number**: This is the serial number for the current configuration. Every time you change the configuration settings, you need to update this number. The format is usually YYYYMMDDxx with xx being a two digit number. Each serial number is higher than the previous one and usually the date is the date when it was changed. The secondary name servers will check the serial number each time they poll, and if the number is updated, they fetch the latest information and update themselves.

- **Refresh**: This value in seconds tells how often the secondary name servers should poll the primary name server to check for updates.

- **Retry**: If there is a connection failure, this number tells the time interval to try again.

- **Expiry**: This is the time that secondary servers need to contact the master before they trash the data it has. If the secondary server is unable to contact the master for latest information, it should direct its queries to the root. This value is specified in seconds.

- **Minimum Time to Live (TTL)**: This value is defined in seconds. This is the default time-to-live for this specific domain.

After SOA, the primary zone file contains hostnames:

```
NS server1.ubuntuserver.org.;
NS server2.ubuntuserver.org.;
```

These are the name servers for the domain. The next line is the MX record, which is the mail server for the domain:

```
MX 10 sever1.ubuntuserver.org.
```

The second word in the preceding line defines the priority of this particular server. Next, we have the A records. A records are the actual mapping from hostnames to IP addresses:

```
ubuntuserver.org    A    10.200.12.140
www                 A    10.200.12.140
server1             A    10.200.12.140
server2             A    10.200.12.160
```

Each hostname can have a maximum of one A record.

# The reverse zone file

Reverse zone files have a mapping from IP address to hostnames. They can be considered as mirrors to the primary zone files. The file lists the IP address first and then the name. This was used in earlier days to reject a service to some clients if they were not able to ping the domain in reverse. Now, this is used to stop e-mail spam by verifying the origins of an e-mail.

First, we create a reverse zone file for our server and put the entry into the `named.conf` file.

```
zone "162.240.10.in-addr.arpa" {
type master;
file "pri.162.240.10.in-addr.arpa";
};
```

The numbers in the IP address follow a pattern. They are in the reverse order. Our server `ubuntuserver.org` is in the `10.240.162` net and it is reversed to get `162.240.10`. Note that the domain `in-addr-arpa` is used by all reverse lookups as the top-level domain. Let's look at a sample reverse zone file now.

We name our file `pri.162.240.10.in-addr.arpa` and the file will be in the same directory where our primary zone file was. Both the zone files look similar at the beginning:

```
@ IN SOA server1.ubuntuserver.org. root.localhost. (
    2015031117; serial-no
    28800; refresh, seconds
    7200; retry seconds
    604800; expiry, seconds
    86400 ); minimum-TTl, seconds
;
  NS server1.ubuntuserver.org;
  NS server2.ubuntuserver.org;
```

In the reverse zone file, there are no A, MX, or CNAME records. We have the PTR records.

# PTR records

PTR are the pointers to a domain name. Now, we will create a PTR record with our `ubuntuserver.org` address. The zone in primary section showed that the IP address for our `ubuntuserver.org` server was `10.200.12.140`. The PTR record specifies the last part of the IP address; here, it is `140` and is defined as follows:

```
140        PTR     ubuntuserver.org.
```

There should be exactly one PTR for every IP address in the domain. Place the PTR records after the name servers in the reverse zone file.

# Summary

In this chapter, we studied various networking concepts. We covered IP address allocation: auto or static. Then, we discussed network sniffing with tcpdump. Next, we talked about binding and bonding. DNS was one of the main topics of this chapter. Then, we saw how to set up the primary and secondary name servers and discussed primary and reverse zone files.

In the next chapter, we will study network authentication, the SSH client, and the SSH server.

# 3
# Network Authentication

In the previous chapter, you learned about setting up the network and topics such DHCP, DNS, and their configuration. In this chapter, we will discuss setting up authentication for users over a network and how to allow users to log in and work on remote servers, to avail of services offered by those servers. The topics covered in this chapter are as follows:

- OpenLDAP
- Kerberos
- Kerberos with LDAP
- Public and private keys
- Passwordless SSH and sshd

## OpenLDAP

**LDAP** is the acronym for **Lightweight Directory Access Protocol**, which provides functionality for connecting to, searching, and modifying the Internet directories. Ubuntu's implementation of LDAP is **OpenLDAP**, the protocol used to access the LDAP directories. We will also discuss how to install OpenLDAP, how to enable logging, how to modify the database and configuration, access control, user and group management, and TLS.

## Installation

We need to install two packages, **slapd** and **ldap-utilities**, for OpenLDAP. slapd will also create a working configuration. A database instance is created to store the configuration data. It will pick the suffix for DN from the hostname domain. This can be changed by changing the /etc/hosts file.

For example, the suffix dc=myubuntu,dc=com will mean the hosts file looks similar to this:

```
GNU nano 2.2.6                  File: /etc/hosts                        Modified

127.0.0.1          localhost
127.0.1.1          hostname.myubuntu.com      hostname
```

The command to install the packages is as follows:

```
sudo apt-get install slapd ldap-utils
```

The configuration database should be visible now under the /etc/ldap/slapd.d folder; it's a collection of text-based **LDAP Data Interchange Format** (LDIF) files. While installing, it will prompt for a new administrative password for the rootDN of this database. You will see something similar to the following screenshot. This is the **directory information tree** (DIT) that is set up during installation.

```
root@server-ubuntu:/etc/ldap/slapd.d/cn=config# ls -ltr
total 28
-rw------- 1 openldap openldap  657 Mar 25 10:00 olcDatabase={-1}frontend.ldif
-rw------- 1 openldap openldap  513 Mar 25 10:00 olcDatabase={0}config.ldif
-rw------- 1 openldap openldap  378 Mar 25 10:00 cn=schema.ldif
-rw------- 1 openldap openldap 1047 Mar 25 10:00 olcDatabase={1}hdb.ldif
-rw------- 1 openldap openldap  396 Mar 25 10:00 olcBackend={0}hdb.ldif
drwxr-x--- 2 openldap openldap 4096 Mar 25 10:00 cn=schema
-rw------- 1 openldap openldap  436 Mar 25 10:00 cn=module{0}.ldif
root@server-ubuntu:/etc/ldap/slapd.d/cn=config# ls -ltr cn\=schema
total 40
-rw------- 1 openldap openldap 15527 Mar 25 10:00 cn={0}core.ldif
-rw------- 1 openldap openldap  2855 Mar 25 10:00 cn={3}inetorgperson.ldif
-rw------- 1 openldap openldap  6491 Mar 25 10:00 cn={2}nis.ldif
-rw------- 1 openldap openldap 11361 Mar 25 10:00 cn={1}cosine.ldif
root@server-ubuntu:/etc/ldap/slapd.d/cn=config#
```

The **slapd-config** database should not be edited directly, as the changes there might corrupt and make the service unusable; instead, use the LDAP utils. You will see something similar when you view the DIT for slapd-config using the LDAP protocol. The command to do this is as follows:

```
sudo ldapsearch -Q -LLL -Y EXTERNAL -H ldapi:/// -b cn=config dn
```

The resulting screen is shown here:

```
skanda@myubuntu:~$ sudo ldapsearch -Q -LLL -Y EXTERNAL -H ldapi:/// -b cn=config
 dn
[sudo] password for skanda:
dn: cn=config

dn: cn=module{0},cn=config

dn: cn=schema,cn=config

dn: cn={0}core,cn=schema,cn=config

dn: cn={1}cosine,cn=schema,cn=config

dn: cn={2}nis,cn=schema,cn=config

dn: cn={3}inetorgperson,cn=schema,cn=config

dn: olcBackend={0}hdb,cn=config

dn: olcDatabase={-1}frontend,cn=config

dn: olcDatabase={0}config,cn=config

dn: olcDatabase={1}hdb,cn=config

skanda@myubuntu:~$ _
```

Let's understand the entries in the previous screenshot and their meanings:

| Entry | Description |
| --- | --- |
| cn=config | Global settings |
| cn=module{0},cn=config | A dynamically loaded module |
| cn=schema,cn=config | Contains hardcoded system-level schema |
| cn={0}core,cn=schema,cn=config | The hard coded core schema |
| cn={1}cosine,cn=schema,cn=config | The cosine schema |
| cn={2}nis,cn=schema,cn=config | The nis schema |
| cn={3}inetorgperson,cn=schema,cn=config | The inetorgperson schema |
| olcBackend={0}hdb,cn=config | The hdb backend storage |
| olcDatabase={-1}frontend,cn=config | Frontend database and default settings for other databases |
| olcDatabase={0}config,con=config | The slapd configuration database |
| olcDatabase={1}hdb,cn=config | Users' database instance |

# Populating the database

Adding content to the database is fairly simple: first create a LDIF file and then use the LDAP utilities to add it. Create a LDIF file similar to the following with the name `new_content.ldif`:

```
dn: ou=People,dc=myubuntu,dc=com
objectClass: organizationalUnit
ou: People
dn: ou=Groups,dc=myubuntu,dc=com
objectClass: organizationalUnit
ou: Groups
dn: cn=dev,ou=Groups,dc=myubuntu,dc=com
objectClass: posixGroup
cn: dev
gidNumber: 5500
dn: uid=skanda,ou=People,dc=myubuntu,dc=com
objectClass: inetOrgPerson
objectClass: posixAccount
objectClass: shadowAccount
uid: skanda
sn: Bhargav
givenName: skanda
cn: skanda Bhargav
displayName: skanda Bhargav
uidNumber: 10400
gidNumber: 5400
userPassword: skandapass
gecos: skanda Bhargav
loginShell: /bin/bash
homeDirectory: /home/skanda
```

The command to add this to the database is as follows:

```
ldapadd -x -D cn=admin,dc=myubuntu,dc=com -W -f new_content.ldif
```

Also, you can check if it was added correctly using the following command:

```
ldapsearch -x -LLL -b dc=myubuntu,dc=com
```

You will see something similar to the following screenshot:

```
skanda@UbuntuServer:~$ sudo ldapsearch -x -LLL -b dc=myubuntu,dc=com
dn: dc=myubuntu,dc=com
objectClass: top
objectClass: dcObject
objectClass: organization
o: myubuntu.com
dc: myubuntu

dn: cn=admin,dc=myubuntu,dc=com
objectClass: simpleSecurityObject
objectClass: organizationalRole
cn: admin
description: LDAP administrator

dn: ou=People,dc=myubuntu,dc=com
objectClass: organizationalUnit
ou: People

dn: ou=Groups,dc=myubuntu,dc=com
objectClass: organizationalUnit
ou: Groups

skanda@UbuntuServer:~$ _
```

# Logging

You need to manually enable the logging for slapd to get more than just minimal logs. Out of the many logging levels provided by slapd, we will try out stats.

First create the file `logging.ldif`:

```
dn: cn=config
changetype: modify
add: olcLogLevel
olcLogLevel: stats
```

Now, change it using the LDAP utility as follows:

```
sudo ldapmodify -Q -Y EXTERNAL -H ldapi:/// -f logging.ldif
```

# Access control

**Access control lists** (ACL) define the configuration for the type of access the users should get. During the installation of the slapd package, some of the ALC were automatically set up.

To view the current access, use the following command:

```
sudo ldapsearch -Q -LLL -Y EXTERNAL -H ldapi:/// -b cn=config
'(olcDatabase={1}hdb)'
```

The output is shown in the following screenshot:

```
skanda@UbuntuServer:~$ sudo ldapsearch -Q -LLL -Y EXTERNAL -H ldapi:/// -b cn=co
nfig '(olcDatabase={1}hdb)'
dn: olcDatabase={1}hdb,cn=config
objectClass: olcDatabaseConfig
objectClass: olcHdbConfig
olcDatabase: {1}hdb
olcDbDirectory: /var/lib/ldap
olcSuffix: dc=myubuntu,dc=com
olcAccess: {0}to attrs=userPassword,shadowLastChange by self write by anonymou
 s auth by dn="cn=admin,dc=myubuntu,dc=com" write by * none
olcAccess: {1}to dn.base="" by * read
olcAccess: {2}to * by self write by dn="cn=admin,dc=myubuntu,dc=com" write by
 * read
olcLastMod: TRUE
olcRootDN: cn=admin,dc=myubuntu,dc=com
olcRootPW: {SSHA}rUm9vRVAYJ18mijvZOZ5YOTMR4+FIvEr
olcDbCheckpoint: 512 30
olcDbConfig: {0}set_cachesize 0 2097152 0
olcDbConfig: {1}set_lk_max_objects 1500
olcDbConfig: {2}set_lk_max_locks 1500
olcDbConfig: {3}set_lk_max_lockers 1500
olcDbIndex: objectClass eq

skanda@UbuntuServer:~$
```

The olcAccess line in the preceding output can be understood as follows:

```
    to attrs=userPassword
        by selfwrite
        by anonymous auth
        by dn="cn=admin,dc=myubuntu,dc=com" write
        by *none
    to attrs=shadowLastChange
        by self write
        by anonymous auth
        by dn="cn=admin,dc=example,dc=com" write
        by * none
```

The explanation for the preceding lines is as follows:

- The `userPassword` attribute is provided with `auth` for anonymous users for the initial connection
- The authentication is possible, as all users have read access
- The rootDN has complete access to the `userPassword` attribute
- If other users need to change their password, then `shadowLastChange` should be accessible to the users after authentication

Now, let's check the frontend database access using the following command:

```
sudo ldapsearch -Q -LLL -Y EXTERNAL -H ldapi:/// -b cn=config
'(olcDatabase={-1}frontend)'
```

The output should be similar to the one shown in the following screenshot:

```
skanda@UbuntuServer:~$ sudo ldapsearch -Q -LLL -Y EXTERNAL -H ldapi:/// -b cn=co
nfig '(olcDatabase={-1}frontend)'
dn: olcDatabase={-1}frontend,cn=config
objectClass: olcDatabaseConfig
objectClass: olcFrontendConfig
olcDatabase: {-1}frontend
olcAccess: {0}to * by dn.exact=gidNumber=0+uidNumber=0,cn=peercred,cn=external
,cn=auth manage by * break
olcAccess: {1}to dn.exact="" by * read
olcAccess: {2}to dn.base="cn=Subschema" by * read
olcSizeLimit: 500

skanda@UbuntuServer:~$ _
```

To display the ACL of the slapd-config database, use the following command:

```
sudo ldapsearch -Q -LLL -Y EXTERNAL -H ldapi:/// -b cn=config
'(olcDatabase={0}config)'
```

The output is shown in the following screenshot:

```
skanda@UbuntuServer:~$ sudo ldapsearch -Q -LLL -Y EXTERNAL -H ldapi:/// -b cn=co
nfig '(olcDatabase={0}config)'
[sudo] password for skanda:
dn: olcDatabase={0}config,cn=config
objectClass: olcDatabaseConfig
olcDatabase: {0}config
olcAccess: {0}to * by dn.exact=gidNumber=0+uidNumber=0,cn=peercred,cn=external
,cn=auth manage by * break

skanda@UbuntuServer:~$
```

To view all the ACLs, use the following command:

```
sudo ldapsearch -Q -LLL -Y EXTERNAL -H ldapi:/// -b cn=config
'(olcAccess=*)'
```

The output is shown in the following screenshot:

```
skanda@UbuntuServer:~$ sudo ldapsearch -Q -LLL -Y EXTERNAL -H ldapi:/// -b cn=co
nfig '(olcAccess=*)'
dn: olcDatabase={-1}frontend,cn=config
objectClass: olcDatabaseConfig
objectClass: olcFrontendConfig
olcDatabase: {-1}frontend
olcAccess: {0}to * by dn.exact=gidNumber=0+uidNumber=0,cn=peercred,cn=external
,cn=auth manage by * break
olcAccess: {1}to dn.exact="" by * read
olcAccess: {2}to dn.base="cn=Subschema" by * read
olcSizeLimit: 500

dn: olcDatabase={0}config,cn=config
objectClass: olcDatabaseConfig
olcDatabase: {0}config
olcAccess: {0}to * by dn.exact=gidNumber=0+uidNumber=0,cn=peercred,cn=external
,cn=auth manage by * break

dn: olcDatabase={1}hdb,cn=config
objectClass: olcDatabaseConfig
objectClass: olcHdbConfig
olcDatabase: {1}hdb
olcDbDirectory: /var/lib/ldap
olcSuffix: dc=myubuntu,dc=com
olcAccess: {0}to attrs=userPassword,shadowLastChange by self write by anonymou
s auth by dn="cn=admin,dc=myubuntu,dc=com" write by * none
olcAccess: {1}to dn.base="" by * read
olcAccess: {2}to * by self write by dn="cn=admin,dc=myubuntu,dc=com" write by
* read
olcLastMod: TRUE
```

# Kerberos

Kerberos is used to enable security for machines and users. Kerberos is easy to set up with LDAP. A user requests a **ticket-granting ticket (TGT)** from the **key distribution center (KDC)** when they log in. The KDC checks for the username in the database, fetches the key and returns TGT with the key. At the client machine, it is decrypted with the help of user password. The password is never sent across the network. Once the system is authenticated, all the services can use it and the user is not required to authenticate again until the TGT is expired.

# Installation

Let's look at the installation and configuration of the Kerberos server. The command to install Kerberos on the Ubuntu Server is as follows:

```
sudo apt-get install krb5-kdc krb5-admin-server libkrb5-dev krb5-config
krb5-user krb5-clients libkadm55
```

During the installation, the terminal will prompt for the **hostname** and the **realm** on which you wish to install the Kerberos server. The last screen will look something similar to the one shown here:

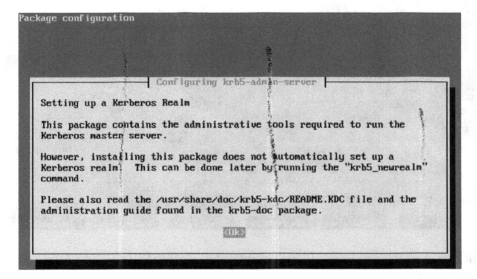

Now, we need to edit the `/etc/krb5.conf` file and change the following settings:

```
MYUBUNTU.COM = {
kdc = UBUNTUSERVER.MYUBUNTU.CON:88
admin_server = UBUNTUSERVER.MYUBUNTU.CON:749
default_domain = MYUBUNTU.COM
}
```

This is shown in the following screenshot:

You need to specify the path for the logging and change the `krb4_convert` switch to `false`. The following screenshot has the values:

```
GNU nano 2.2.6            File: /etc/krb5.conf              Modified


[domain_realm]
        .ubuntu.com = UBUNTU.COM
        ubuntu.com = UBUNTU.COM
        .mit.edu = ATHENA.MIT.EDU
        mit.edu = ATHENA.MIT.EDU
        .media.mit.edu = MEDIA-LAB.MIT.EDU
        media.mit.edu = MEDIA-LAB.MIT.EDU
        .csail.mit.edu = CSAIL.MIT.EDU
        csail.mit.edu = CSAIL.MIT.EDU
        .whoi.edu = ATHENA.MIT.EDU
        whoi.edu = ATHENA.MIT.EDU
        .stanford.edu = stanford.edu
        .slac.stanford.edu = SLAC.STANFORD.EDU
        .toronto.edu = UTORONTO.CA
        .utoronto.ca = UTORONTO.CA

[login]
        krb4_convert = false
        krb4_get_tickets = false
[logging]
        kdc= FILE:/var/log/kerberos/krb5kdc.log
        admin_server= FILE:/var/log/kerberos/kadmin.log
        default = FILE:/var/log/kerberos/krb5lib.log

^G Get Help   ^O WriteOut   ^R Read File  ^Y Prev Page  ^K Cut Text   ^C Cur Pos
^X Exit       ^J Justify    ^W Where Is   ^V Next Page  ^U UnCut Text ^  To Spell
```

It's time to start the server now. The command to start the KDC and Kerberos admin server is as follows:

```
sudo /etc/init.d/krb5-admin-server start; sudo /etc/init.d/krb5-kdc start
```

You may see the following error on the terminal:

```
kadmind: No such file or directory while initializing, aborting
```

We will now solve this issue. The first step is to create a new realm with the following command:

```
sudo krb5_newrealm
```

It should be run only once, and it will ask for a master password. Be sure to remember this password. You will see a screen similar to the one shown here:

```
skanda@UbuntuServer:~$ sudo krb5_newrealm
This script should be run on the master KDC/admin server to initialize
a Kerberos realm.  It will ask you to type in a master key password.
This password will be used to generate a key that is stored in
/etc/krb5kdc/stash.  You should try to remember this password, but it
is much more important that it be a strong password than that it be
remembered.  However, if you lose the password and /etc/krb5kdc/stash,
you cannot decrypt your Kerberos database.
Loading random data
Initializing database '/var/lib/krb5kdc/principal' for realm 'MYUBUNTU.COM',
master key name 'K/M@MYUBUNTU.COM'
You will be prompted for the database Master Password.
It is important that you NOT FORGET this password.
Enter KDC database master key:
Re-enter KDC database master key to verify:
 * Starting Kerberos KDC krb5kdc                                    [ OK ]
 * Starting Kerberos administrative servers kadmind                 [ OK ]


Now that your realm is set up you may wish to create an administrative
principal using the addprinc subcommand of the kadmin.local program.
Then, this principal can be added to /etc/krb5kdc/kadm5.acl so that
you can use the kadmin program on other computers.  Kerberos admin
principals usually belong to a single user and end in /admin.  For
example, if jruser is a Kerberos administrator, then in addition to
the normal jruser principal, a jruser/admin principal should be
created.

Don't forget to set up DNS information so your clients can find your
KDC and admin servers.  Doing so is documented in the administration
```

Create the following directories and change the permission:

```
sudo mkdir /var/log/kerberos
sudo touch /var/log/kerberos/{krb5kdc,kadmin,krb5lib}.log
sudo chmod -R 750  /var/log/kerberos
```

Change the authorization for the admin in the `/etc/krb5kdc/kadm5.acl` file:

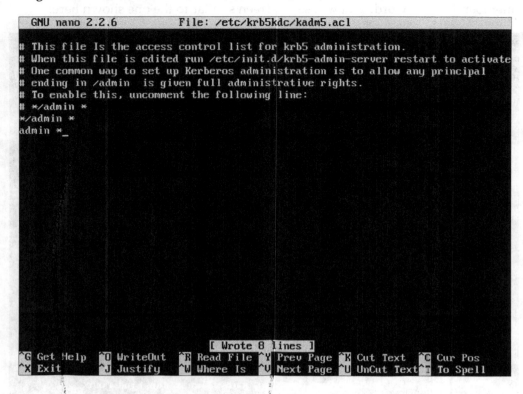

Then, restart the services KDC and Kerberos admin server. The command to do this is as follows:

```
sudo /etc/init.d/krb5-admin-server restart; sudo /etc/init.d/krb5-kdc
restart
```

If all goes well, you will see the following screen:

```
skanda@UbuntuServer:~$ sudo /etc/init.d/krb5-admin-server restart ; sudo /etc/in
it.d/krb5-kdc restart
 * Restarting Kerberos administrative servers kadmind                    [ OK ]
 * Restarting Kerberos KDC krb5kdc                                       [ OK ]
skanda@UbuntuServer:~$
```

# Database setup

For the initial setup, we have to authenticate and make the changes to the database locally as **root**. This is because Kerberos is not yet available and we cannot populate the database using the Kerberos service. Once the initial setup is done and the admin user is set up, all subsequent changes to the database will be handled via the Kerberos service using the `kadmin -p` command.

Log in as root and execute the following commands to perform the initial setup using `admin.local`. The first command is to create a database, and the next command is for admin changes and the last one is to add a new key to the keytab:

```
kadmin.local -q "ktadd -k /etc/krb5kdc/kadm5.keytab kadmin/admin"

kadmin.local -q "ktadd -k /etc/krb5kdc/kadm5.keytab kadmin/changepw"

kadmin.local -q "addprinc krbadmin@MYUBUNTU.COM"
```

Once the commands are successful, you will see a screen similar to the one shown in the following screenshot. You will be asked to enter a password for the new user `krbadmin`.

```
root@UbuntuServer:/etc/krb5kdc# kadmin.local -q "ktadd -k /etc/krb5kdc/kadm5.key
tab kadmin/admin"
Authenticating as principal root/admin@MYUBUNTU.COM with password.
Entry for principal kadmin/admin with kvno 2, encryption type aes256-cts-hmac-sh
a1-96 added to keytab WRFILE:/etc/krb5kdc/kadm5.keytab.
Entry for principal kadmin/admin with kvno 2, encryption type arcfour-hmac added
 to keytab WRFILE:/etc/krb5kdc/kadm5.keytab.
Entry for principal kadmin/admin with kvno 2, encryption type des3-cbc-sha1 adde
d to keytab WRFILE:/etc/krb5kdc/kadm5.keytab.
Entry for principal kadmin/admin with kvno 2, encryption type des-cbc-crc added
to keytab WRFILE:/etc/krb5kdc/kadm5.keytab.
root@UbuntuServer:/etc/krb5kdc# kadmin.local -q "ktadd -k /etc/krb5kdc/kadm5.key
tab kadmin/changepw"
Authenticating as principal root/admin@MYUBUNTU.COM with password.
Entry for principal kadmin/changepw with kvno 2, encryption type aes256-cts-hmac
-sha1-96 added to keytab WRFILE:/etc/krb5kdc/kadm5.keytab.
Entry for principal kadmin/changepw with kvno 2, encryption type arcfour-hmac ad
ded to keytab WRFILE:/etc/krb5kdc/kadm5.keytab.
Entry for principal kadmin/changepw with kvno 2, encryption type des3-cbc-sha1 a
dded to keytab WRFILE:/etc/krb5kdc/kadm5.keytab.
Entry for principal kadmin/changepw with kvno 2, encryption type des-cbc-crc add
ed to keytab WRFILE:/etc/krb5kdc/kadm5.keytab.
root@UbuntuServer:/etc/krb5kdc# kadmin.local -q "addprinc krbadmin@MYUBUNTU.COM"
Authenticating as principal root/admin@MYUBUNTU.COM with password.
WARNING: no policy specified for krbadmin@MYUBUNTU.COM; defaulting to no policy
Enter password for principal "krbadmin@MYUBUNTU.COM":
Re-enter password for principal "krbadmin@MYUBUNTU.COM":
Principal "krbadmin@MYUBUNTU.COM" created.
root@UbuntuServer:/etc/krb5kdc# _
```

Make the appropriate changes in the `/etc/krb5kdc/kadm5.acl` file to allow the newly created admin to have all the access. Refer to the following screenshot:

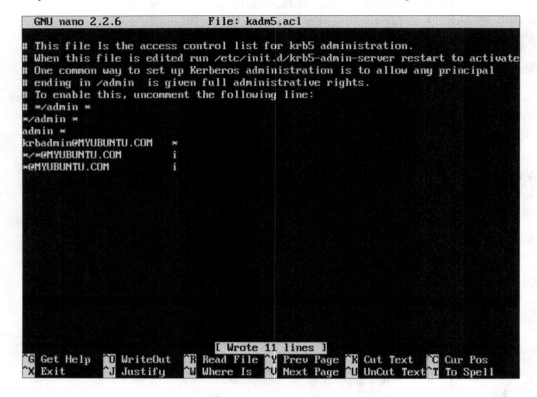

Edit the `/etc/krb5kdc/kdc.conf` file, set MYUBUNTU.COM as the realm, and ensure that the database, keytab, stash, and ACL location match as per the database creation. The following screenshot can guide you:

```
root@UbuntuServer:/etc/krb5kdc# /etc/init.d/krb5-admin-server restart
 * Restarting Kerberos administrative servers kadmind                    [ OK ]
root@UbuntuServer:/etc/krb5kdc# cat /etc/krb5kdc/kdc.conf
[kdcdefaults]
    kdc_ports = 750,88

[realms]
    MYUBUNTU.COM = {
        database_name = /var/lib/krb5kdc/principal
        admin_keytab = FILE:/etc/krb5kdc/kadm5.keytab
        acl_file = /etc/krb5kdc/kadm5.acl
        key_stash_file = /etc/krb5kdc/stash
        kdc_ports = 750,88
        max_life = 10h 0m 0s
        max_renewable_life = 7d 0h 0m 0s
        master_key_type = des3-hmac-sha1
        supported_enctypes = aes256-cts:normal arcfour-hmac:normal des3-hmac-sha
1:normal des-cbc-crc:normal des:normal des:v4 des:norealm des:onlyrealm des:afs3
        default_principal_flags = +preauth
    }
root@UbuntuServer:/etc/krb5kdc# _
```

Then, restart the Kerberos server to apply the new controls. The command to do so is as follows:

```
sudo /etc/init.d/krb5-admin-server restart; sudo /etc/init.d/krb5-kdc
restart
```

Now, let's test and ensure our Kerberos server is up and running properly. We will no longer use kadmin.local; all the changes will be via the krbadmin user we created:

```
kadmin -p krbadmin
kinit krbadmin
klist
```

You will be asked to enter password for the krbadmin user, and then you will see a list of authorized tickets. Here's a screenshot of the kadmin console:

```
skanda@UbuntuServer:~$ kadmin -p krbadmin
Couldn't open log file /var/log/kerberos/kadmin.log: Permission denied
Authenticating as principal krbadmin with password.
Password for krbadmin@MYUBUNTU.COM:
kadmin:  listprincs
K/M@MYUBUNTU.COM
kadmin/admin@MYUBUNTU.COM
kadmin/changepw@MYUBUNTU.COM
kadmin/ubuntuserver.myubuntu.com@MYUBUNTU.COM
krbadmin@MYUBUNTU.COM
krbtgt/MYUBUNTU.COM@MYUBUNTU.COM
kadmin:
```

# Setting up the Kerberos client

The following command will help you install the client and also the ntpdate packages. The latter package is to make sure the time is synchronized for the client and server authentication to be successful.

```
sudo apt-get install krb5-user ntpdate
```

Once the packages are installed, you need to modify the /etc/krb5.conf file to match the configuration in your server. For example, the following will be the contents of the configuration file for the client:

```
[libdefaults]
        default_realm = MYUBUNTU.COM
[realms]
        MYUBUNTU.COM = {
          kdc = ubuntuserver.myubuntu.com
```

```
            admin_server = ubuntuserver.myubuntu.com
    }
[domain_realm]
myubuntu.com = MYUBUNTU.COM
.myubuntu.com = MYUBUNTU.COM
```

# Kerberos SSH and logon

In this section, we will set up both the client and server to use Kerberos for SSH logon. We will use PAM for local as well as SSH logons. The command to install Kerberos is as follows:

```
sudo apt-get install libpam-krb5 openssh-server libsasl2-dev libsasl2-
modules-gssapi-mit
```

Next, we need to edit the /etc/pam.d/common-auth and /etc/pam.d/common-session files as follows:

```
skanda@UbuntuServer:~$ tail /etc/pam.d/common-auth
# prime the stack with a positive return value if there isn't one already;
# this avoids us returning an error just because nothing sets a success code
# since the modules above will each just jump around
# auth     required                        pam_permit.so
# and here are more per-package modules (the "Additional" block)
auth       optional                        pam_cap.so
# end of pam-auth-update config
auth       sufficient      pam_krb5.so     use_first_pass  ignore_root_forwardable
auth       required        pam_unix.so     nullok_secure   try_first_pass

skanda@UbuntuServer:~$ tail /etc/pam.d/common-session
# See "man pam_umask".
### session optional                       pam_umask.so
# and here are more per-package modules (the "Additional" block)
### session     optional                   pam_krb5.so minimum_uid=1000
### session     required    pam_unix.so
### session     optional    pam_systemd.so

session         sufficient  pam_unix.so
session         suffieicnt  pam_krb5.so     ignore_root
# end of pam-auth-update config
skanda@UbuntuServer:~$
```

Now, let's set up SSH login to use Kerberos. Edit the `/etc/ssh/ssh_config` file:

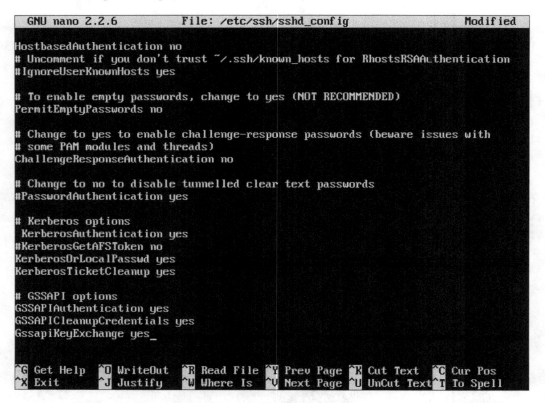

Pay close attention to `Kerberos options` and `GSSAPI options` in this file. Next, edit the `/etc/ssh/ssh_config` file (not the `sshd_config` file!) and set the following flags:

```
GSSAPIAuthentication yes
GSSAPIDelegateCredentials yes
```

These changes need to be made in all the machines that you intend to use for SSH with Kerberos enabled. Then, restart the SSH server in every machine that you have edited for the change to take effect:

```
sudo /etc/init.d/ssh restart
```

Next, you need to add the keytab on the client so that SSH transfers the credentials to Kerberos. Run the following commands in the client machine:

```
kadmin -p krbadmin
kadmin: addprinc -randkey host/client.myubuntu.com
kadmin: ktadd host/client.myubuntu.com
kadmin: addprinc test@MYUBUNTU.com
```

You can test this setup by logging in with the new test user via SSH. The machine will be Kerberized on successful login.

# Integrating LDAP with Kerberos

In this section, we will discuss the process to integrate LDAP with Kerberos in the Ubuntu Server.

# Installation

In this section, we will discuss how to set up LDAP with Kerberos. First, add the LDAP admin and LDAP server to the Kerberos server using the following command via `kadmin`:

```
kadmin - p kradmin
```

Inside `kdamin`, execute the following commands:

```
kadmin:    add princ ldapadm@MYUBUNTU.COM
kadmin:    add princ -randkey ldap/server.myubuntu.com
kadmin:    ktadd -k /etc/ldap/ldap.keytab  ldap/server.myubuntu.com
```

The first command will create the LDAP admin user, and you will be asked for a password. We then create a separate keytab at the `/etc/ldap/ldap.keytab` location so as to keep LDAP different from the system-specific keytab. Then, change the file permissions and owner so that LDAP becomes the owner of this keytab:

```
chown openldap:openldap /etc/ldap/ldap.keytab
```

Ensure that the slapd process is looking for the right keytab, and add this line to the `/etc/default/slapd` file:

```
    export KRB5_KTNAME=/etc/ldap/ldap.keytab
```

Restart the slapd server to make sure the changes take effect:

```
sudo /etc/init.d/slapd restart
```

# Database setup

We have seen the LDAP admin setup in the previous sections of this chapter. Now, we add the ldapadm user into the database. First, create a file with the name setup.ldif. We will use the base domain (here, dc=myubuntu).

Use the ldapadd command to add the setup.ldif file is as follows:

```
ldapadd -c -D "cn=admin,dc=myubuntu,dc=com" -W -f setup.ldif
# setup.ldif
dn: dc=myubuntu,dc=com
objectclass: organization
objectclass: dcObject
objectclass: top
o: myubuntu Company
dc: myubuntu
description: root entry
dn: ou=people,dc=myubuntu,dc=com
objectclass: organizationalUnit
ou: people
description: Users
dn: uid=ldapadm,ou=people,dc=myubuntu,dc=com
objectClass: inetOrgPerson
objectClass: posixAccount
objectClass: shadowAccount
cn: LDAP admin account
uid: ldapadm
uidNumber: 1002
gidNumber: 100
homeDirectory: /etc/ldap
loginShell: /bin/false
```

Restart the slapd process. From next time, you can use the `kinit ldapadm` command to add, modify, or delete entries:

```
kinit username; ldapsearch -H ldaps://server.myubuntu.com
```

Test the setup using the preceding command. If it does not work, you may need to check for any of these conditions to troubleshoot:

- The `/etc/ldap/cacert.pem` file should be readable by all; change permissions if it is not.

- Check `/etc/hosts` to make sure the hostname is resolved correctly. The client will try for `server.myubuntu.com`, so this should be present in the hosts file.

- If you encounter the `key version for principal in keytable is incorrect` error, it means the keytab at Kerberos server and master have a mismatch. Run the following commands from the LDAP host:

```
kterm ldap/server.myubuntu.com

delprinc ldap/server.myubuntu.com

addprinc -randkey ldap/server.myubuntu.com

ktadd ldap/server.myubuntu.com
```

# OpenSSH, public, and private keys – passwordless SSH

It's time now to look at SSH and its usage.

## The SSH client and the server

The **SSH** (acronym for **secure shell**) is made of a set of tools for secure and encrypted connections between server and clients. The older tools such as telnet, rlogin, and rsh should be discarded as they are prone to hacks as they do not encrypt the login session thereby leaving your username and password vulnerable. SSH is different as it encrypts the connection and also it authenticates both ways.

The transport layer in the network stack is encrypted with a cryptographic handshake and hence the connection is secure. The authentication is via either user ID/password or a public/private key between the server and client.

Install the client and server in your machines using the following commands:

```
sudo apt-get install openssh-client
sudo apt-get install openssh-server
```

The server package needs to be installed only on those machines to which you want to log in to.

# Setting up passwordless SSH

The normal practice among users is to SSH into a machine using the following command syntax:

```
ssh user@192.168.1.6
```

Here, `user` is the user ID and after hitting the *Enter* key, the user is expected to enter the password. We will now see how to log in to a machine using the public/private key pair. First, generate the keys at the client machine. The command to generate both private and public keys is the same. It will create the keys by default in the user's home directory under the `.ssh` folder:

```
ssh-keygen -t rsa
```

So, for me, with username `skanda`, the private and public keys will be stored in the folder `/home/skanda/.ssh`. If you list the directory, you will see two files: `id_rsa` and `id_rsa.pub`. Here, the one with the `.pub` extension is the public key, which we will exchange with other systems for authentication. The private key will stay within the system and will be used to authenticate the incoming connections. The folder is hidden and hence is preceded with a period(.). The permissions for the `./ssh` folder should be 700.

Next, we need to copy this user's public key to the server to which we intend to establish a secured passwordless connection. The preferred and recommended way is to use the `ssh-copyid` command. You may use `scp` too, but then you need to be careful so as to append the key to the file called `authorized_keys` at the server and not overwrite it. The command is as follows:

```
ssh-copyid -i .ssh/id_rsa.pub server@192.168.1.5
```

Your client can now authenticate and log in to the server machine without the need of any password. The same process needs to be followed for other machines as well.

To troubleshoot, use the following command to diagnose the errors:

```
ssh -v
```

The preceding command will present the debug information about the connection attempt.

# Disabling password authentication

Many people use weak passwords. It is possible that a hacker may be able to get a password by guessing when he gets hold of a SSH server. Also, if you want to make sure only the systems you authorize should be used to connect to the server, disabling the password-based authentication must be practiced. The user will be discouraged from using a password to log in, thereby making your systems secure. It would be recommended to use SSH key-based authentication.

To disable the password-based authentication, modify the /etc/ssh/ssh_config file as follows:

```
PasswordAuthentication no
```

Now, only the system whose public key is shared with your server will be able to authenticate from the authorized user ID.

# Allowing or denying users to SSH

You can control which users or groups are allowed to SSH into your server. This will ensure that people with weak security practices and people who do not need SSH access to the server can be denied.

To allow a user be able to SSH, we need to change the following line in /etc/ssh/ssh_config, with the following value:

```
AllowUsers Skanda Client
```

The preceding line means that users Skanda and Client are allowed to SSH into the server. All other users will be denied. However, to deny a few users and allow all others, use the following line:

```
DenyUsers Bhargav Guest
```

# Greeting users with a banner

You can welcome and display server-specific information to the users with a banner. Each time a user logs into the server, this message can be displayed. This is usually helpful when you want to warn the user about a special server, such as the production server where the user should not be modifying anything. First, change the line in the /etc/ssh/ssh_config file as follows:

```
Banner /etc/issue.net
```

Next, go and edit the /etc/issue.net file and fill in the relevant information. That's it, all the users logging in will get the message at the start of their session. This does not affect connectivity or add additional security; it can be used for informational purpose only.

# Summary

In this chapter, we discussed LDAP, Kerberos installation and configuration, setting up LDAP with Kerberos. We used Kerberos security for SSH logins, discussed SSH server and passwordless SSH setup between two machines, discussed how to disable password-based authentication and limit the users who can SSH into the system. Finally, we saw how to greet users with banners.

In the next chapter, we will study the monitoring and optimization of our Ubuntu Server. We will discuss CPU load, storage, network, and monitoring with tools such as Nagios, Munin, and more.

# Monitoring and Optimization

This chapter deals with centrally monitoring your set of systems and managing the individual machines. There are many tools available, but we will discuss Nagios, Puppet, and ClusterSSH. We will see how we can centrally monitor using Nagios, Puppet will help us to handle configuration management from a central location, and we will use ClusterSSH to repeat commands over the network simultaneously.

## Nagios

First, let's learn about Nagios. We will discuss setting up Nagios, how to add hosts to Nagios, how to make use of templates in Nagios, and how to set up services using hostgroups. We will also see how to use Nagios for alerts, write our own plugins to monitor, the NPRE plugin for Nagios, and how to execute Nagios from external machines.

## The Nagios setup

Nagios provides you with a web-based interface and once it is set up correctly, you can monitor your system centrally. It gives you information and you can control that as well. Nagios uses very less resources and hence it's low on maintenance. Setting up Nagios is easy: install it on a server and add all the clients that you want to monitor. Nagios service does the work of checking whether the clients are reachable using Ping or SSH, whether HTTP/LDAP/NFS are working, and so on. The beauty of this is you need not install any special software or packages on the client machines that are being monitored.

Let's see how we can install Nagios 3 on the Ubuntu Server. Execute the following command:

```
sudo apt-get install nagios3 nagios-plugins
```

In addition to the Nagios service, we are also installing the associated plugins here. We will discuss the plugins in the later part of this chapter. The output of the preceding command is as follows:

```
  nagios3-core php5-cli php5-common php5-json php5-readline postfix
  python-crypto python-ldb python-ntdb python-samba python-talloc python-tdb
  rpcbind samba-common samba-common-bin samba-libs smbclient snmp ssl-cert
  whois
Suggested packages:
  apache2-doc apache2-suexec-pristine apache2-suexec-custom php-pear
  cups-common libgd-tools javascript-common libcrypt-des-perl
  libdigest-hmac-perl libio-socket-inet6-perl lm-sensors snmp-mibs-downloader
  nagios-plugins-contrib nagios-nrpe-plugin php5-user-cache procmail
  postfix-mysql postfix-pgsql postfix-ldap postfix-pcre sasl2-bin
  dovecot-common postfix-cdb mail-reader postfix-doc python-crypto-dbg
  python-crypto-doc heimdal-clients cifs-utils openssl-blacklist
The following NEW packages will be installed:
  apache2 apache2-bin apache2-data apache2-utils bsd-mailx fontconfig-config
  fonts-dejavu-core libapache2-mod-php5 libapr1 libaprutil1
  libaprutil1-dbd-sqlite3 libaprutil1-ldap libavahi-client3
  libavahi-common-data libavahi-common3 libcups2 libdbi1 libfontconfig1 libgd3
  libgssglue1 libjbig0 libjpeg-turbo8 libjpeg8 libjs-jquery libldb1
  libmysqlclient18 libnet-snmp-perl libntdb1 libpq5 libsensors4 libsmbclient
  libsnmp-base libsnmp30 libtalloc2 libtdb1 libtevent0 libtiff5 libtirpc1
  libvpx1 libwbclient0 libxpm4 mysql-common nagios-images nagios-plugins
  nagios-plugins-basic nagios-plugins-common nagios-plugins-standard nagios3
  nagios3-cgi nagios3-common nagios3-core php5-cli php5-common php5-json
  php5-readline postfix python-crypto python-ldb python-ntdb python-samba
  python-talloc python-tdb rpcbind samba-common samba-common-bin samba-libs
  smbclient snmp ssl-cert whois
0 upgraded, 70 newly installed, 0 to remove and 126 not upgraded.
Need to get 22.6 MB of archives.
After this operation, 94.1 MB of additional disk space will be used.
Do you want to continue? [Y/n]
```

Enter an admin password when prompted, as shown in the following screenshot. Also, you can choose No to answer the question for backward compatibility with version 1 of Nagios.

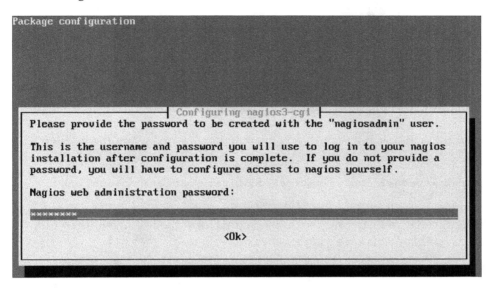

You must have apache2 installed in your server to work along with Nagios. After installing Nagios, check for a symlink from /etc/apache2/conf.d/nagios3.conf to /etc/nagios3/ apache2.conf. A letter l at the first position depicts that it is a link. This means that the configuration from Nagios will be put along in your web server config. You can confirm the same by referring to the next screenshot. First, run these commands:

```
cd /etc/apache2/conf-available/
ls -ltr
```

The result is shown here:

```
skanda@UbuntuServer:~$ cd /etc/apache2/conf-available/
skanda@UbuntuServer:/etc/apache2/conf-available$ ls -ltr
total 20
-rw-r--r-- 1 root root 2190 Jan  3 2014 security.conf
-rw-r--r-- 1 root root  189 Jan  3 2014 other-vhosts-access-log.conf
-rw-r--r-- 1 root root 3224 Jan  3 2014 localized-error-pages.conf
-rw-r--r-- 1 root root  315 Jan  3 2014 charset.conf
-rw-r--r-- 1 root root  455 Jan  7 2014 serve-cgi-bin.conf
lrwxrwxrwx 1 root root   26 Jan  9 2014 nagios3.conf -> ../../nagios3/apache2.c
onf
skanda@UbuntuServer:/etc/apache2/conf-available$ _
```

If the symbolic link is not visible, go ahead and create one using the following command:

```
ln -s /etc/apache2/conf.d/nagios3.conf /etc/nagios3/apache2.conf
```

Here are the default settings for the basic server setup, which will monitor the server itself (localhost). You can find the defined contacts in the following directory: /etc/nagios3/conf.d/contacts_nagios2.cfg.

Change the e-mail from root@localhost.com to the e-mail address you want the alerts to be sent. The default settings look as shown in the following screenshot:

```
###############################################################################
###############################################################################
#
# CONTACTS
#
###############################################################################
###############################################################################

# In this simple config file, a single contact will receive all alerts.

define contact{
        contact_name                    root
        alias                           Root
        service_notification_period     24x7
        host_notification_period        24x7
        service_notification_options    w,u,c,r
        host_notification_options       d,r
        service_notification_commands   notify-service-by-email
        host_notification_commands      notify-host-by-email
        email                           root@localhost
        }



###############################################################################
###############################################################################
#
# CONTACT GROUPS
#
```

After you have edited the file, check for the syntax in the config using the following command:

```
nagios3 -v /etc/nagios3/nagios.cfg
```

The output is as follows:

```
        Checked 4 host groups.
Checking service groups...
        Checked 0 service groups.
Checking contacts...
        Checked 1 contacts.
Checking contact groups...
        Checked 1 contact groups.
Checking service escalations...
        Checked 0 service escalations.
Checking service dependencies...
        Checked 0 service dependencies.
Checking host escalations...
        Checked 0 host escalations.
Checking host dependencies...
        Checked 0 host dependencies.
Checking commands...
        Checked 153 commands.
Checking time periods...
        Checked 4 time periods.
Checking for circular paths between hosts...
Checking for circular host and service dependencies...
Checking global event handlers...
Checking obsessive compulsive processor commands...
Checking misc settings...

Total Warnings: 0
Total Errors:   0

Things look okay - No serious problems were detected during the pre-flight check
skanda@UbuntuServer:/etc/nagios3/conf.d$ _
```

You should be able to see something similar to the preceding screenshot. The screenshot shows there are no warnings and no errors, so we are good to go. Reload Nagios for the settings to take effect. The command to restart the Nagios service is as follows:

```
/etc/init.d/nagios3 reload
```

Now, connect to the web page using the IP address of the server and **nagios3** as the service. I connected to the Nagios web with `http://192.168.1.5/nagios3/`. It will ask for the admin username and admin password that you set while installation. Once logged in, click on **Tactical Overview** on the left-hand side menu. You should be able to see something similar to the following screenshot:

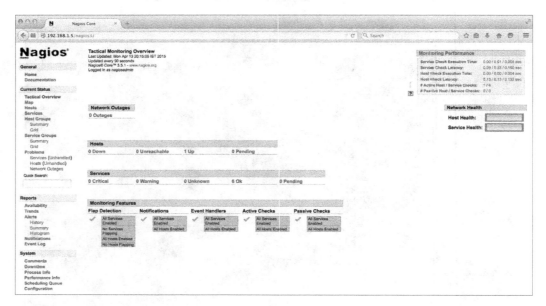

In the **Tactical Monitoring Overview** screen, you will see the overview and states for hosts and services. The states can be one of the following:

- **Pending**: This means checking is going on
- **OK (green)**: This means all is well
- **Yellow**: This means warning
- **Red**: This means critical

Clicking on a link will open an expanded view and will show the additional details, as shown here:

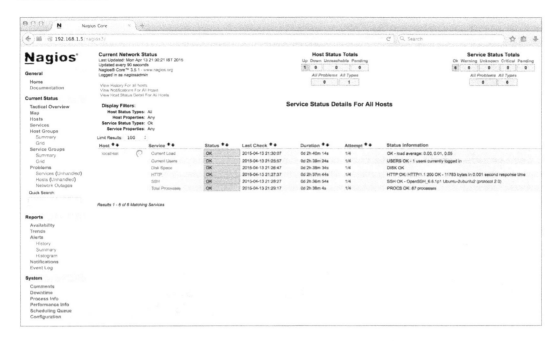

# Adding another host in Nagios

Till now, we were monitoring the server system itself. Now, we will see how to add another host (machine) to the Nagios service and monitor it centrally. To do so, create a configuration file in the server machine and name it using the hostname that you want to monitor. For example, if you want to add a machine with hostname `myuser` to be monitored, the name of file will be `host-myuser.cfg` and the contents will be as follows:

```
define host{
    use          generic-host
    host_name    myuser
    address      192.168.1.8
    }
```

This is the bare minimum, as most of the information required for the configuration is taken from the host template. We will discuss templates in Nagios in the next section. For Nagios to start monitoring this new host, you will have to reload. The command to reload is as follows:

```
/etc/init.d/nagios3 reload
```

It may take a little longer to reload, as it is collecting statistics from the newly added host machine to show up on the web page. You may add other machines in the same manner for monitoring under Nagios service.

# Nagios templates

You can save a lot of effort by making use of templates provided by Nagios. Templates are a set of standard configuration that you want to apply for a set of machines at once. The default host definition and service definition can be found in the /etc/nagios3/conf.d/localhost_nagios2.cfg file. You can see something similar to the following screenshot:

```
skanda@UbuntuServer:~$ cat /etc/nagios3/conf.d/localhost_nagios2.cfg
# A simple configuration file for monitoring the local host
# This can serve as an example for configuring other servers;
# Custom services specific to this host are added here, but services
# defined in nagios2-common_services.cfg may also apply.
#

define host{
        use                     generic-host            ; Name of host template
to use
        host_name               localhost
        alias                   localhost
        address                 127.0.0.1
        }

# Define a service to check the disk space of the root partition
# on the local machine.  Warning if < 20% free, critical if
# < 10% free space on partition.

define service{
        use                     generic-service         ; Name of servic
e template to use
        host_name               localhost
        service_description     Disk Space
        check_command           check_all_disks!20%!10%
        }


# Define a service to check the number of currently logged in
```

To refer to a template, you need to put it with the keyword use. Having templates is always a better idea, as you can control the configuration from a central location rather than having to modify each and every host machine dependent file when you are updating. It adds to the maintainability.

The generic-host template is located in the conf.d/gneric-host_nagios2.cfg file. As you can see in the following screenshot, it has a set of defaults for notification enabling, events, and so on. All these can be overridden in the host definitions if required.

```
skanda@UbuntuServer:~$ cat /etc/nagios3/conf.d/generic-host_nagios2.cfg
# Generic host definition template - This is NOT a real host, just a template!

define host{
        name                            generic-host      ; The name of this host
template
        notifications_enabled           1                 ; Host notifications are enabled
        event_handler_enabled           1                 ; Host event handler is enabled
        flap_detection_enabled          1                 ; Flap detection is enabled
        failure_prediction_enabled      1                 ; Failure prediction is enabled
        process_perf_data               1                 ; Process performance data
        retain_status_information       1                 ; Retain status information acro
ss program restarts
        retain_nonstatus_information    1                 ; Retain non-status information
across program restarts
                check_command                             check-host-alive
                max_check_attempts                        10
                notification_interval                     0
                notification_period                       24x7
                notification_options                      d,u,r
                contact_groups                            admins
        register                        0                 ; DONT REGISTER THIS DEFINITION
- ITS NOT A REAL HOST, JUST A TEMPLATE!
        }
skanda@UbuntuServer:~$
```

Similarly, take a look at the host-service template. The template is defined in the `conf.d/generic-service_nagios2.cfg` file. You will be able to see something similar to the following screenshot:

```
skanda@UbuntuServer:~$ cat /etc/nagios3/conf.d/generic-service_nagios2.cfg
# generic service template definition
define service{
        name                            generic-service ; The 'name' of this ser
vice template
        active_checks_enabled           1       ; Active service checks are enab
led
        passive_checks_enabled          1       ; Passive service checks are ena
bled/accepted
        parallelize_check               1       ; Active service checks should b
e parallelized (disabling this can lead to major performance problems)
        obsess_over_service             1       ; We should obsess over this ser
vice (if necessary)
        check_freshness                 0       ; Default is to NOT check servic
e 'freshness'
        notifications_enabled           1       ; Service notifications are enab
led
        event_handler_enabled           1       ; Service event handler is enabl
ed
        flap_detection_enabled          1       ; Flap detection is enabled
        failure_prediction_enabled      1       ; Failure prediction is enabled
        process_perf_data               1       ; Process performance data
        retain_status_information       1       ; Retain status information acro
ss program restarts
        retain_nonstatus_information    1       ; Retain non-status information
across program restarts
                notification_interval   0               ; Only send noti
fications on status change by default.
                is_volatile             0
                check_period            24x7
```

# Nagios hostgroups and services

We had previously added a machine with the name myuser to our Nagios service for monitoring. We haven't added any service check or status check. There are two ways to do this. One is by adding the services and status in the individual configuration files. But this would mean a lot of effort, as you would be required to repeat the same across all the configurations for corresponding host machines in your cluster.

Alternatively, you can take the advantage of templates and use hostgroups. Then, you can define a service for a set of hosts rather than a single host. Modify the `conf.d/hostgroups_nagios2.cfg` file and add a name that you think will best fit the group:

```
skanda@UbuntuServer:~$ cat /etc/nagios3/conf.d/hostgroups_nagios2.cfg
# Some generic hostgroup definitions

# A simple wildcard hostgroup
define hostgroup {
        hostgroup_name    all
                alias            All Servers
                members          *
        }

# A list of your Debian GNU/Linux servers
define hostgroup {
        hostgroup_name   debian-servers
                alias            Debian GNU/Linux Servers
                members          localhost
        }

# A list of your web servers
define hostgroup {
        hostgroup_name   http-servers
                alias            HTTP servers
                members          localhost
        }

# A list of your ssh-accessible servers
define hostgroup {
        hostgroup_name   ssh-servers
                alias            SSH servers
                members          localhost
        }
```

Also, you can create a new group altogether. When defining a new hostgroup, the only required fields are `hostgroup_name` and `alias`. Every other field is optional. For example, the following code snippet will create a new hostgroup:

```
define hostgroup {
        hostgroup_name  debian-servers
        alias           Debian GNU/Linux Servers
        members         localhost,webserver,ldapserver
        }
```

Now, let's set up some services to be monitored for this hostgroup. You have to change the `conf.d/services_nagios2.cfg` file and add the following service checks. All you are doing here is checking whether the hosts will respond to pings and if SSH is working alright:

```
define service {
        hostgroup_name            debian-servers
        service_description       SSH
        check_command             check_ssh
        use                       generic-service
        notification_interval     0
}
define service {
        hostgroup_name            debian-servers
        service_description       PING
        check_command             check_ping!100.0,20%!500.0,60%
        use                       generic-service
        notification_interval     0
}
```

The Nagios service will monitor the machines in the groups for the services we defined in the `check_command` statement with `generic-service` settings and fire an alert if it encounters an issue.

# Nagios setup alerts

It isn't always possible to go and check the web page to identify any problems. It is advisable to set up alerts and have it sent to your e-mail address whenever any problems are detected in any of the machines. We had set the contacts earlier in the `/etc/nagios3/conf.d/contacts_nagios2.cfg` file. At the end of the file, you will see an admin contact group (for easier maintainability).

Let's now see the default settings for a service to send e-mail for any errors encountered. You will appreciate the usefulness of the generic-service definition. Edit the `/etc/nagios3/conf.d/generic-service_nagios2.cfg` file and add the following lines there:

```
notification_interval     1440
is_volatile               0
check_period              24x7
normal_check_interval     5
retry_check_interval      1
```

```
max_check_attempts          5
notification_period         24x7
notification_options        w,u,c,r
contact_groups              admins
```

 The preceding code is not an exhaustive list. For more commands, refer to https://assets.nagios.com/ downloads/nagioscore/docs/nagioscore/3/en/ objectdefinitions.html#service.

Save the file and reload the Nagios service. The generic-service file should be something similar to the following screenshot:

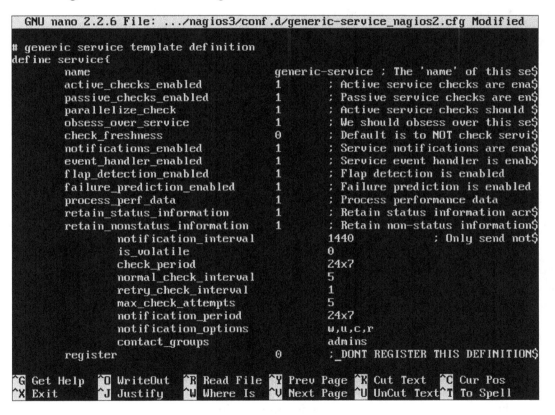

Let's understand what each of the lines means:

- `notification_interval`: This is a reminder. Here, `1440` means 24 hours.

- `check_period`: This specifies when the services should be running. Here `24x7` means always.

- `normal_check_interval`: This is the time period between each check in minutes.

- `retry_check_interval`: In case of failure, this is the time to wait before checking again (in minutes).

- `max_check_attempts`: This specifies how many times to retry before concluding something is wrong.

- `notification_period`: This is the time period when alerts should be mailed. Here, it is set for *all the time.*

- `notification_options`: This specifies for which states of the system an alert should be sent. The types are as follows:
    - d: This means the host is down
    - u: This means the host is unreachable
    - r: This means the host is recovered
    - f: This means the host starts and stops flapping
    - w: This means the service is in the warning state
    - u: This means the service is in an unknown state
    - c: This means the service is in a critical state

- `contact_groups`: This specifies which contacts are to be notified for alerts.

You can test the working of alerts by turning off any of the monitored services in any host; you will receive an alert. Turn the service back on again, and you will get an e-mail alert saying the service is up.

# Writing a Nagios plugin

There are a lot of plugins provided by Nagios to make it extensible in many ways. Check out `http://nagios-plugins.org/` and you will be able to download and use the plugins. If you have downloaded the plugins, go and check for them in the `/usr/lib/nagios/plugins` folder. To check the help for a particular plugin, use the following command:

```
/usr/lib/nagios/plugins/plugin_name - h
```

Here's a screenshot of the `plugins` folder:

```
skanda@UbuntuServer:~$ ls /usr/lib/nagios/plugins/
check_apt          check_icmp          check_nntps        check_snmp
check_breeze       check_ide_smart     check_nt           check_spop
check_by_ssh       check_ifoperstatus  check_ntp          check_ssh
check_clamd        check_ifstatus      check_ntp_peer     check_ssmtp
check_cluster      check_imap          check_ntp_time     check_swap
check_dbi          check_ircd          check_nwstat       check_tcp
check_dhcp         check_jabber        check_oracle       check_time
check_dig          check_ldap          check_overcr       check_udp
check_disk         check_ldaps         check_pgsql        check_ups
check_disk_smb     check_load          check_ping         check_users
check_dns          check_log           check_pop          check_wave
check_dummy        check_mailq         check_procs        negate
check_file_age     check_mrtg          check_real         urlize
check_flexlm       check_mrtgtraf      check_rpc          utils.pm
check_ftp          check_mysql         check_rta_multi    utils.sh
check_host         check_mysql_query   check_sensors
check_hpjd         check_nagios        check_simap
check_http         check_nntp          check_smtp
skanda@UbuntuServer:~$
```

You can also write your own plugins. The `/usr/lib/nagios/plugins/utils.sh` file has few functions and variables that you can use in your plugin. The following plugin will check if a process whose name is passed as argument is running:

```
01 #! /bin/sh
02
03 PATH=/bin:/sbin:/usr/bin:/usr/sbin:/usr/local/bin:/usr/local/sbin
04
05 PROGNAME=`basename $0`
06 PROGPATH=`echo $0 | sed -e 's,[\\/][^\\/][^\\/]*$,,'`
07 REVISION=`echo '$Revision: 1 $' | sed -e 's/[^0-9.]//g'`
08
09 process=$1
10
11 . $PROGPATH/utils.sh
12
13 print_usage() {
14    echo "Usage: $PROGNAME process-to-check"
15 }
16
17 print_help() {
18    print_revision $PROGNAME $REVISION
```

```
19   echo ""
20   print_usage
21   echo ""
22   echo "This plugin checks if the given process is running,
        using ps and grep."
23   echo ""
24   support
25   exit 0
26 }
27
28 case "$process" in
29   --help)
30     print_help
31     exit 0
32     ;;
33   -h)
34     print_help
35     exit 0
36     ;;
37   --version)
38     print_revision $PROGNAME $REVISION
39     exit 0
40     ;;
41   -V)
42     print_revision $PROGNAME $REVISION
43     exit 0
44     ;;
45   *)
46     processdata=`ps -A | grep $process 2>&1`
47     status=$?
48     if test ${status} -ne 0 ; then
49       echo Process not found
50       exit 2
51     fi
52     else
53       echo Process running
54       exit 0
55     fi
56     ;;
57 esac
```

We are using the variables and subroutines from the `utils.sh` file by sourcing it. These actions are performed in lines 1 to 27. The lines 27 to 44 check for an argument and validate if the argument is correct. The actual work of checking is done in lines 45 to 55, while line 46 checks the process and 47 returns the exit code. Exit codes are understood as follows:

- 0: This means success
- 1: This means warning
- 2: This means alert

# The NRPE plugin

By default, Nagios will monitor whether hosts are up and will check for the services that you define in the configuration files. The **NRPE** plugin, short for **Nagios remote plugin executor**, will help you monitor resources in remote machines. You can also monitor the CPU usage and disk space utilization. For NRPE, you should perform two tasks. First, install the NRPE plugin on your server where the Nagios server is running. Then, install the NRPE server on the remote machines you want to monitor.

Execute the following command on the Nagios server machine:

```
sudo apt-get install nagios-nrpe-plugin
```

Execute the following command on the remote machines:

```
sudo apt-get install nagios-nrpe-server
```

After installing the service on both the machines, we need to test out the connections. Run the following command from the server where your Nagios server is running:

```
/usr/lib/nagios/plugins/checknrpe -H myuser -c check_users
```

The preceding plugin will check for the number of users logged in to the remote machine `myuser`. Check the `/etc/nagios-plugins/config/check_nrpe.cfg` file on the server machine. Here's what it will look like:

```
skanda@UbuntuServer:~$ cd /etc/nagios-plugins/config/
skanda@UbuntuServer:/etc/nagios-plugins/config$ ls
apt.cfg          dns.cfg        hppjd.cfg       mailq.cfg       ntp.cfg       rpc-nfs.cfg
breeze.cfg       dummy.cfg      http.cfg        mrtg.cfg        pgsql.cfg     snmp.cfg
check_nrpe.cfg   flexlm.cfg     ifstatus.cfg    mysql.cfg       ping.cfg      ssh.cfg
dhcp.cfg         fping.cfg      ldap.cfg        netware.cfg     procs.cfg     tcp_udp.cfg
disk.cfg         ftp.cfg        load.cfg        news.cfg        radius.cfg    telnet.cfg
disk-smb.cfg     games.cfg      mail.cfg        nt.cfg          real.cfg      users.cfg
skanda@UbuntuServer:/etc/nagios-plugins/config$ cat check_nrpe.cfg
# this command runs a program $ARG1$ with arguments $ARG2$
define command {
        command_name      check_nrpe
        command_line      /usr/lib/nagios/plugins/check_nrpe -H $HOSTADDRESS$ -c $
ARG1$ -a $ARG2$
}

# this command runs a program $ARG1$ with no arguments
define command {
        command_name      check_nrpe_1arg
        command_line      /usr/lib/nagios/plugins/check_nrpe -H $HOSTADDRESS$ -c $
ARG1$
}
skanda@UbuntuServer:/etc/nagios-plugins/config$ _
```

If you want to monitor additional services running on the remote machines, then edit the `/etc/nagios3/conf.d/services_nagios2.cfg` file in the remote machine and add the following lines:

```
# SMTP doesn't need any arguments passed into the check_smtp
# program, so we use check_nrpe_1arg
define service {
    service_description    SMTP
    use                    generic-service
    hostgroup_name         nrpe
    check_command          check_nrpe_1arg!check_smtp
}
define service {
    service_description    LOAD
    use                    generic-service
    hostgroup_name         nrpe
    check_command          check_nrpe_1arg!check_load
}
# check_disk takes an argument, /, so we use check_nrpe
define service {
```

```
    service_description      DISK
    use                      generic-service
    hostgroup_name           nrpe
    check_command            check_nrpe!check_disk!/
}
```

Restart the Nagios service and you will be able to monitor the additional services on the remote machine.

# Enabling external commands

By default, Nagios will only let you monitor the services on a host from the web interface. If you want to do some operations such as stop or start a service from a web interface, you first need to enable it. First, stop the Nagios service on the server using the following command:

**sudo /etc/init.d/nagios3 stop**

Now, edit the nagios.cfg file and set the value to 1 where you see check_external_commands:

```
  GNU nano 2.2.6          File: /etc/nagios3/nagios.cfg          Modified

# You can either supply a group name or a GID.

nagios_group=nagios


# EXTERNAL COMMAND OPTION
# This option allows you to specify whether or not Nagios should check
# for external commands (in the command file defined below).  By default
# Nagios will *not* check for external commands, just to be on the
# cautious side.  If you want to be able to use the CGI command interface
# you will have to enable this.
# Values: 0 = disable commands, 1 = enable commands

check_external_commands=1_


# EXTERNAL COMMAND CHECK INTERVAL
# This is the interval at which Nagios should check for external commands.
# This value works of the interval_length you specify later.  If you leave
# that at its default value of 60 (seconds), a value of 1 here will cause
# Nagios to check for external commands every minute.  If you specify a
# number followed by an "s" (i.e. 15s), this will be interpreted to mean
# actual seconds rather than a multiple of the interval_length variable.

^G Get Help   ^O WriteOut   ^R Read File  ^Y Prev Page  ^K Cut Text   ^C Cur Pos
^X Exit       ^J Justify    ^W Where Is   ^V Next Page  ^U UnCut Text ^T To Spell
```

You will have to set permissions on /var/nagios3/rw for apache2 to read/write. Use the following commands:

```
sudo dpkg-statoverride --update --add nagios www-data 2710 /var/lib/
nagios3/rw
```

```
sudo dpkg-statoverride --update --add nagios nagios 751 /var/lib/nagios3
```

You will have to restart the Nagios service for the changes to take effect. Log in to the Nagios web interface. Click on the services in the **Tactical Overview** section. Select any of the services; here, I am selecting **Current Users**. On the right-hand side, you will see the commands box. You can click on any of those and run the commands right from the web interface. The following screenshot shows the **Service Commands** box on the right-hand side:

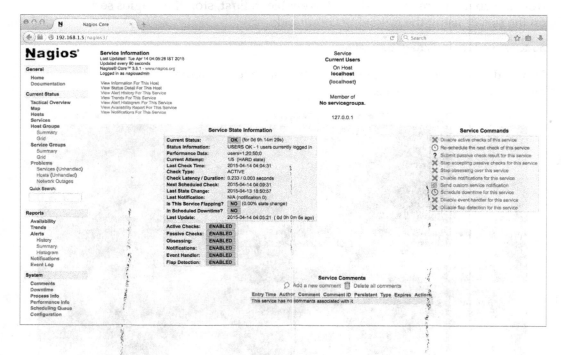

If you are logged in as an admin (nagiosadmin) to the web interface, you can also stop or restart the Nagios service using the **Process Information** page. This is shown in the following screenshot:

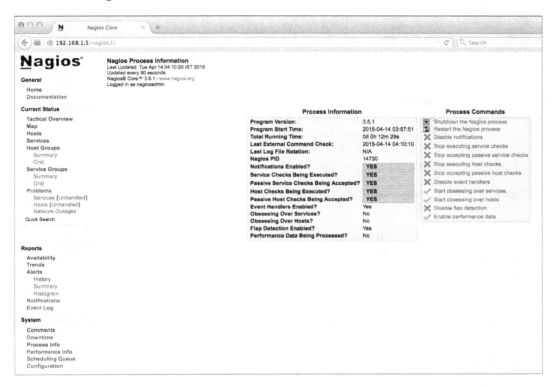

# Puppet

A challenge for most of the system administrators is having the config set up in all the machines in the same manner. The installation can be central, but this does not guarantee the configurations will be consistent across all machines. Over a period of time, some machine configuration files might have been changed or moved to a different location. This is where Puppet comes to the rescue.

Puppet is a system that helps you centrally manage the configuration across machines and helps avoid problems of locating the config files in each of the remote machines and then changing the configuration in each of them one by one. Puppet master is a service set up on a server to centrally track and maintain the configuration files on all your client nodes. Every client will have a daemon running, which periodically reports to the Puppet master and also makes the changes in the client config files. Puppet is primarily an open source system; however, there is an enterprise version available as well.

You need to be careful with one issue though. If you manually change the configuration files in any of the client machines, Puppet master will change it to the settings it had previously set. For any changes that have to stay, you need to centrally set the configuration. If you want to test a service on a client, then it is advisable to first turn off Puppet monitoring on that host and carry out the testing.

Puppet identifies every entity that it monitors as a resource. The resources are put into following categories:

- Files (ownership, mode, content, and existence can all be managed)
- Users and groups
- Packages
- Services
- Commands and scripts (Puppet can execute these under particular conditions)
- Crontabs
- Mounts

# Installing Puppet

To install Puppet on your Ubuntu Server, use the following command:

```
sudo apt-get install puppetmaster
```

Puppet also installs a set of other packages. The following screenshot shows a set of dependent packages:

```
skanda@UbuntuServer:~$ sudo apt-get install puppetmaster
[sudo] password for skanda:
Reading package lists... Done
Building dependency tree
Reading state information... Done
The following extra packages will be installed:
  augeas-lenses debconf-utils facter libaugeas0 libruby1.9.1 libyaml-0-2
  puppet-common puppetmaster-common ruby ruby-augeas ruby-hiera ruby-json
  ruby-rgen ruby-safe-yaml ruby-shadow ruby1.9.1
Suggested packages:
  augeas-doc virt-what augeas-tools ruby-selinux ruby-rrd librrd-ruby
  puppet-el ruby-ldap ruby-stomp stompserver vim-puppet ri ruby-dev
  mcollective-common ruby1.9.1-examples ri1.9.1 graphviz ruby1.9.1-dev
  ruby-switch
The following NEW packages will be installed:
  augeas-lenses debconf-utils facter libaugeas0 libruby1.9.1 libyaml-0-2
  puppet-common puppetmaster puppetmaster-common ruby ruby-augeas ruby-hiera
  ruby-json ruby-rgen ruby-safe-yaml ruby-shadow ruby1.9.1
0 upgraded, 17 newly installed, 0 to remove and 126 not upgraded.
Need to get 4,252 kB of archives.
After this operation, 21.0 MB of additional disk space will be used.
Do you want to continue? [Y/n] Y_
```

After installation is complete, you can find the main config for Puppet in the /etc/puppet/puppet.conf file:

```
skanda@UbuntuServer:~$ sudo cat /etc/puppet/puppet.conf
[main]
logdir=/var/log/puppet
vardir=/var/lib/puppet
ssldir=/var/lib/puppet/ssl
rundir=/var/run/puppet
factpath=$vardir/lib/facter
templatedir=$confdir/templates
prerun_command=/etc/puppet/etckeeper-commit-pre
postrun_command=/etc/puppet/etckeeper-commit-post

[master]
# These are needed when the puppetmaster is run by passenger
# and can safely be removed if webrick is used.
ssl_client_header = SSL_CLIENT_S_DN
ssl_client_verify_header = SSL_CLIENT_VERIFY

skanda@UbuntuServer:~$
```

The username for the Puppet service is puppet. The following directory's owner needs to be the user named puppet. Use this command:

```
chown puppet { /var/log/puppet, /var/lib/puppet }
```

Let's set up a basic file server config file so that the service can store and access file content. The file will be located in /etc/puppet/fileserver.conf:

```
  GNU nano 2.2.6          File: /etc/puppet/fileserver.conf          Modified

# This file consists of arbitrarily named sections/modules
# defining where files are served from and to whom

# Define a section 'files'
# Adapt the allow/deny settings to your needs. Order
# for allow/deny does not matter, allow always takes precedence
# over deny
[files]
  path /etc/puppet/files
  allow *.example.com
  deny *.evil.example.com
  allow 192.168.0.0/24

[plugins]
#  allow *.example.com
#  deny *.evil.example.com
#  allow 192.168.0.0/24




                            [ Read 17 lines ]
^G Get Help    ^O WriteOut    ^R Read File  ^Y Prev Page  ^K Cut Text    ^C Cur Pos
^X Exit        ^J Justify     ^W Where Is   ^V Next Page  ^U UnCut Text  ^T To Spell
```

The preceding settings say where the files will be stored on the Puppet master machine and which all machines have access and which do not. IP addresses can also be specified. You will have to use the mkusers and nonodes flags when you run the Puppet master daemon server for the first time. The command is as follows:

```
/usr/bin/puppetmasterd --mkusers --nonodes
```

# Setting up the client

Install the Puppet client on client machines using the following command:

```
sudo apt-get install puppet
```

Then, you need to set the Puppet server in the `/etc/puppet/puppetd.conf` file:

```
server = puppetserver.myubuntu.com
```

However, you need to set up the manifest before you can run the client.

# Setting up the manifest

The Puppet master gets all the information and the manifest file will be run on all the client machines. You can view the file at `/etc/puppet/manifests/site.pp`. The following code snippet will enable properties specific to the `/etc/sudoers` file specified here for all client machines:

```
file { "/etc/sudoers":
    owner => "root",
    group => "root",
    mode => "440"
}
```

It's time to test the setup and check whether Puppet master is performing well.

First, edit the `/etc/sudoers` file on any of the client machines. Change any attribute or value in the file and save it. Just make sure it is different from what you have set in the server file `site.pp`. Run the following command on the Puppet master server:

```
puppetmasterd --verbose
```

Now, run the client Puppet on the client machine:

```
puppetd --waitforcert 60 --test
```

Clients need to authenticate to the master using a certificate. You may encounter errors with the message related to certificates. Run the following command on the Puppet master server to let the server sign the client's certificate:

```
puppetca --sign client.example.com
```

The client will pick the certificate and run after 60 seconds. Now, go to the `/etc/sudoers` file in the client machine. You will notice that it has changed to the one defined in the Puppet master `site.pp` file. Puppet will manage attributes as well.

# ClusterSSH

Most system administrators would want to execute a set of commands over a large number of client machines. With **ClusterSSH (cssh)**, admins can set up cluster *sets* of hosts and log in to all of them once using SSH. Once you log in to the cssh terminal, all the commands that you type in your server window will be replicated across all the nodes. You can monitor this with the help of **xterm** and see what's going on. If you want to run a specific command on any of the connected machines via xterm, click on that window and only that host will run your commands now.

To install ClusterSSH, use the following command:

```
sudo apt-get install clusterssh
```

Next, you need to generate a global configuration file. The command is as follows:

```
sudo cssh -u > /etc/csshrc
```

Now, set up a system-wide cluster definition. To do this, change the /etc/clusters file and add the servers, as follows:

```
    servers server1 server2 server3
```

The preceding line will create a server group with server1, server2, and server3 as members. Next, start the ClusterSSH service using the following command:

```
cssh servers
```

You will see three windows open via SSH, one per server.

If you want to log in as a specific user in each of these machines, say root, then prefix each of the machines with the username. For example, the following modification will let you log in as root to each of the three servers:

```
servers root@server1 root@server2 root@server3
```

The best way to use ClusterSSH is to have the key-based SSH set up between the machines.

If you have categorized your machines in the /etc/clusters file and for some reason want to connect to all the machines (maybe for a security patch update), then you can connect to all machines using the following commands:

```
servers server1 server2 server3
desktops desktop4 desktop5
all servers desktops
```

Execute the following command to connect all of the five machines:

```
sudo cssh all
```

# Summary

In this chapter, we discussed how to set up Nagios and monitor hosts from a central place. We looked at using Nagios templates, hostgroups, and services for managing client machines. We also discussed setting up Nagios alerts, controlling the Nagios process, and executing commands from the web interface. We learned about writing Nagios plugins and working with the NRPE plugin for CPU as well as disk usage monitoring. Then, we discussed Puppet, which is used to centrally manage the configuration. We tested our Puppet setup. Then, we saw how ClusterSSH can be used to replicate commands over a set of host machines and monitor them using xterm.

In the next chapter, you will learn about process management. You will learn about running processes, monitoring processes, and background processes.

# 5
# Process Management

So far in this book, we have discussed topics such as package management, networking and DNS, network authentication, monitoring, and optimization. In this chapter, we will discuss process management, the various stages in a process, process priorities, and background and foreground jobs.

Let's go through some terminologies related to process management:

- **Process**: This is any piece of software that is currently in running state.
- **PID**: This is the process ID, and every process has one.
- **PPID**: This is the process ID of the parent that started this process. Parents normally start child processes.
- `init`: This is the first process and has process ID 1. The kernel starts this process and `init` does not have a parent process.
- `kill`: This is the command used to stop a process forcefully.
- `daemon`: These are the processes that usually start when system is started and are running forever.
- `zombie`: This is a process that has been killed already, yet shows up in the list of processes in the system. Note that zombie processes cannot be killed.

## The basics of process management

Let's now look at some basic process management commands and tools.

# $$ and $PPID

Let's look at some shell variables that carry information about processes. The $$ is a special variable in shell that stores the process ID of the current process. The process ID of its parent is in the $PPID variable. Here's an example to check $$ and $PPID:

```
skanda@UbuntuServer:~$ echo $$ $PPID
1623 1389
skanda@UbuntuServer:~$
```

Note that you cannot assign values to these special shell variables.

# pidof

If you want to know the ID of a process but you have only its name, you can use the command shown in the following screenshot:

```
skanda@UbuntuServer:~$ pidof apache2
1360 1359 1358 1357 1356 1353
skanda@UbuntuServer:~$ _
```

Here, you can see we have listed out the process ID for the apache2 process. You can specify any process name and will see the process IDs with the pidof command.

# Parent and child

In the previous sections, we saw the terminologies and also brief information on parent process. Essentially, every process is started by its parent; in UNIX, processes follow the parent-child relation. Let's now demonstrate this by calling a new bash from bash. We will see the child now becomes parent for another process when it starts.

First, let's print the process ID of the current bash process and its parent's process ID. We use the same variables $$ and $PPID for this:

```
echo $$ $PPID
```

The output is shown in the following screenshot:

```
skanda@UbuntuServer:~$ echo $$ $PPID
1623 1389
skanda@UbuntuServer:~$ _
```

Next, we'll start a new bash. This will start a new child process. Here, the child and parent process names are same, namely bash, but the process IDs will be different. After starting a new bash, let's print the $$ and $PPID values:

```
bash
echo $$ $PPID
```

The output is shown in the following screenshot:

```
skanda@UbuntuServer:~$ bash
skanda@UbuntuServer:~$ echo $$ $PPID
1880 1623
skanda@UbuntuServer:~$ _
```

As you can see in the preceding screenshot, the process ID and parent process ID are displayed. Go back one step and check what the process ID was earlier. Yes, you will surely notice that the parent process ID of the current process is same as the process ID of previous bash before starting a new bash process. This will be helpful when debugging and diagnosing child and parent processes.

The following screenshot puts this together. We end the current bash process with the `exit` command and again check the process ID.

```
skanda@UbuntuServer:~$ echo $$ $PPID
1623 1389
skanda@UbuntuServer:~$ bash
skanda@UbuntuServer:~$ echo $$ $PPID
2019 1623
skanda@UbuntuServer:~$ exit
exit
skanda@UbuntuServer:~$ echo $$ $PPID
1623 1389
skanda@UbuntuServer:~$ _
```

As we can see in the preceding screenshot, the process ID for the first bash process is 1623. Then, we launch another bash process from this current bash process. The new bash gets a different process ID; here, we see the process ID assigned is 2019. Also, the parent process ID for this new bash process is 1623, which is nothing but the process ID for the previous bash process. Again, we exit from child bash process and come back to parent bash process. On checking the process ID, we can confirm that it is the same 1623, which we saw earlier.

# fork() and exec()

A parent process starts a child process in the following two phases:

- `fork`: In this phase, the parent process creates an identical copy of itself.
- `exec`: In this phase, the child process replaces the forked process.

When `fork` is executed, the parent duplicates the following to its child process:

- Environment
- Controlling terminal
- umask
- Root directory
- Signal mask
- Resource limits
- Current working directory

The `fork()` and `exec()` calls are used in cases when there is a need for one program to run another program in parallel.

# exec

You can skip the `fork` operation and directly start a process with `exec` command. Let's see this with an example. First, let's get the process ID of the current bash process. Then, start a new shell process, the korn shell. The command to start the korn shell is as follows:

```
ksh
```

Once the korn shell is started, we again get the process ID and parent process ID with the following command:

```
echo $$ $PPID
```

The output is shown in the following screenshot:

```
skanda@UbuntuServer:~$ echo $$
13212
skanda@UbuntuServer:~$ ksh
$ echo $$ $PPID
13226 13212
$ exec bash
skanda@UbuntuServer:~$ echo $$ $PPID
13226 13212
skanda@UbuntuServer:~$ exit
exit
skanda@UbuntuServer:~$ echo $$
13212
skanda@UbuntuServer:~$
```

Now, we will start a new bash process but this time we will bypass `fork`, which means there is mirroring of the same process. Instead, the bash process will use the same process ID as that of ksh. The screenshot shows the complete picture. Note that the process ID of the korn shell process and the process ID of the new bash shell process are the same. Hence, we can say that we successfully initiated a new process directly with `exec` and skipped the `fork`.

# ps

The `ps` is the command to get information on the processes running on Linux systems. If you type `ps` without any options, it will show you a small subset of the currently running process, namely **shell** and **ps**. You will see a screen similar to the following screenshot when you run the `ps` command:

```
skanda@UbuntuServer:~$ ps
  PID TTY          TIME CMD
15099 tty1     00:00:00 bash
15820 tty1     00:00:00 ps
skanda@UbuntuServer:~$
```

There are four items listed: `PID` is the process ID, `TTY` is the terminal from which user has logged in, `TIME` is the CPU time taken by the current process and is shown in minutes and seconds, and `CMD` is the command name that was used to launch this process.

If you want the complete information of all the currently running processes on your machine, you can use the following command:

```
ps -aux | less
```

We use three options along with the ps command here: -a tells the ps command to display processes from all users and -u stands for showing detailed process information. You may relate it to difference between ls and ls -l. The -x option will show processes for which there is no controlling terminal. These are mainly the daemons that are started at boot process and not launched by any user or event. We pipe the output through less, as the result of the ps -aux command can be quite long. Keys to navigate the less command's output are Space and *B*. The output of this command is shown in the following screenshot:

| USER | PID | %CPU | %MEM | VSZ | RSS | TTY | STAT | START | TIME | COMMAND |
|------|-----|------|------|-----|-----|-----|------|-------|------|---------|
| root | 1 | 0.0 | 0.0 | 33488 | 2808 | ? | Ss | May05 | 0:01 | /sbin/init |
| root | 2 | 0.0 | 0.0 | 0 | 0 | ? | S | May05 | 0:00 | [kthreadd] |
| root | 3 | 0.0 | 0.0 | 0 | 0 | ? | S | May05 | 0:01 | [ksoftirqd/0] |
| root | 5 | 0.0 | 0.0 | 0 | 0 | ? | S< | May05 | 0:00 | [kworker/0:0H] |
| root | 7 | 0.0 | 0.0 | 0 | 0 | ? | S | May05 | 0:09 | [rcu_sched] |
| root | 8 | 0.0 | 0.0 | 0 | 0 | ? | S | May05 | 0:08 | [rcuos/0] |
| root | 9 | 0.0 | 0.0 | 0 | 0 | ? | S | May05 | 0:10 | [rcuos/1] |
| root | 10 | 0.0 | 0.0 | 0 | 0 | ? | S | May05 | 0:00 | [rcu_bh] |
| root | 11 | 0.0 | 0.0 | 0 | 0 | ? | S | May05 | 0:00 | [rcuob/0] |
| root | 12 | 0.0 | 0.0 | 0 | 0 | ? | S | May05 | 0:00 | [rcuob/1] |
| root | 13 | 0.0 | 0.0 | 0 | 0 | ? | S | May05 | 0:00 | [migration/0] |
| root | 14 | 0.0 | 0.0 | 0 | 0 | ? | S | May05 | 0:06 | [watchdog/0] |
| root | 15 | 0.0 | 0.0 | 0 | 0 | ? | S | May05 | 0:07 | [watchdog/1] |
| root | 16 | 0.0 | 0.0 | 0 | 0 | ? | S | May05 | 0:00 | [migration/1] |
| root | 17 | 0.0 | 0.0 | 0 | 0 | ? | S | May05 | 0:00 | [ksoftirqd/1] |
| root | 19 | 0.0 | 0.0 | 0 | 0 | ? | S< | May05 | 0:00 | [kworker/1:0H] |
| root | 20 | 0.0 | 0.0 | 0 | 0 | ? | S< | May05 | 0:00 | [khelper] |
| root | 21 | 0.0 | 0.0 | 0 | 0 | ? | S | May05 | 0:00 | [kdevtmpfs] |
| root | 22 | 0.0 | 0.0 | 0 | 0 | ? | S< | May05 | 0:00 | [netns] |
| root | 23 | 0.0 | 0.0 | 0 | 0 | ? | S< | May05 | 0:00 | [writeback] |
| root | 24 | 0.0 | 0.0 | 0 | 0 | ? | S< | May05 | 0:00 | [kintegrityd] |
| root | 25 | 0.0 | 0.0 | 0 | 0 | ? | S< | May05 | 0:00 | [bioset] |
| root | 26 | 0.0 | 0.0 | 0 | 0 | ? | S< | May05 | 0:01 | [kworker/u5:0] |
| root | 27 | 0.0 | 0.0 | 0 | 0 | ? | S< | May05 | 0:00 | [kblockd] |
| root | 28 | 0.0 | 0.0 | 0 | 0 | ? | S< | May05 | 0:00 | [ata_sff] |
| root | 29 | 0.0 | 0.0 | 0 | 0 | ? | S | May05 | 0:00 | [khubd] |
| root | 30 | 0.0 | 0.0 | 0 | 0 | ? | S< | May05 | 0:00 | [md] |
| root | 31 | 0.0 | 0.0 | 0 | 0 | ? | S< | May05 | 0:00 | [devfreq_wq] |

:

You will see a screen similar to the preceding screenshot. The output has the following columns:

- USER: This is the user who started the process.
- PID: This is the process ID.
- %CPU: This is percentage of CPU used by this process.
- %MEM: This is the percentage of RAM used by this process.
- VSZ: This is the virtual size in KB units.
- RSS: This is the resident set size in KB units.
- TTY: This is the terminal type.
- STAT: This is the state code for the process, that is, the current state of the process. Refer to the next bullet points to understand what each code means.
- START: This is the time when process started.
- TIME: This is the active time of the process.
- COMMAND: This is the command which started the process.

The following are the codes for process states that can be seen in the STAT column:

- D: This means the process is in an uninterruptible sleep
- N: This means the process has low priority
- R: This means the process is runnable or waiting in the run queue
- S: This means the process is sleeping
- T: This means the process is stopped
- Z: This means the process is a zombie

Now, let's see another command that can be used for a similar task, that is, viewing the process information:

```
ps -ef
```

The preceding command will show a listing of fewer items in columns:

```
skanda@UbuntuServer:~$ ps -ef
UID        PID  PPID  C STIME TTY          TIME CMD
root         1     0  0 May05 ?        00:00:01 /sbin/init
root         2     0  0 May05 ?        00:00:00 [kthreadd]
root         3     2  0 May05 ?        00:00:01 [ksoftirqd/0]
root         5     2  0 May05 ?        00:00:00 [kworker/0:0H]
root         7     2  0 May05 ?        00:00:09 [rcu_sched]
root         8     2  0 May05 ?        00:00:09 [rcuos/0]
root         9     2  0 May05 ?        00:00:10 [rcuos/1]
root        10     2  0 May05 ?        00:00:00 [rcu_bh]
root        11     2  0 May05 ?        00:00:00 [rcuob/0]
root        12     2  0 May05 ?        00:00:00 [rcuob/1]
root        13     2  0 May05 ?        00:00:00 [migration/0]
root        14     2  0 May05 ?        00:00:06 [watchdog/0]
root        15     2  0 May05 ?        00:00:07 [watchdog/1]
root        16     2  0 May05 ?        00:00:00 [migration/1]
root        17     2  0 May05 ?        00:00:00 [ksoftirqd/1]
root        19     2  0 May05 ?        00:00:00 [kworker/1:0H]
root        20     2  0 May05 ?        00:00:00 [khelper]
root        21     2  0 May05 ?        00:00:00 [kdevtmpfs]
root        22     2  0 May05 ?        00:00:00 [netns]
root        23     2  0 May05 ?        00:00:00 [writeback]
root        24     2  0 May05 ?        00:00:00 [kintegrityd]
root        25     2  0 May05 ?        00:00:00 [bioset]
root        26     2  0 May05 ?        00:00:01 [kworker/u5_0]
root        27     2  0 May05 ?        00:00:00 [kblockd]
root        28     2  0 May05 ?        00:00:00 [ata_sff]
root        29     2  0 May05 ?        00:00:00 [khubd]
root        30     2  0 May05 ?        00:00:00 [md]
root        31     2  0 May05 ?        00:00:00 [devfreq_wq]
```

UID is the username of the owner for that process. STIME shows the start time for the process; it shows only date if process was started more than 24 hours ago. You can also use the -1 option with the ps command to get a long listing. You will see a screen similar to the following screenshot:

```
skanda@UbuntuServer:~$ ps -el
F S   UID   PID  PPID  C PRI  NI ADDR SZ WCHAN   TTY          TIME CMD
4 S     0     1     0  0  80   0 -  8372 poll_s  ?        00:00:01 init
1 S     0     2     0  0  80   0 -     0 kthrea  ?        00:00:00 kthreadd
1 S     0     3     2  0  80   0 -     0 smpboo  ?        00:00:01 ksoftirqd/0
1 S     0     5     2  0  60 -20 -     0 worker  ?        00:00:00 kworker/0:0H
1 S     0     7     2  0  80   0 -     0 rcu_gp  ?        00:00:09 rcu_sched
1 S     0     8     2  0  80   0 -     0 rcu_no  ?        00:00:09 rcuos/0
1 S     0     9     2  0  80   0 -     0 rcu_no  ?        00:00:10 rcuos/1
1 S     0    10     2  0  80   0 -     0 rcu_gp  ?        00:00:00 rcu_bh
1 S     0    11     2  0  80   0 -     0 rcu_no  ?        00:00:00 rcuob/0
1 S     0    12     2  0  80   0 -     0 rcu_no  ?        00:00:00 rcuob/1
1 S     0    13     2  0 -40   - -     0 smpboo  ?        00:00:00 migration/0
5 S     0    14     2  0 -40   - -     0 smpboo  ?        00:00:06 watchdog/0
5 S     0    15     2  0 -40   - -     0 smpboo  ?        00:00:07 watchdog/1
1 S     0    16     2  0 -40   - -     0 smpboo  ?        00:00:00 migration/1
1 S     0    17     2  0  80   0 -     0 smpboo  ?        00:00:00 ksoftirqd/1
1 S     0    19     2  0  60 -20 -     0 worker  ?        00:00:00 kworker/1:0H
1 S     0    20     2  0  60 -20 -     0 rescue  ?        00:00:00 khelper
5 S     0    21     2  0  80   0 -     0 devtmp  ?        00:00:00 kdevtmpfs
1 S     0    22     2  0  60 -20 -     0 rescue  ?        00:00:00 netns
1 S     0    23     2  0  60 -20 -     0 rescue  ?        00:00:00 writeback
1 S     0    24     2  0  60 -20 -     0 rescue  ?        00:00:00 kintegrityd
1 S     0    25     2  0  60 -20 -     0 rescue  ?        00:00:00 bioset
1 S     0    26     2  0  60 -20 -     0 worker  ?        00:00:01 kworker/u5:0
1 S     0    27     2  0  60 -20 -     0 rescue  ?        00:00:00 kblockd
1 S     0    28     2  0  60 -20 -     0 rescue  ?        00:00:00 ata_sff
1 S     0    29     2  0  80   0 -     0 hub_th  ?        00:00:00 khubd
1 S     0    30     2  0  60 -20 -     0 rescue  ?        00:00:00 md
1 S     0    31     2  0  60 -20 -     0 rescue  ?        00:00:00 devfreq_wq
```

Here, you will see additional columns. You only need to pay attention to the NI and SZ columns. The NI column depicts the nice value. We will discuss more on nice values in the later sections of this chapter. It is the priority of the process — the lesser the number, the higher the priority. 0 is the default value for NI on most Linux systems. SZ shows the size of process in memory. The unit of SZ is 4 KB.

# pstree

A nice way to view the processes in a tree-like structure is by using the `pstree` command. The output will be similar to the following screenshot:

```
skanda@UbuntuServer:~$ pstree
init─┬─acpid
     ├─apache2───5*[apache2]
     ├─atd
     ├─cron
     ├─dbus-daemon
     ├─dhclient
     ├─5*[getty]
     ├─kadmind
     ├─krb5kdc
     ├─login───bash───pstree
     ├─master─┬─pickup
     │        └─qmgr
     ├─nagios3───{nagios3}
     ├─nrpe
     ├─puppet───2*[{puppet}]
     ├─rpcbind
     ├─rsyslogd───3*[{rsyslogd}]
     ├─slapd───2*[{slapd}]
     ├─sshd
     ├─systemd-logind
     ├─systemd-udevd
     ├─upstart-file-br
     ├─upstart-socket-
     └─upstart-udev-br
skanda@UbuntuServer:~$ _
```

# ps fx

To view the parent-child relationship between processes, you can use the following command:

```
ps fx
```

In the following screenshot, you can see that we are starting bash process and checking their process IDs. Then, we use the `ps fx` command to view the parent-child relationship:

```
skanda@UbuntuServer:~$ echo $$ $PPID
15099 15000
skanda@UbuntuServer:~$ bash
skanda@UbuntuServer:~$ echo $$ $PPID
15113 15099
skanda@UbuntuServer:~$ bash
skanda@UbuntuServer:~$ echo $$ $PPID
15128 15113
skanda@UbuntuServer:~$ ps fx
  PID TTY      STAT   TIME COMMAND
15099 tty1     S      0:00 -bash
15113 tty1     S      0:00  \_ bash
15128 tty1     S      0:00     \_ bash
15155 tty1     R+     0:00        \_ ps fx
skanda@UbuntuServer:~$ exit
exit
skanda@UbuntuServer:~$ ps fx
  PID TTY      STAT   TIME COMMAND
15099 tty1     S      0:00 -bash
15113 tty1     S      0:00  \_ bash
15159 tty1     R+     0:00     \_ ps fx
skanda@UbuntuServer:~$
```

# ps -C and pgrep

Sometimes, you may want to know the PID for a process from its name.
The following commands can be used to do exactly the same:

```
ps -C <process name>
```

Alternatively, you can use the following command:

```
pgrep <process name>
```

In the following screenshot, you can see the process ID of the sleep process:

```
skanda@UbuntuServer:~$ sleep 1000 &
[1] 17385
skanda@UbuntuServer:~$ pgrep sleep
17385
skanda@UbuntuServer:~$ ps -C sleep
  PID TTY          TIME CMD
17385 tty1     00:00:00 sleep
skanda@UbuntuServer:~$ _
```

# top

The `top` command is widely used in Linux machines to monitor the processes. The `top` command shows the processor activity in real time. It orders the running processes by CPU time, memory, and run time. You can manipulate the processes right from the top screen. To start top, use the following command:

`top`

The `top` screen looks like this:

```
top - 02:17:31 up 1 day, 19:21,  1 user,  load average: 0.00, 0.01, 0.05
Tasks:  93 total,   1 running,  92 sleeping,   0 stopped,   0 zombie
%Cpu(s):  0.0 us,  0.2 sy,  0.0 ni, 99.5 id,  0.2 wa,  0.2 hi,  0.0 si,  0.0 st
KiB Mem:   3537820 total,   658268 used,  2879552 free,   118540 buffers
KiB Swap:  2699260 total,        0 used,  2699260 free.   397792 cached Mem

  PID USER      PR  NI    VIRT    RES    SHR S  %CPU %MEM     TIME+ COMMAND
17531 skanda    20   0   23536   1540   1116 R   0.3  0.0   0:00.66 top
    1 root      20   0   33488   2808   1484 S   0.0  0.1   0:01.39 init
    2 root      20   0       0      0      0 S   0.0  0.0   0:00.00 kthreadd
    3 root      20   0       0      0      0 S   0.0  0.0   0:01.34 ksoftirqd/0
    5 root       0 -20       0      0      0 S   0.0  0.0   0:00.00 kworker/0:+
    7 root      20   0       0      0      0 S   0.0  0.0   0:09.91 rcu_sched
    8 root      20   0       0      0      0 S   0.0  0.0   0:09.53 rcuos/0
    9 root      20   0       0      0      0 S   0.0  0.0   0:11.05 rcuos/1
   10 root      20   0       0      0      0 S   0.0  0.0   0:00.00 rcu_bh
   11 root      20   0       0      0      0 S   0.0  0.0   0:00.00 rcuob/0
   12 root      20   0       0      0      0 S   0.0  0.0   0:00.00 rcuob/1
   13 root      rt   0       0      0      0 S   0.0  0.0   0:00.34 migration/0
   14 root      rt   0       0      0      0 S   0.0  0.0   0:06.28 watchdog/0
   15 root      rt   0       0      0      0 S   0.0  0.0   0:07.84 watchdog/1
   16 root      rt   0       0      0      0 S   0.0  0.0   0:00.56 migration/1
   17 root      20   0       0      0      0 S   0.0  0.0   0:00.13 ksoftirqd/1
   19 root       0 -20       0      0      0 S   0.0  0.0   0:00.00 kworker/1:+
   20 root       0 -20       0      0      0 S   0.0  0.0   0:00.00 khelper
   21 root      20   0       0      0      0 S   0.0  0.0   0:00.00 kdevtmpfs
   22 root       0 -20       0      0      0 S   0.0  0.0   0:00.00 netns
   23 root       0 -20       0      0      0 S   0.0  0.0   0:00.00 writeback
   24 root       0 -20       0      0      0 S   0.0  0.0   0:00.00 kintegrityd
   25 root       0 -20       0      0      0 S   0.0  0.0   0:00.00 bioset
```

If you need help with the functions available in the `top` process, type h from inside the process. You will see the following screen:

```
Help for Interactive Commands - procps-ng version 3.3.9
Window 1:Def: Cumulative mode Off. System: Delay 3.0 secs; Secure mode Off.

  Z,B,E,e   Global: 'Z' colors; 'B' bold; 'E'/'e' summary/task memory scale
  l,t,m     Toggle Summary: 'l' load avg; 't' task/cpu stats; 'm' memory info
  0,1,2,3,I Toggle: '0' zeros; '1/2/3' cpus or numa node views; 'I' Irix mode
  f,F,X     Fields: 'f'/'F' add/remove/order/sort; 'X' increase fixed-width

  L,&,<,> . Locate: 'L'/'&' find/again; Move sort column: '<'/'>' left/right
  R,H,V,J . Toggle: 'R' Sort; 'H' Threads; 'V' Forest view; 'J' Num justify
  c,i,S,j . Toggle: 'c' Cmd name/line; 'i' Idle; 'S' Time; 'j' Str justify
  x,y     . Toggle highlights: 'x' sort field; 'y' running tasks
  z,b     . Toggle: 'z' color/mono; 'b' bold/reverse (only if 'x' or 'y')
  u,U,o,O . Filter by: 'u'/'U' effective/any user; 'o'/'O' other criteria
  n,#,^O  . Set: 'n'/'#' max tasks displayed; Show: Ctrl+'O' other filter(s)
  C,...   . Toggle scroll coordinates msg for: up,down,left,right,home,end

  k,r       Manipulate tasks: 'k' kill; 'r' renice
  d or s    Set update interval
  W,Y       Write configuration file 'W'; Inspect other output 'Y'
  q         Quit
          ( commands shown with '.' require a visible task display window )
Press 'h' or '?' for help with Windows,
Type 'q' or <Esc> to continue █
```

The `top` process recognizes interactive commands and these are single key commands. Some of the important ones are as follows:

- Space: This updates the screen immediately
- *Ctrl* + *L*: This redraws the screen
- *h* or *?*: This displays the help screen as shown in the previous screenshot
- *k*: This kills a process
- *i*: This is the key to ignore or show zombie and idle processes
- *n* or *#*: This allows you to choose the number of processes to show on the top screen
- *q*: This means quit
- *r*: This means re-nice. This is used to change the priority of a process. Only root users can enter negative values.

# Signaling processes

It's time to look at some of the signaling processes in Ubuntu Server.

## kill

The `kill` command is used to stop or kill a process. The command is used as follows:

`kill <PID>`

Here, `PID` is the process ID of the process running on the Linux machine.

## Listing all signals

If you need to view all the available signals that can be passed to a process, use the following command:

`kill -l`

Please note that the option provided with `kill` is the letter l and not digit 1. You will see a screen similar to the following screenshot:

```
skanda@UbuntuServer:~$ kill -l
 1) SIGHUP        2) SIGINT        3) SIGQUIT       4) SIGILL       5) SIGTRAP
 6) SIGABRT       7) SIGBUS        8) SIGFPE        9) SIGKILL     10) SIGUSR1
11) SIGSEGV      12) SIGUSR2      13) SIGPIPE      14) SIGALRM     15) SIGTERM
16) SIGSTKFLT    17) SIGCHLD      18) SIGCONT      19) SIGSTOP     20) SIGTSTP
21) SIGTTIN      22) SIGTTOU      23) SIGURG       24) SIGXCPU     25) SIGXFSZ
26) SIGVTALRM    27) SIGPROF      28) SIGWINCH     29) SIGIO       30) SIGPWR
31) SIGSYS       34) SIGRTMIN     35) SIGRTMIN+1   36) SIGRTMIN+2  37) SIGRTMIN+3
38) SIGRTMIN+4   39) SIGRTMIN+5   40) SIGRTMIN+6   41) SIGRTMIN+7  42) SIGRTMIN+8
43) SIGRTMIN+9   44) SIGRTMIN+10  45) SIGRTMIN+11  46) SIGRTMIN+12 47) SIGRTMIN+13
48) SIGRTMIN+14  49) SIGRTMIN+15  50) SIGRTMAX-14  51) SIGRTMAX-13 52) SIGRTMAX-12
53) SIGRTMAX-11  54) SIGRTMAX-10  55) SIGRTMAX-9   56) SIGRTMAX-8  57) SIGRTMAX-7
58) SIGRTMAX-6   59) SIGRTMAX-5   60) SIGRTMAX-4   61) SIGRTMAX-3  62) SIGRTMAX-2
63) SIGRTMAX-1   64) SIGRTMAX
skanda@UbuntuServer:~$ _
```

Let's look at some of the important signals next. The processes can receive the signals from other processes or users.

# kill -1 or SIGHUP

Users can use `kill -1` with digit 1 to force a process to reload its configuration. For example, if you want bash to reload its configuration, you can execute the following commands:

```
sudo su
ps -C init
kill -1 1
```

The output is shown in the following screenshot:

```
skanda@UbuntuServer:~$ sudo su
root@UbuntuServer:/home/skanda# ps -C init
  PID TTY          TIME CMD
    1 ?        00:00:01 init
root@UbuntuServer:/home/skanda# kill -1 1
root@UbuntuServer:/home/skanda# _
```

Here, we reinitialized the init process. Note that you need to be logged in as root user to kill the init process. The init process always has PID value as 1.

# kill -15 or SIGTERM

When you use `kill` without any options, it defaults to `-15`. The SIGTERM command is the standard `kill` command, and it is same as providing `-15` as option. Both the following commands are same:

```
kill -15 1555
kill 1555
```

# kill -9 or SIGKILL

The `kill -9` command is a special type of `kill`. The `kill` command with option `-9` will never be sent to the process. This is the same reason why developers can't intercept this `kill` in their processes. When you send `kill` with this signal, it goes to the kernel directly. This is also called as secured kill. The kernel shoots down the process, whose process ID was passed along with the `kill` command. This command can be used when the process isn't responding to any commands or signals. But you should be careful, as forcefully killing a process may mean an abrupt stop and also you may end up losing some work that was in progress.

The syntax for this command is as follows:

```
kill -9 1555
```

# SIGSTOP and SIGCONT

The SIGSTOP and SIGCONT commands are used to pause and start a running process. The SIGSTOP command, which is the kill -19 command, will make the process go into a suspended state. This process will no longer be using the CPU cycles, but will be present in memory. When you want to start the process or get it out of suspended state, the kill -18 command can be used. The kill -18 command is SIGCONT telling the process to continue. The syntax to use these commands is as follows:

```
kill -19 <PID>
kill -18 <PID>
```

# pkill

If you do not know the PID of a process and want to kill the process by its name, then pkill is the command that you have been looking for.

Let's see this in action in the following screenshot:

```
skanda@UbuntuServer:~$ sleep 1000 &
[1] 21005
skanda@UbuntuServer:~$ ps -C sleep
  PID TTY          TIME CMD
21005 tty1     00:00:00 sleep
skanda@UbuntuServer:~$ pkill sleep
[1]+  Terminated              sleep 1000
skanda@UbuntuServer:~$ ps -C sleep
  PID TTY          TIME CMD
skanda@UbuntuServer:~$ _
```

In the preceding screenshot, we first start a process sleep and let it run in the background. Then, we check if it is running. We issue the following command to kill the process by its name:

```
pkill sleep
```

Then, we go ahead and check the process using the ps command.

# killall

Suppose there are multiple instances of the same process running, and you want to kill them all. Use the `killall` command to issue a `kill` statement to all processes with same name as follows:

```
killall <process name>
```

This results in the following output:

```
skanda@UbuntuServer:~$ ps -C sleep
  PID TTY          TIME CMD
skanda@UbuntuServer:~$ sleep 1000 &
[1] 21145
skanda@UbuntuServer:~$ sleep 1000 &
[2] 21146
skanda@UbuntuServer:~$ sleep 1000 &
[3] 21147
skanda@UbuntuServer:~$ sleep 1000 &
[4] 21151
skanda@UbuntuServer:~$ ps -C sleep
  PID TTY          TIME CMD
21145 tty1     00:00:00 sleep
21146 tty1     00:00:00 sleep
21147 tty1     00:00:00 sleep
21151 tty1     00:00:00 sleep
skanda@UbuntuServer:~$ killall sleep
[1]   Terminated              sleep 1000
[2]   Terminated              sleep 1000
[3]-  Terminated              sleep 1000
[4]+  Terminated              sleep 1000
skanda@UbuntuServer:~$ ps -C sleep
  PID TTY          TIME CMD
skanda@UbuntuServer:~$
```

# Process priorities

We will look at setting and changing process priorities in this section. We will now look at the `renice` and `nice` commands.

# renice

We saw in the earlier section that processes have a priority and nice value associated with them. The `top` command screen shows the nice value under `NI` column. You can change the priority of an already running process using the `renice` command. This will change the CPU resource cycles that the process uses. Here's the syntax to change the priority of an already running process:

```
renice +5 1555
```

If you are running this command as a normal user, the values you can assign are 0 to 20. Only root user can set a negative nice value. Lesser the number, higher the priority. But be very careful while setting a negative value to any process, as it may affect your Linux system seriously and it might then be impossible for you to use the keyboard or SSH into the system. By default, the kernel attributes almost all processes with a nice value of 0.

## nice

The `renice` and `nice` commands are very similar; the only difference is that the `nice` command is used when starting a process for which you want to set a priority. The syntax to set a nice value to a process while starting is as follows:

```
nice +2 <script file name>
```

Again, the same rules apply here as that of `renice`. Normal users cannot assign nice values less than 0. You can verify values of the process for which you changed the nice values from the `top` command screen.

# Background processes

We will now look at background processes and discuss how to start, view, and stop them.

## jobs

There are times when processes may be running in the background. To view the processes that are running in the background, use the following command:

```
jobs
```

By default, this is blank as you might not have jobs running in the background.

## & (ampersand)

You might want to start a process directly in background. To do so, suffix the ampersand (&) symbol after the process name when starting it. You might have observed this in the earlier sections of this chapter. Let's start the `sleep` process in the background now. The command to do so is as follows:

```
sleep 1000 &
```

Now, let's check whether the process was started successfully and is running in the background using the `jobs` command:

```
skanda@UbuntuServer:~$ jobs
skanda@UbuntuServer:~$ sleep 1000 &
[1] 24826
skanda@UbuntuServer:~$ sleep 1000 &
[2] 24827
skanda@UbuntuServer:~$ jobs
[1]-  Running                 sleep 1000 &
[2]+  Running                 sleep 1000 &
skanda@UbuntuServer:~$
```

Here, we first checked for any processes running in the background using the `jobs` command. Initially, it showed nothing, which means no jobs are running in the background. Next, we start the `sleep` process twice, both running in background. Then, we check for these background jobs if they are running using the `jobs` command. We see them in the output, which confirms that they are running in the background.

# jobs -p

Assume you have some jobs running in the background. You now want to know the process IDs of these background-running jobs. The command to view them is as follows:

`jobs -p`

Let's check this for the jobs that we ran in background in the previous section:

```
skanda@UbuntuServer:~$ jobs
skanda@UbuntuServer:~$ sleep 1000 &
[1] 24826
skanda@UbuntuServer:~$ sleep 1000 &
[2] 24827
skanda@UbuntuServer:~$ jobs
[1]-  Running                 sleep 1000 &
[2]+  Running                 sleep 1000 &
skanda@UbuntuServer:~$ jobs -p
24826
24827
skanda@UbuntuServer:~$ ps `jobs -p`
  PID TTY      STAT   TIME COMMAND
24826 tty1     S      0:00 sleep 1000
24827 tty1     S      0:00 sleep 1000
skanda@UbuntuServer:~$ _
```

You can see the process ID in the `jobs -p` command's output and the process ID when those `sleep` jobs were started, and both are same.

# Suspended state with Ctrl + Z

You can suspend some processes by hitting the key-combination *Ctrl + Z* while the process is running. In the following screenshot, we can see the `vi` process in suspended state when we start it and suspend it:

```
"new_file.txt" [New File]                                    0,0-1          All

[1]+  Stopped                    vi new_file.txt
skanda@UbuntuServer:~$ jobs
[1]+  Stopped                    vi new_file.txt
skanda@UbuntuServer:~$ _
```

You can see in the preceding screenshot that the state of the `vi` process is now stopped.

# bg

In the previous section, we saw jobs being put in the suspended state. You can start the jobs that are suspended in the background using the `bg` command. Let's see a small example. We will suspend a `sleep` job and check whether we can start it again with the `bg` command. Take a look at the following screenshot:

```
skanda@UbuntuServer:~$ sleep 4000 &
[2] 25099
skanda@UbuntuServer:~$ sleep 3000
^Z
[3]+  Stopped                    sleep 3000
skanda@UbuntuServer:~$ jobs
[1]-  Stopped                    vi new_file.txt
[2]   Running                    sleep 4000 &
[3]+  Stopped                    sleep 3000
skanda@UbuntuServer:~$ bg 3
[3]+ sleep 3000 &
skanda@UbuntuServer:~$ jobs
[1]+  Stopped                    vi new_file.txt
[2]   Running                    sleep 4000 &
[3]-  Running                    sleep 3000 &
skanda@UbuntuServer:~$ _
```

As you can see in the preceding screenshot, we started a sleep job in background, then another sleep job normally. Then, we hit *Ctrl + Z* and suspended the sleep job. We then checked the state of different background jobs using the jobs command. Then, we used the bg command with the ID of the background job to reactivate it. Again, we verified the state of jobs using the jobs command and saw the state of job with ID 3 change.

# fg

The fg command is used to get background jobs to the foreground. We first check for the background job ID that you want to bring to the foreground using the jobs command:

```
skanda@UbuntuServer:~$ jobs
[2]-   Running                    sleep 4000 &
[3]+   Running                    sleep 3000 &
skanda@UbuntuServer:~$ fg 3
sleep 3000
```

Taking the same example from previous section, we see two jobs running in background. These are sleep jobs with ID 2 and 3. Next, we use the fg command with the parameter 3, which is the job ID and bring the job to foreground. The command will run for that duration and you will see the blinking cursor. The procedure to bring any background running job to foreground is the same.

# Summary

In this chapter, you learned about process management. We studied the various stages in a process, process priorities, and background and foreground jobs. We discussed many commands associated with a process, such as ps, top, fg, bg, jobs, and more. We also discussed how to change the process priorities with their nice values, both at start of the job and also while the job is running.

In the next chapter, we will study shell management, tools, user management, and more.

# 6
# Shell Management, Tools, and User Management

In this chapter, we will discuss shell management, tools, and user management. Shell management will help administrators set up shell for remote access to server without monitors, schedule jobs on the server for their condition maintenance, and also collect information in logs for any troubleshooting. We will also look at optimizing the shell. Lastly, we will learn about user management, permissions, and file access.

## The Secure Shell server

Systems talk to each other over a network. People use their machines to log in to remote terminals to access and/or process information on those servers. In order for the communication to be safe, we require a security mechanism in place. UNIX networking initially worked on clear text, and the information could be read if the transmission was not encrypted. Now, SSH solves this by implementing encryption at both ends of the connection. SSH has strong encryption, which makes it difficult for the people trying to crack in.

## Installing the SSH server

When you install the server, the client for SSH is also installed. It is preferred to install the server package even if all you need is client only. There are many benefits of having the server package of SSH installed. The command to install the SSH server is as follows:

```
sudo apt-get install openssh-server
```

This is shown in the following screenshot:

```
skanda@UbuntuServer:~$ sudo apt-get install openssh-server
[sudo] password for skanda:
Reading package lists... Done
Building dependency tree
Reading state information... Done
openssh-server is already the newest version.
0 upgraded, 0 newly installed, 0 to remove and 143 not upgraded.
skanda@UbuntuServer:~$ _
```

After the SSH server package is installed, it is set to start by default. This will start at runlevel 2 instead of runlevel 1. So, it will start in the single user mode. If the server were configured to boot into recovery mode, then SSH would not be possible for administrating the remote server.

# Configuration

By default, most of the configuration for basic operation is set automatically. You may be required to open the port 22 TCP/IP if firewall or security blocks are in place. The configuration files for the SSH server can be found in following locations:

- /etc/default/ssh
- /etc/ssh/sshd_config

The first file is shown in the following screenshot:

```
skanda@UbuntuServer:~$ cd /etc/default/
skanda@UbuntuServer:/etc/default$ cat ssh
# Default settings for openssh-server. This file is sourced by /bin/sh from
# /etc/init.d/ssh.

# Options to pass to sshd
SSHD_OPTS=
skanda@UbuntuServer:/etc/default$ _
```

# Default settings for the SSH server

The SSH script in /etc/init.d/ssh is responsible for starting the SSH daemon located in /usr/sbin/sshd. It reads the custom configuration, if any, from the configuration file /etc/default/ssh. You may limit access to IPv4 or IPv6 address, have your own configuration file, or even choose to use a different TCP/IP port address.

# The SSH configuration file

The configuration file for the SSH server is located at /etc/ssh/sshd_config. We will look at the important settings in this file and also look at their default values:

```
#Banner /etc/issue.net
skanda@UbuntuServer:/etc/ssh$ cat sshd_config
# Package generated configuration file
# See the sshd_config(5) manpage for details

# What ports, IPs and protocols we listen for
Port 22
# Use these options to restrict which interfaces/protocols sshd will bind to
#ListenAddress ::
#ListenAddress 0.0.0.0
Protocol 2
# HostKeys for protocol version 2
HostKey /etc/ssh/ssh_host_rsa_key
HostKey /etc/ssh/ssh_host_dsa_key
HostKey /etc/ssh/ssh_host_ecdsa_key
HostKey /etc/ssh/ssh_host_ed25519_key
#Privilege Separation is turned on for security
UsePrivilegeSeparation yes

# Lifetime and size of ephemeral version 1 server key
KeyRegenerationInterval 3600
ServerKeyBits 1024

# Logging
SyslogFacility AUTH
LogLevel INFO

# Authentication:
LoginGraceTime 120
PermitRootLogin without-password
```

As you can see from the preceding screenshot, first we have the port number. The default TCP/IP port for the SSH service is 22. Comment this line if you wish to use a different port address, and mention the new port address in the /etc/default/ssh file.

```
Port 22
```

If this server is one of your gateways, then uncomment the following two settings and specify the address you want the server to listen to. By default, it would listen to all addresses if not changed:

```
#ListenAddress ::
#ListenAddress 0.0.0.0
```

The next line tells which version of SSH to use. You should ideally be using version 2, which is lot more secure than the previous version:

```
Protocol 2
```

The next two lines are for the host keys. These are created during installation and access for read/write is limited to root alone. These names refer to encryption algorithms, RSA, and DSA:

```
HostKey /etc/ssh/ssh_host_rsa_key
HostKey /etc/ssh/ssh_host_dsa_key
```

To minimize the risk due to unprivileged process access, keep the following setting to true:

```
UsePrivilegeSeparation yes
```

Enable logging to send all log messages corresponding to authentication to the location /var/log/secure. Each successful login or failure event is logged in the log files:

```
SyslogFacility AUTH
LogLevel INFO
```

The next set of directives is for authentication. LoginGraceTime is measured in seconds. It is the time given for a user to enter the password before closing the connection. By default, access to root administration is allowed. However, it is a best practice to disable it. The next setting checks the user ownership over a directory and prevents other users from accessing files of a user who has not set any permission:

```
LoginGraceTime 120
PermitRootLogin yes
StrictModes yes
```

You may ignore the RSAAuthentication line as it is required only for SSH protocol version 1. The next line, PubkeyAuthentication, is for enabling or disabling the support of private/public authentication keys. We will discuss this in the next stage. AuthorizedKeysFile specifies the location of authorized encryption login keys, which is usually a user's home subdirectory. All these are default values:

```
RSAAuthentication yes
PubkeyAuthentication yes
#AuthorizedKeysFile      %h/.ssh/authorized_keys
```

Have a look at the following screenshot:

```
KeyRegenerationInterval 3600
ServerKeyBits 1024

# Logging
SyslogFacility AUTH
LogLevel INFO

# Authentication:
LoginGraceTime 120
PermitRootLogin without-password
StrictModes yes

RSAAuthentication yes
PubkeyAuthentication yes
#AuthorizedKeysFile      %h/.ssh/authorized_keys

# Don't read the user's ~/.rhosts and ~/.shosts files
IgnoreRhosts yes
# For this to work you will also need host keys in /etc/ssh_known_hosts
RhostsRSAAuthentication no
# similar for protocol version 2
HostbasedAuthentication no
# Uncomment if you don't trust ~/.ssh/known_hosts for RhostsRSAAuthentication
#IgnoreUserKnownHosts yes

# To enable empty passwords, change to yes (NOT RECOMMENDED)
PermitEmptyPasswords no

# Change to yes to enable challenge-response passwords (beware issues with
# some PAM modules and threads)
```

Also, it is advisable not to allow users to use an empty password. So, you need to set the following settings:

```
PermitEmptyPasswords no
ChallengeResponseAuthentication no
```

The `PasswordAuthentication` setting will be commented, but it is definitely important. This is the default value. You should disable it only if you do not want the SSH server to transmit passwords over network. Wondering how to log in then? Wait for the key-based authentication section. The `PasswordAuthentication` setting specifies whether local passwords can be used for authentication:

```
# PasswordAuthentication yes
PasswordAuthentication = yes
```

The next set of flags will help you enable remote access on GUI based windows:

```
X11Forwarding yes
X11DisplayOffset 10
```

If you want the connection to the server to be restored in the event of an interruption in a wireless network, then set the following setting as `yes`:

```
TCPKeepAlive yes
```

You can control the maximum number of SSH connections to the server with the following setting. The next line after that is the message you want to display to the user at login. You may customize the message in the file specified as part of value.

```
#MaxStartups 10:30:60
#Banner /etc/issue.net
```

SFTP is the encrypted and secure method of FTP over SSH connections. You should be enabling it and then setting it as follows:

```
Subsystem sftp   /usr/lib/openssh/sftp-server
```

The PAM utilities can be used if the following directive is set to yes:

```
UsePAM yes
```

These settings are shown in the following screenshot:

```
GSSAPIAuthentication yes
GSSAPICleanupCredentials yes
GssapiKeyExchange yes

X11Forwarding yes
X11DisplayOffset 10
PrintMotd no
PrintLastLog yes
TCPKeepAlive yes
#UseLogin no

#MaxStartups 10:30:60
#Banner /etc/issue.net

# Allow client to pass locale environment variables
AcceptEnv LANG LC_*

Subsystem sftp /usr/lib/openssh/sftp-server

# Set this to 'yes' to enable PAM authentication, account processing,
# and session processing. If this is enabled, PAM authentication will
# be allowed through the ChallengeResponseAuthentication and
# PasswordAuthentication.  Depending on your PAM configuration,
# PAM authentication via ChallengeResponseAuthentication may bypass
# the setting of "PermitRootLogin without-password".
# If you just want the PAM account and session checks to run without
# PAM authentication, then enable this but set PasswordAuthentication
# and ChallengeResponseAuthentication to 'no'.
UsePAM yes
skanda@UbuntuServer:/etc/ssh$ _
```

# Using passphrases

You can strengthen your security by not allowing passwords to be transmitted over a network. For this, you will need to set the password authentication to no in the preceding file (from previous section). We will change this at the last step after setting up passphrases:

```
PasswordAuthentication no
```

Now, we will use a pair of keys to set up passphrases. A pair of public and private keys will do the authentication work for you and passwords won't be required between two machines. The process is simple.

First, log in to the client machine. Next, generate the public/private key pair on client machine using the following command:

```
ssh-keygen -t rsa
```

The preceding command will create two files in the user's `home` directory under the `./ssh` folder. It will ask for a location where you want to save the files. By default, it will show `./ssh` under the user's `home` directory. Just press *Enter* so that the default location is selected. Next, it will prompt you to enter a passphrase to your set of public/private key pair. Enter a passphrase; if you leave it blank, it is possible that any person who gets a hold of the client machine can get into the server, which may be problematic in some cases:

```
Enter file in which to save the key (/home/skanda/.ssh/id_rsa):

Enter passphrase (empty for no passphrase):
Enter same passphrase again:
Your identification has been saved in /home/skanda/.ssh/id_rsa.
Your public key has been saved in /home/skanda/.ssh/id_rsa.pub.
The key fingerprint is:
```

This is shown in the following screenshot:

By default, it uses 1024-bit encryption that is good enough for most cases. However, if you feel the need for a stronger encryption, you can specify the encryption strength as follows. Note that the higher the bits you ask for, the more the amount of time taken will be. The command is as follows:

```
ssh-keygen -t rsa -b 4096
```

We have generated the key pair. The next step is to add the public key to the server for which you want access to. This can be done in three ways. Use the following command to copy the public key to server's known hosts folder:

```
ssh-copy-id -i .ssh/id_rsa.pub 192.168.1.5
```

The option -i stands for identity file, that is, it specifies which public key file will be copied. The IP address is the server's IP address to which you want to add the client's public key for pairing. You will be prompted for the server's password. Once the pairing is done, you will be able to SSH into the server without the need for a password.

The second way is to copy it to the server machine over SFTP and then append the key into the **authorized keys** file. Be careful here; do not erase the file contents already present in the file.

The last method is to copy your public key to a USB flash drive (pen drive) and then copy it into the server machine. Append the public key file to the authorized keys file.

After you get your public key successfully added to the authorized keys file, you can try logging in to the server from the client. If all goes well, you will not be prompted for a password. If it asks you to enter your password, it means that the previous operation was not successful. Repeat the process again. If you were able to log in to the server without password, then your passphrases setup is successful. Now, you can go ahead and set the following setting to false, which will make sure that the server will accept connection only if private/public keys match and will not authenticate on password:

```
PasswordAuthentication no
```

This has to be changed in the /etc/ssh/sshd_config file.

# Scheduling jobs with cron

The cron system has brought relief to system administrators, without which they had to wake up and run jobs at specified times in order to run a server smoothly. For example, if there is a requirement to clear the /tmp directory every Sunday midnight before the business begins next day (Monday morning), it makes absolutely no sense for an administrator to be awake and carry out the job manually at midnight. Thanks to cron, jobs can now be scheduled, that is, they can start at scheduled times. **cron** and **at** are daemons that help achieve this. Linux's cron is a little different compared to that of Unix, as cron in Unix wakes only at the time when it has to launch a program.

The cron and at daemons should be installed by default on your Ubuntu Server. Systems are designed to check for user specified cron jobs in the /var/spool/cron directory, as shown in the following screenshot. Also, cron checks the /etc/crontab and the /etc/cron.d directory for computer jobs.

```
skanda@UbuntuServer:~$ ls -ltr /var/spool/cron/
total 12
drwx-wx--T 2 root    crontab 4096 Feb  9  2013 crontabs
drwxrwx--T 2 daemon daemon  4096 Oct 21  2013 atspool
drwxrwx--T 2 daemon daemon  4096 Mar 25 22:53 atjobs
skanda@UbuntuServer:~$
```

Let's take a look at the /etc/crontab configuration file. Comments start with #. The SHELL and PATH are variables that can be set. Time serves as an alarm for running the commands specified in the file.

Let's understand the following line from the /etc/crontab file:

```
# m h dom mon dow user command
```

Here is the representation of each of the columns in the preceding line:

| Column heading | Description |
|---|---|
| m | Minute |
| h | Hour |
| dom | Day of month |
| mon | Calendar month |
| dow | Day of week |
| user | User running the job |
| command | Command to run the job |

A star or an asterisk (*) means the job will be run for all standard values for that particular column. For example, an * under month will represent all values 1 to 12. The /etc/crontab is shown in the following screenshot:

```
skanda@UbuntuServer:~$ cat /etc/crontab
# /etc/crontab: system-wide crontab
# Unlike any other crontab you don't have to run the `crontab'
# command to install the new version when you edit this file
# and files in /etc/cron.d. These files also have username fields,
# that none of the other crontabs do.

SHELL=/bin/sh
PATH=/usr/local/sbin:/usr/local/bin:/sbin:/bin:/usr/sbin:/usr/bin

# m h dom mon dow user   command
17 *    * * *    root    cd / && run-parts --report /etc/cron.hourly
25 6    * * *    root    test -x /usr/sbin/anacron || ( cd / && run-parts --repor
t /etc/cron.daily )
47 6    * * 7    root    test -x /usr/sbin/anacron || ( cd / && run-parts --repor
t /etc/cron.weekly )
52 6    1 * *    root    test -x /usr/sbin/anacron || ( cd / && run-parts --repor
t /etc/cron.monthly )
#
skanda@UbuntuServer:~$ _
```

Standard jobs in Linux are run from the /etc/crontab file on an hourly, daily, weekly, and monthly basis. The scripts for these files are present in the corresponding folders /etc/cron.hourly, /etc/cron.daily, /etc/cron.weekly, and /etc/cron.monthly, respectively. The schedule for jobs which do not fall under any of these is put into the /etc/cron.d directory:

```
/etc/cron.hourly:
total 0

/etc/cron.weekly:
total 16
-rwxr-xr-x 1 root root 730 Feb 23  2014 apt-xapian-index
-rwxr-xr-x 1 root root 211 Apr 10  2014 update-notifier-common
-rwxr-xr-x 1 root root 771 Apr 10  2014 man-db
-rwxr-xr-x 1 root root 427 Apr 16  2014 fstrim

/etc/cron.daily:
total 64
-rwxr-xr-x 1 root root  2417 May 13  2013 popularity-contest
-rwxr-xr-x 1 root root   355 Jun  4  2013 bsdmainutils
-rwxr-xr-x 1 root root   435 Jun 20  2013 mlocate
-rwxr-xr-x 1 root root   372 Jan 23  2014 logrotate
-rwxr-xr-x 1 root root   249 Feb 17  2014 passwd
-rwxr-xr-x 1 root root   314 Feb 18  2014 aptitude
-rwxr-xr-x 1 root root   256 Mar  7  2014 dpkg
-rwxr-xr-x 1 root root   376 Apr  4  2014 apport
-rwxr-xr-x 1 root root   214 Apr 10  2014 update-notifier-common
-rwxr-xr-x 1 root root  1261 Apr 10  2014 man-db
-rwxr-xr-x 1 root root 15481 Apr 10  2014 apt
-rwxr-xr-x 1 root root   328 Jul 18  2014 upstart
-rwxr-xr-x 1 root root   625 Mar 10 18:37 apache2

/etc/cron.d:
total 4
-rw-r--r-- 1 root root 510 Mar 17 02:30 php5
skanda@UbuntuServer:~$ _
```

# Scheduling user cron jobs

Normal users can make use of the cron daemons to schedule and run user specific jobs. Here are the four switches that deal with crontab:

- `-u user`: The root user can edit the crontab file of another user.
- `-l`: This is used to list the entries in the crontab.
- `-r`: This is used to remove cron entries.
- `-e`: This is used to edit a crontab entry.

Users can configure account-specific cron jobs using the following command:

```
crontab -e
```

This will open the Nano editor, which is the default editor in Ubuntu for editing a crontab file. The format to be followed for the user-specific cron file will be the same as that of the system-level `/etc/crontab` configuration file. However, the username is not required:

```
  GNU nano 2.2.6          File: /tmp/crontab.dWXONK/crontab

# Edit this file to introduce tasks to be run by cron.
#
# Each task to run has to be defined through a single line
# indicating with different fields when the task will be run
# and what command to run for the task
#
# To define the time you can provide concrete values for
# minute (m), hour (h), day of month (dom), month (mon),
# and day of week (dow) or use '*' in these fields (for 'any').#
# Notice that tasks will be started based on the cron's system
# daemon's notion of time and timezones.
#
# Output of the crontab jobs (including errors) is sent through
# email to the user the crontab file belongs to (unless redirected).
#
# For example, you can run a backup of all your user accounts
# at 5 a.m every week with:
# 0 5 * * 1 tar -zcf /var/backups/home.tgz /home/
#
# For more information see the manual pages of crontab(5) and cron(8)
#
# m h  dom mon dow   command

^G Get Help  ^O WriteOut  ^R Read File  ^Y Prev Page  ^K Cut Text   ^C Cur Pos
^X Exit      ^J Justify   ^W Where Is   ^V Next Page  ^U UnCut Text ^T To Spell
```

You will see a window similar to the preceding screenshot when you edit a user-specific crontab configuration file.

# Configuring jobs using at

We discussed cron in the previous section. It is used to schedule and run jobs at regular intervals. The **at** utility is used to schedule jobs for one-time execution. An example of one-time scheduling may be formatting a media drive. The jobs which are scheduled using the at daemon can be seen in the following directory `/var/spool/cron/atspool`.

The command to schedule a job using the at utility is as follows:

```
$ at now + 1 hour
at> touch report_file
at> Ctrl-D
```

Take a look at the following screenshot:

```
skanda@UbuntuServer:~$ at now + 1 hour
warning: commands will be executed using /bin/sh
at> touch report_file
at> <EOT>
job 1 at Sat Jun  6 12:13:00 2015
skanda@UbuntuServer:~$ atq
1         Sat Jun  6 12:13:00 2015 a skanda
skanda@UbuntuServer:~$ atrm 1
skanda@UbuntuServer:~$ atq
skanda@UbuntuServer:~$
```

To come out of the at prompt, hit the *Ctrl + D* keys. If you want to view the list of jobs spooled for the at daemon, use the command `atq`. To remove a job scheduled by at, use the command `atrm` with the queue number that you viewed with the `atq` command. The preceding screenshot shows the same.

Some of the examples for the at schedule are listed in the following table:

| Period | Example | Description |
|---|---|---|
| Minutes | at now + 40 minutes | Start the job in 40 minutes |
| Hours | at now + 5 hours | Start the job in 5 hours |
| Days | at now + 3 days | Start the job in 72 hours |
| Weeks | at now + 2 weeks | Start the job in 14 days |
| n/a | at teatime | Start the job at 4.00 p.m. |
| n/a | at 2:00 06/22/15 | Start the job at 2 a.m. on June 6, 2015 |

# Job schedule security

System administrators can limit the user's access to cron and at daemons. For cron, the settings need to be implemented in the /etc/cron.allow and /etc/cron. deny files. If these files are not present, then cron usage is not restricted. If there are usernames present in the allow file, then only these users are allowed to use the cron daemon to schedule jobs. Conversely, if the deny files has usernames, then all users expect the ones mentioned can make use of the cron daemon. The right way to populate these files is to mention one username per line.

Similarly, access to the at daemon can be controlled. The configuration files for this are /etc/at.allow and /etc/at.deny, as shown in the following screenshot:

```
skanda@UbuntuServer:~$ sudo ls /etc/at*
/etc/at.deny
skanda@UbuntuServer:~$ sudo cat /etc/at.deny
alias
backup
bin
daemon
ftp
games
gnats
guest
irc
lp
mail
man
nobody
operator
proxy
qmaild
qmaill
qmailp
qmailq
qmailr
qmails
sync
sys
www-data
skanda@UbuntuServer:~$ _
```

By default, the configuration file /etc/at.deny has a standard list of services, as shown in the preceding screenshot. If an unauthorized user breaks into any of these, they will not be able to run at jobs.

# Optimizing the shell

By default, Ubuntu configures the root and the first user created to the bash shell. This is the traditional shell. Any users created from this shell will also be given the same bash shell. We will discuss the configuration files and commands related to the bash shell. The system-wide settings files can be located in the folder /etc. Some of the most important ones are bash.bashrc, bash_completion, profile, and scripts stored in the /etc/bash_completion.d folder:

```
skanda@UbuntuServer:~$ ls /etc/bas*
/etc/bash.bashrc  /etc/bash_completion

/etc/bash_completion.d:
apache2              axi-cache  gem1.9.1  initramfs-tools  pon  upstart
apport_completion    debconf    grub      insserv          ufw
skanda@UbuntuServer:~$
```

The same files are supplemented and you can override them as hidden files in each users' home directory. The files are .bashrc, .bash_history, .bash_logout, and .profile, as shown in the following screenshot:

```
skanda@UbuntuServer:~$ ls -ltra
total 64
drwxr-xr-x 3 root   root   4096 Mar 25 22:54 ..
-rw-r--r-- 1 skanda skanda  675 Mar 25 22:54 .profile
-rw-r--r-- 1 skanda skanda 3637 Mar 25 22:54 .bashrc
-rw-r--r-- 1 skanda skanda  220 Mar 25 22:54 .bash_logout
drwx------ 2 skanda skanda 4096 Mar 25 22:57 .cache
-rwxrwxrwx 1 root   root    584 Mar 26 06:53 new_content.ldif
-rwxrwxrwx 1 root   root     67 Mar 26 07:22 log_enable.ldif
-rw------- 1 root   root     10 Apr 14 03:51 .nano_history
-rw------- 1 skanda skanda   86 May  6 14:25 .sh_history
-rw------- 1 skanda skanda  593 May  7 22:41 .viminfo
drwx------ 2 skanda skanda 4096 Jun  5 09:30 .ssh
-rw------- 1 skanda skanda 9772 Jun  5 11:43 .bash_history
drwxr-xr-x 4 skanda skanda 4096 Jun  6 10:52 .
-rw-r--r-- 1 skanda skanda   66 Jun  6 10:52 .selected_editor
skanda@UbuntuServer:~$
```

# Bash profiles

We will look at the two files that are the configuration files for the bash shell. They are stored in /etc and named bash.bashrc and profile.

# The /etc/bash.bashrc file

Ubuntu uses the /etc/bash.bashrc file for aliases and functions throughout the system. You can open the file and view the contents to get an understanding of what parameters are set for the users of this system:

```
skanda@UbuntuServer:~$ sudo cat /etc/bash.bashrc
[sudo] password for skanda:
# System-wide .bashrc file for interactive bash(1) shells.

# To enable the settings / commands in this file for login shells as well,
# this file has to be sourced in /etc/profile.

# If not running interactively, don't do anything
[ -z "$PS1" ] && return

# check the window size after each command and, if necessary,
# update the values of LINES and COLUMNS.
shopt -s checkwinsize

# set variable identifying the chroot you work in (used in the prompt below)
if [ -z "${debian_chroot:-}" ] && [ -r /etc/debian_chroot ]; then
    debian_chroot=$(cat /etc/debian_chroot)
fi

# set a fancy prompt (non-color, overwrite the one in /etc/profile)
PS1='${debian_chroot:+($debian_chroot)}\u@\h:\w\$ '

# Commented out, don't overwrite xterm -T "title" -n "icontitle" by default.
# If this is an xterm set the title to user@host:dir
#case "$TERM" in
#xterm*|rxvt*)
#    PROMPT_COMMAND='echo -ne "\033]0;${USER}@${HOSTNAME}: ${PWD}\007"'
#    ;;
#*)
#    ;;
```

Some of the parameters we can see in the file are as follows:

- Assigning a prompt using the PS1 variable. This appears at start of line before the cursor at command prompt.
- The settings for automatic command completion from /etc/bash_completion
- Message to be displayed when user is logging with sudo access.

The same settings are called in each user's home directory by .bashrc. There might be some additional settings in the user's home directory files of .bash_history and .bash_logout.

# The /etc/profile file

This file is used by Ubuntu for system-wide environment and startup files. Let's look at the /etc/profile file. You will see a similar file in your Ubuntu Server:

```
skanda@UbuntuServer:~$ sudo cat /etc/profile
# /etc/profile: system-wide .profile file for the Bourne shell (sh(1))
# and Bourne compatible shells (bash(1), ksh(1), ash(1), ...).

if [ "$PS1" ]; then
  if [ "$BASH" ] && [ "$BASH" != "/bin/sh" ]; then
    # The file bash.bashrc already sets the default PS1.
    # PS1='\h:\w\$ '
    if [ -f /etc/bash.bashrc ]; then
      . /etc/bash.bashrc
    fi
  else
    if [ "`id -u`" -eq 0 ]; then
      PS1='# '
    else
      PS1='$ '
    fi
  fi
fi

# The default umask is now handled by pam_umask.
# See pam_umask(8) and /etc/login.defs.

if [ -d /etc/profile.d ]; then
  for i in /etc/profile.d/*.sh; do
    if [ -r $i ]; then
      . $i
    fi
  done
  unset i
```

We can see the profile sets a command prompt as the value for the PS variable.

# Variables in bash

There are quite a few standard environment variables for bash. To check the default values for them, use the env command. One of the most important variables in bash is the PATH. When you try to run a command, the directories listed in $PATH will be automatically searched. So, you will not be required to include the complete path to the command if the parent directories' path exists in the $PATH variable. Run the env command:

```
env
```

The output of this command is shown in the following screenshot:

```
skanda@UbuntuServer:~$ env
SHELL=/bin/bash
TERM=linux
HUSHLOGIN=FALSE
USER=skanda
LS_COLORS=rs=0:di=01;34:ln=01;36:mh=00:pi=40;33:so=01;35:do=01;35:bd=40;33;01:cd
=40;33;01:or=40;31;01:su=37;41:sg=30;43:ca=30;41:tw=30;42:ow=34;42:st=37;44:ex=0
1;32:*.tar=01;31:*.tgz=01;31:*.arj=01;31:*.taz=01;31:*.lzh=01;31:*.lzma=01;31:*.
tlz=01;31:*.txz=01;31:*.zip=01;31:*.z=01;31:*.Z=01;31:*.dz=01;31:*.gz=01;31:*.lz
=01;31:*.xz=01;31:*.bz2=01;31:*.bz=01;31:*.tbz=01;31:*.tbz2=01;31:*.tz=01;31:*.d
eb=01;31:*.rpm=01;31:*.jar=01;31:*.war=01;31:*.ear=01;31:*.sar=01;31:*.rar=01;31
:*.ace=01;31:*.zoo=01;31:*.cpio=01;31:*.7z=01;31:*.rz=01;31:*.jpg=01;35:*.jpeg=0
1;35:*.gif=01;35:*.bmp=01;35:*.pbm=01;35:*.pgm=01;35:*.ppm=01;35:*.tga=01;35:*.x
bm=01;35:*.xpm=01;35:*.tif=01;35:*.tiff=01;35:*.png=01;35:*.svg=01;35:*.svgz=01;
35:*.mng=01;35:*.pcx=01;35:*.mov=01;35:*.mpg=01;35:*.mpeg=01;35:*.m2v=01;35:*.mk
v=01;35:*.webm=01;35:*.ogm=01;35:*.mp4=01;35:*.m4v=01;35:*.mp4v=01;35:*.vob=01;3
5:*.qt=01;35:*.nuv=01;35:*.wmv=01;35:*.asf=01;35:*.rm=01;35:*.rmvb=01;35:*.flc=0
1;35:*.avi=01;35:*.fli=01;35:*.flv=01;35:*.gl=01;35:*.dl=01;35:*.xcf=01;35:*.xwd
=01;35:*.yuv=01;35:*.cgm=01;35:*.emf=01;35:*.axv=01;35:*.anx=01;35:*.ogv=01;35:*
.ogx=01;35:*.aac=00;36:*.au=00;36:*.flac=00;36:*.mid=00;36:*.midi=00;36:*.mka=00
;36:*.mp3=00;36:*.mpc=00;36:*.ogg=00;36:*.ra=00;36:*.wav=00;36:*.axa=00;36:*.oga
=00;36:*.spx=00;36:*.xspf=00;36:
MAIL=/var/mail/skanda
PATH=/usr/local/sbin:/usr/local/bin:/usr/sbin:/usr/bin:/sbin:/bin:/usr/games:/us
r/local/games
PWD=/home/skanda
LANG=en_US.UTF-8
SHLVL=1
HOME=/home/skanda
LOGNAME=skanda
```

You can add a new path for a directory to the path variable. If you want to add /etc into the $PATH variable, then execute the following commands on the shell:

**PATH=$PATH:/etc**

**export PATH**

**echo $PATH**

However, if you want to set a user's path, then add the following line to that particular user's .profile file in the home directory:

```
PATH=$PATH:/etc
```

# User management and file permissions

We will discuss user management concepts such as creating a user, assigning permissions, and deleting a user in this section. Then, we will discuss file permissions for user and groups.

# User management in Ubuntu

In this section, we will discuss how to add users, delete users, give them permissions, and more.

## Adding and removing users

To add a new user to your Ubuntu Server, use the following command:

```
sudo adduser user2
```

You will be asked to enter some details apart from the username and password for the new user. To delete a user, use the following commands:

```
sudo deluser user2
sudo rm -r /home/user2
```

Pay attention here, this operation does not delete the home directory of the user. Adding and deleting groups is similar to that of users. Here's the syntax to add and remove groups:

```
sudo addgroup groupname
sudo delgroup groupname
```

Now, to add a user to a group, execute the following command:

```
sudo adduser user2 groupname
```

# Managing file permissions

Linux is known for its security offered on file access, with read, write, and execute. You can set the default permissions using umask. A user who creates a file will become the owner initially, but this can be changed too. We will look at different commands such as chmod, chown, and chgrp in the following sections in order to efficiently manage the permissions for file access.

## Understanding file permissions

File permissions in Linux are very easy to understand. Let's look at an example here:

```
ls -l /etc/ssh
```

The output of this command is shown in the following screenshot. The first 10 characters are of importance to us while discussing permissions. The first character states this is a file or directory; d stands for directory, whereas a stands for a regular file, b is for the block device, and c is the hardware. The next set of nine characters is for file permissions. We will read those in sets of three. The first set of three bits is file owner's permission, next set of three bits is group permissions, and the last set of three bits is access permissions for others. Here, r is read, w is write, and x is execute.

```
skanda@UbuntuServer:~$ ls -l /etc/ssh/
total 284
-rw-r--r-- 1 root root 242091 May 12  2014 moduli
-rw-r--r-- 1 root root   1690 Mar 27 10:22 ssh_config
-rw-r--r-- 1 root root   2561 Mar 27 10:21 sshd_config
-rw------- 1 root root    672 Mar 27 09:35 ssh_host_dsa_key
-rw-r--r-- 1 root root    607 Mar 27 09:35 ssh_host_dsa_key.pub
-rw------- 1 root root    227 Mar 27 09:35 ssh_host_ecdsa_key
-rw-r--r-- 1 root root    179 Mar 27 09:35 ssh_host_ecdsa_key.pub
-rw------- 1 root root    411 Mar 27 09:35 ssh_host_ed25519_key
-rw-r--r-- 1 root root     99 Mar 27 09:35 ssh_host_ed25519_key.pub
-rw------- 1 root root   1675 Mar 27 09:35 ssh_host_rsa_key
-rw-r--r-- 1 root root    399 Mar 27 09:35 ssh_host_rsa_key.pub
-rw-r--r-- 1 root root    338 Mar 27 09:35 ssh_import_id
skanda@UbuntuServer:~$ _
```

# Changing permissions with chmod

The chmod command uses the numeric way of representation for permissions associated with file for owner, group, and others. Octal base is used and the number 1 represents one set of 3 bits, so 3 Octal numbers with chmod will define the 9 bits we saw in the preceding section. This is explained in the following table:

| r, w, x Permissions | Binary | Octal |
|---|---|---|
| - - - | 000 | 0 |
| - -x | 001 | 1 |
| -w- | 010 | 2 |
| -wx | 011 | 3 |
| r- - | 100 | 4 |
| r-x | 101 | 5 |
| rw- | 110 | 6 |
| rwx | 111 | 7 |

Here are the values for read, write, and execute: r is 4, w is 2, and x is 1. Let's create a new file in the home directory and change the permissions using the chmod command:

```
touch test_file
ls -l test_file
chmod 755 test_file
ls -l test_file
```

This is shown in the following screenshot:

```
skanda@UbuntuServer:~$ touch test_file
skanda@UbuntuServer:~$ ls -l test_file
-rw-r--r-- 1 skanda skanda 0 Jun  7 06:46 test_file
skanda@UbuntuServer:~$ chmod 755 test_file
skanda@UbuntuServer:~$ ls -l test_file
-rwxr-xr-x 1 skanda skanda 0 Jun  7 06:46 test_file
skanda@UbuntuServer:~$ _
```

Here, we changed the access permissions for groups and others. We made the file executable. Only 3 Octal digits can change the entire 9 bits of file permissions access.

One more method exists to change the file access permissions. Suppose you want to give group write permissions for the preceding file. You can use the following command to change only write bits for users in the group:

```
chmod g+w test_file
```

The letters for user, group, and others are u, g, and o respectively. The access letters for read, write, and execute are r, w, and x, respectively. The symbols + and - are used to add or remove an access permission. This method is used in cases when you want to change only 1 access and for one user type only. Have a look at the following screenshot:

```
skanda@UbuntuServer:~$ touch test_file
skanda@UbuntuServer:~$ ls -l test_file
-rw-r--r-- 1 skanda skanda 0 Jun  7 06:46 test_file
skanda@UbuntuServer:~$ chmod 755 test_file
skanda@UbuntuServer:~$ ls -l test_file
-rwxr-xr-x 1 skanda skanda 0 Jun  7 06:46 test_file
skanda@UbuntuServer:~$ chmod g+w test_file
skanda@UbuntuServer:~$ ls -l test_file
-rwxrwxr-x 1 skanda skanda 0 Jun  7 06:46 test_file
skanda@UbuntuServer:~$
```

# Modifying ownership using chown and chgrp

To change the user and group owner for a file, use the chown and chgrp commands, respectively. Let's try these two commands. We will create a user named user2, a new group named testgroup, and change user and group owner for the preceding file named test_file:

```
sudo adduser user2

sudo addgroup test_group

ls -ltr test_file

sudo chown user2 test_file

sudo chgrp test_group test_file

ls -ltr test_file
```

As we can see in the following screenshot, we first created a new user, user2. Then, we created a new group test_group. Next, we changed the owner of the file to user2 using the chown command. Finally, we successfully changed the group owner to test_group with the chgrp command. For verification, we executed the ls -ltr command with the parameter test_file file name before and after executing the chown and chgrp commands. We could clearly see the difference and hence our executions were successful.

```
skanda@UbuntuServer:~$ sudo adduser user2
[sudo] password for skanda:
Adding user `user2' ...
Adding new group `user2' (1001) ...
Adding new user `user2' (1001) with group `user2' ...
Creating home directory `/home/user2' ...
Copying files from `/etc/skel' ...
Current Kerberos password:
Current Kerberos password:
passwd: Authentication token manipulation error
passwd: password unchanged
Try again? [y/N] n
Changing the user information for user2
Enter the new value, or press ENTER for the default
        Full Name []: user2
        Room Number []:
        Work Phone []:
        Home Phone []:
        Other []:
Is the information correct? [Y/n] Y
skanda@UbuntuServer:~$ sudo addgroup test_group
Adding group `test_group' (GID 1002) ...
Done.
skanda@UbuntuServer:~$ ls -ltr test_file
-rwxrwxr-x 1 skanda skanda 0 Jun  7 06:46 test_file
skanda@UbuntuServer:~$ sudo chown user2 test_file
skanda@UbuntuServer:~$ sudo chgrp test_group test_file
skanda@UbuntuServer:~$ ls -ltr test_file
-rwxrwxr-x 1 user2 test_group 0 Jun  7 06:46 test_file
skanda@UbuntuServer:~$ _
```

# Setting default permissions with umask

In Linux, whenever a new file is created, the execution permissions for it will be disabled by default. This is to ensure security, as less executable files mean less chances of breaking through the system. Each time a new file is created, its permissions are set based on the values specified in umask. For example, if the umask value is set to 133, then the new file will have permission as *777 - 133 = 644*. This means the user or owner has read/write permission, the group owner has only read permission, and others have read permission only. Use the following command to see the umask value in your Ubuntu Server:

```
umask
```

To change the value of umask, run the command with the value you want to set. If we want to change the umask value to 022, we can run the command as follows:

```
umask 0022
```

The first bit, which is 0, is not used, so you can ignore it. One important point to remember is that even though you set umask values to make a file executable at creation, Ubuntu no longer allows a file to have executable permissions at the point of file creation. You will have to manually change the permission using the chmod command.

# Special file permissions

Sometimes, it is imperative to provide all users in the system with access to some programs. But giving read, write, and execute permissions to every user can be risky. One way is to set SUID and SGID permission for a file. **SUID** stands for **set user ID** and **SGID** is short for **set group ID**. SUID, SGID and sticky bits are special permissions for a file. Let's check how the permissions look for a file with SUID set:

```
ls -l /usr/bin/passwd
```

The output is shown in the following screenshot. You can see an s character instead of x for the user's execute permission. Even though the user owner and group owner is root, all users in your system will have execute permission for this file. The rules are similar for the SGID bit as well.

```
skanda@UbuntuServer:~$ ls -l /usr/bin/passwd
-rwsr-xr-x 1 root root 47032 Feb 17  2014 /usr/bin/passwd
skanda@UbuntuServer:~$ ls -l /
total 81
drwxr-xr-x   2 root root  4096 May  6 14:22 bin
drwxr-xr-x   4 root root  1024 Mar 25 22:53 boot
drwxr-xr-x  15 root root  4100 Jun 10 17:40 dev
drwxr-xr-x 102 root root  4096 Jun 10 17:48 etc
drwxr-xr-x   4 root root  4096 Jun 10 17:47 home
lrwxrwxrwx   1 root root    33 Mar 25 22:45 initrd.img -> boot/initrd.img-3.13.0
-32-generic
drwxr-xr-x  21 root root  4096 Mar 26 18:43 lib
drwxr-xr-x   2 root root  4096 Mar 26 18:43 lib64
drwx------   2 root root 16384 Mar 25 22:45 lost+found
drwxr-xr-x   3 root root  4096 Mar 25 22:45 media
drwxr-xr-x   2 root root  4096 Apr 11  2014 mnt
drwxr-xr-x   2 root root  4096 Jul 23  2014 opt
dr-xr-xr-x 107 root root     0 Jun 10 17:40 proc
drwx------   2 root root  4096 Mar 26 00:35 root
drwxr-xr-x  24 root root   860 Jun 10 17:43 run
drwxr-xr-x   2 root root 12288 Apr 13 18:48 sbin
drwxr-xr-x   2 root root  4096 Jul 23  2014 srv
dr-xr-xr-x  13 root root     0 Jun 10 17:40 sys
drwxrwxrwt   2 root root  4096 Jun 10 18:25 tmp
drwxr-xr-x  10 root root  4096 Mar 25 22:45 usr
drwxr-xr-x  13 root root  4096 Apr 13 18:48 var
lrwxrwxrwx   1 root root    30 Mar 25 22:45 vmlinuz -> boot/vmlinuz-3.13.0-32-ge
neric
skanda@UbuntuServer:~$ _
```

We can check for the sticky bit for a directory with the `ls -l /` command. If you observe carefully, you will see a character t in place of x at the last permission bit for the /tmp directory. This means all users will have permission to access the /tmp folder.

You can change the SUID bit for a file. Here's the command to add SUID to our test_file:

```
sudo chmod u+s test_file
```

For changing the SGID bit, use the command chmod with the g+s option along with file name as parameter:

```
sudo chmod g+s test_file
```

The sticky bit is normally applicable to folders. This ensures that users will have permissions to add or remove files from the directory. You can set the sticky bit on a file with the following command:

```
sudo chmod o+t directory
```

# Summary

In this chapter, we discussed how to create a Secure Shell server. Then, we discussed scheduling jobs using cron, optimized the shell, and managed user profiles. In the end, we studied file access, Octal, and special file permissions.

The next chapter deals with virtualization, how to implement virtualization, and the benefits of virtualization. You will learn about KVM, Xen, and Qemu.

# 7
# Virtualization

This chapter deals with virtualization techniques—why virtualization is important and how administrators can install and serve users with services via virtualization. We will learn about KVM, Xen, and Qemu. So sit back and let's take a spin into the virtual world of Ubuntu.

## What is virtualization?

Virtualization is a technique by which you can convert a set of files into a live running machine with an OS. It is easy to set up one machine and much easier to clone and replicate the same machine across hardware. Also, each of the clones can be customized based on requirements. We will look at setting up a virtual machine using Kernel-based Virtual Machine, Xen, and Qemu in the sections that follow.

Today, people are using the power of virtualization in different situations and environments. Developers use virtualization in order to have an independent environment in which they safely test and develop applications without affecting other working environments. Administrators are using virtualization to separate services and also commission or decommission services as and when required or requested.

By default, Ubuntu supports the **Kernel-based Virtual Machine** (**KVM**), which has built-in extensions for AMD and Intel-based processors. Xen and Qemu are the options suggested where you have hardware that does not have extensions for virtualization.

# libvirt

The libvirt library is an open source library that is helpful for interfacing with different virtualization technologies. One small task before starting with libvirt is to check your hardware support extensions for KVM. The command to do so is as follows:

```
kvm-ok
```

You will see a message stating whether or not your CPU supports hardware virtualization. An additional task would be to verify the BIOS settings for virtualization and activate it.

# Installation

Use the following command to install the package for libvirt:

```
sudo apt-get install kvm libvirt-bin
```

Next, you will need to add the user to the group `libvirt`. This will ensure that user gets additional options for networking. The command is as follows:

```
sudo adduser $USER libvirtd
```

We are now ready to install a guest OS. Its installation is very similar to that of installing a normal OS on the hardware. If your virtual machine needs a **graphical user interface (GUI)**, you can make use of an application **virt-viewer** and connect using VNC to the virtual machine's console. We will be discussing the virt-viewer and its uses in the later sections of this chapter.

## virt-install

virt-install is a part of the python-virtinst package. The command to install this package is as follows:

```
sudo apt-get install python-virtinst
```

One of the ways of using virt-install is as follows:

```
sudo virt-install -n new_my_vm -r 256 -f new_my_vm.img \
-s 4 -c jeos.iso --accelerate \
--connect=qemu:///system --vnc \
--noautoconsole -v
```

Let's understand the preceding command part by part:

- -n: This specifies the name of virtual machine that will be created
- -r: This specifies the RAM amount in MBs
- -f: This is the path for the virtual disk
- -s: This specifies the size of the virtual disk
- -c: This is the file to be used as virtual CD, but it can be an .iso file as well
- --accelerate: This is used to make use of kernel acceleration technologies
- --vnc: This exports the guest console via vnc
- --noautoconsole: This disables autoconnect for the virtual machine console
- -v: This creates a fully virtualized guest

Once virt-install is launched, you may connect to console with virt-viewer utility from remote connections or locally using GUI.

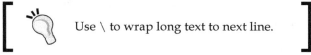

Use \ to wrap long text to next line.

# virt-clone

One of the applications to clone a virtual machine to another is virt-clone. Cloning is a process of creating an exact replica of the virtual machine that you currently have. Cloning is helpful when you need a lot of virtual machines with same configuration. Here is an example of cloning a virtual machine:

```
sudo virt-clone -o my_vm -n new_vm_clone -f /path/to/ new_vm_clone.img
--connect=qemu:///sys
```

Let's understand the preceding command part by part:

- -o: This is the original virtual machine that you want to clone
- -n: This is the new virtual machine name
- -f: This is the new virtual machine's file path
- --connect: This specifies the hypervisor to be used

# Managing the virtual machine

Let's see how to manage the virtual machine we installed using virt.

## virsh

Numerous utilities are available for managing virtual machines and libvirt; virsh is one such utility that can be used via command line. Here are a few examples:

- The following command lists the running virtual machines:

```
virsh -c qemu:///system list
```

- The following command starts a virtual machine:

```
virsh -c qemu:///system start my_new_vm
```

- The following command starts a virtual machine at boot:

```
virsh -c qemu:///system autostart my_new_vm
```

- The following command restarts a virtual machine:

```
virsh -c qemu:///system reboot my_new_vm
```

- You can save the state of virtual machine in a file. It can be restored later. Note that once you save the virtual machine, it will not be running anymore. The following command saves the state of the virtual machine:

```
virsh -c qemu://system save my_new_vm my_new_vm-290615.state
```

- The following command restores a virtual machine from saved state:

```
virsh -c qemu:///system restore my_new_vm-290615.state
```

- The following command shuts down a virtual machine:

```
virsh -c qemu:///system shutdown my_new_vm
```

- The following command mounts a CD-ROM in the virtual machine:

```
virsh -c qemu:///system attach-disk my_new_vm /dev/cdrom /media/cdrom
```

## The virtual machine manager

A GUI-type utility for managing virtual machines is virt-manager. You can manage both local and remote virtual machines. The command to install the package is as follows:

```
sudo apt-get install virt-manager
```

The virt-manager works on a GUI environment. Hence, it is advisable to install it on a remote machine other than the production cluster, as production cluster should be used for doing the main tasks. The command to connect the virt-manager to a local server running libvirt is as follows:

```
virt-manager -c qemu:///system
```

If you want to connect the virt-manager from a different machine, then first you need to have SSH connectivity. This is required as libvirt will ask for a password on the machine. Once you have set up passwordless authentication, use the following command to connect manager to server:

```
virt-manager -c qemu+ssh://virtnode1.ubuntuserver.com/system
```

Here, the virtualization server is identified with the hostname ubuntuserver.com.

# The virtual machine viewer

A utility for connecting to your virtual machine's console is virt-viewer. This requires a GUI to work with the virtual machine.

Use the following command to install virt-viewer:

```
sudo apt-get install virt-viewer
```

Now, connect to your virtual machine console from your workstation using the following command:

```
virt-viewer -c qemu:///system my_new_vm
```

You may also connect to a remote host using SSH passwordless authentication by using the following command:

```
virt-viewer -c qemu+ssh://virtnode4.ubuntuserver.com/system my_new_vm
```

# JeOS and vmbuilder

Let's now look at JeOS and vmbuilder to build our own VM image.

## JeOS

**JeOS**, short for **Just Enough Operation System**, is pronounced as "Juice" and is an operating system in the Ubuntu flavor. It is specially built for running virtual applications. JeOS is no longer available as a downloadable ISO CD-ROM. However, you can pick up any of the following approaches:

- Get a server ISO of the Ubuntu OS. While installing, hit *F4* on your keyboard. You will see a list of items and select the one that reads **Minimal installation**. This will install the JeOS variant.
- Build your own copy with vmbuilder from Ubuntu.

The kernel of JeOS is specifically tuned to run in virtual environments. It is stripped off of the unwanted packages and has only the base ones. JeOS takes advantage of the technological advancement in VMware products. A powerful combination of limited size with performance optimization is what makes JeOS a preferred OS over a full server OS in a large virtual installation.

Also, with this OS being so light, the updates and security patches will be small and only limited to this variant. So, the users who are running their virtual applications on the JeOS will have less maintenance to worry about compared to a full server OS installation.

## vmbuilder

The second way of getting the JeOS is by building your own copy of Ubuntu; you need not download any ISO from the Internet. The beauty of vmbuilder is that it will get the packages and tools based on your requirements. Then, build a virtual machine with these and the whole process is quick and easy. Essentially, vmbuilder is a script that will automate the process of creating a virtual machine, which can be easily deployed. Currently, the virtual machines built with vmbuilder are supported on KVM and Xen hypervisors.

Using command-line arguments, you can specify what additional packages you require, remove the ones that you feel aren't necessary for your needs, select the Ubuntu version, and do much more. Some developers and admins contributed to the vmbuilder and changed the design specifics, but kept the commands same. Some of the goals were as follows:

- Reusability by other distributions
- Plugin feature added for interactions, so people can add logic for other environments
- A web interface along with CLI for easy access and maintenance

# Setup

Firstly, we will need to set up libvirt and KVM before we use vmbuilder. libvirt was covered in the previous section. Let's now look at setting up KVM on your server.

We will install some additional packages along with the KVM package, and one of them is for enabling X server on the machine. The command that you will need to run on your Ubuntu Server is as follows:

```
sudo apt-get install qemu-kvm libvirt-bin ubuntu-vm-builder bridge-utils
```

The output of this command will be as follows:

```
skanda@UbuntuServer:~$ sudo apt-get install qemu-kvm libvirt-bin ubuntu-vm-build
er bridge-utils
Reading package lists... Done
Building dependency tree
Reading state information... Done
The following extra packages will be installed:
  acl build-essential cgroup-lite dctrl-tools debootstrap devscripts diffstat
  distro-info-data dnsmasq-base dpkg-dev dput ebtables fakeroot file g++
  g++-4.8 gettext hardening-includes intltool-debian iproute ipxe-qemu kpartx
  libaio1 libalgorithm-diff-perl libalgorithm-diff-xs-perl
  libalgorithm-merge-perl libapt-pkg-perl libarchive-zip-perl libasound2
  libasound2-data libasprintf-dev libasyncns0 libauthen-sasl-perl
  libautodie-perl libbluetooth3 libboost-system1.54.0 libboost-thread1.54.0
  libbrlapi0.6 libcaca0 libclone-perl libcommon-sense-perl libcroco3
  libdigest-hmac-perl libdistro-info-perl libdpkg-perl libemail-valid-perl
  libencode-locale-perl liberror-perl libexporter-lite-perl libfakeroot
  libfdt1 libfile-basedir-perl libfile-fcntllock-perl libfile-listing-perl
  libflac8 libfont-afm-perl libgettextpo-dev libgettextpo0 libhtml-form-perl
  libhtml-format-perl libhtml-parser-perl libhtml-tagset-perl
  libhtml-tree-perl libhttp-cookies-perl libhttp-daemon-perl libhttp-date-perl
  libhttp-message-perl libhttp-negotiate-perl libio-html-perl libio-pty-perl
  libio-socket-inet6-perl libio-socket-ssl-perl libio-stringy-perl
  libipc-run-perl libipc-system-simple-perl libjson-perl libjson-xs-perl
  liblist-moreutils-perl liblwp-mediatypes-perl liblwp-protocol-https-perl
  libmagic1 libmailtools-perl libmnl0 libnet-dns-perl libnet-domain-tld-perl
  libnet-http-perl libnet-ip-perl libnet-smtp-ssl-perl libnet-ssleay-perl
  libnetcf1 libnetfilter-conntrack3 libnl-route-3-200 libnspr4 libnss3
  libnss3-nssdb libogg0 libparse-debcontrol-perl libpciaccess0
  libperlio-gzip-perl libpixman-1-0 libpulse0 librados2 librbd1
  libsdl1.2debian libseccomp2 libsndfile1 libsocket6-perl libspice-server1
```

Let's look at what each of the packages mean:

- `libvirt-bin`: This is used by libvirtd for administration of KVM and Qemu
- `qemu-kvm`: This runs in the background
- `ubuntu-vm-builder`: This is a tool for building virtual machines from the command line
- `bridge-utils`: This enables networking for various virtual machines

## Adding users to groups

You will have to add the user to the `libvirtd` command; this will enable them to run virtual machines. The command to add the current user is as follows:

```
sudo adduser `id -un` libvirtd
```

The output is as follows:

```
Setting up vbetool (1.1-3) ...
Setting up wdiff (1.2.1-2) ...
Setting up debootstrap (1.0.59ubuntu0.3) ...
Setting up kpartx (0.4.9-3ubuntu7.2) ...
Setting up libauthen-sasl-perl (2.1500-1) ...
Setting up python3-magic (1:5.14-2ubuntu3.3) ...
Setting up libnss3-nssdb (2:3.19.2-0ubuntu0.14.04.1) ...
Setting up libnss3:amd64 (2:3.19.2-0ubuntu0.14.04.1) ...
Setting up librados2 (0.80.9-0ubuntu0.14.04.2) ...
Setting up librbd1 (0.80.9-0ubuntu0.14.04.2) ...
Setting up libwww-perl (6.05-2) ...
Setting up liblwp-protocol-https-perl (6.04-2ubuntu0.1) ...
Setting up libparse-debcontrol-perl (2.005-4) ...
Setting up qemu-system-x86 (2.0.0+dfsg-2ubuntu1.13) ...
qemu-kvm start/running
Setting up qemu-utils (2.0.0+dfsg-2ubuntu1.13) ...
Processing triggers for ureadahead (0.100.0-16) ...
Setting up libvirt-bin (1.2.2-0ubuntu13.1.12) ...
Adding group `libvirtd' (GID 119) ...
Done.
libvirt-bin start/running, process 9174
Setting up libvirt-bin dnsmasq configuration.
Setting up qemu-kvm (2.0.0+dfsg-2ubuntu1.13) ...
Setting up python-vm-builder (0.12.4+bzr489-0ubuntu2) ...
Setting up ubuntu-vm-builder (0.12.4+bzr489-0ubuntu2) ...
Processing triggers for libc-bin (2.19-0ubuntu6) ...
Processing triggers for ureadahead (0.100.0-16) ...
skanda@UbuntuServer:~$ sudo adduser `id -un` libvirtd
The user `skanda' is already a member of `libvirtd'.
skanda@UbuntuServer:~$ _
```

# Installing vmbuilder

Download the latest vmbuilder called python-vm-builder. You may also use the older ubuntu-vm-builder, but there are slight differences in the syntax.

The command to install python-vm-builder is as follows:

```
sudo apt-get install python-vm-builder
```

The output will be as follows:

```
skanda@UbuntuServer:~$ sudo apt-get install python-vm-builder
Reading package lists... Done
Building dependency tree
Reading state information... Done
python-vm-builder is already the newest version.
python-vm-builder set to manually installed.
0 upgraded, 0 newly installed, 0 to remove and 173 not upgraded.
skanda@UbuntuServer:~$
```

# Defining the virtual machine

While defining the virtual machine that you want to build, you need to take care of the following two important points:

- Do not assume that the enduser will know the technicalities of extending the disk size of virtual machine if the need arises. Either have a large virtual disk so that the application can grow or document the process to do so. However, it would be better to have your data stored in an external storage device.

- Allocating RAM is fairly simple. But remember that you should allocate your virtual machine an amount of RAM that is safe to run your application.

To check the list of parameters that vmbuilder provides, use the following command:

```
vmbuilder -h
```

The result is shown in the following screenshot:

```
skanda@UbuntuServer:~$ vmbuilder
2015-07-12 07:30:12,531 INFO     : logging to file: /tmp/tmpv5HNFw
Usage: vmbuilder hypervisor distro [options]

vmbuilder: error: You need to specify at least the hypervisor type and the distr
o
skanda@UbuntuServer:~$ vmbuilder -h
2015-07-12 07:30:20,252 INFO     : logging to file: /tmp/tmpADOEXo
Usage: vmbuilder hypervisor distro [options]

Options:
  -h, --help            show this help message and exit
  --version             Show version information

  Build options:
    --debug             Show debug information
    -v, --verbose       Show progress information
    -q, --quiet         Silent operation
    -o, --overwrite     Remove destination directory before starting build
    -c CONFIG, --config=CONFIG
                        Configuration file
    --templates=DIR     Prepend DIR to template search path.
    -d DESTDIR, --destdir=DESTDIR
                        Destination directory
    --only-chroot       Only build the chroot. Don't install it on disk images
                        or anything.
    --chroot-dir=CHROOT_DIR
                        Build the chroot in directory.
    --existing-chroot=EXISTING_CHROOT
                        Use existing chroot.
```

The two main parameters are virtualization technology, also known as hypervisor, and targeted distribution.

The distribution we are using is Ubuntu 14.04, which is also known as **trusty** because of its codename. The command to check the release version is as follows:

```
lsb_release -a
```

The output is as follows:

```
skanda@UbuntuServer:~$ lsb_release -a
No LSB modules are available.
Distributor ID: Ubuntu
Description:    Ubuntu 14.04.1 LTS
Release:        14.04
Codename:       trusty
skanda@UbuntuServer:~$
```

Let's build a virtual machine on the same version of Ubuntu. Here's an example of building a virtual machine with vmbuilder:

```
sudo vmbuilder kvm ubuntu --suite trusty --flavour virtual --arch amd64
-o --libvirt qemu:///system
```

Now, we will discuss what the parameters mean:

- `--suite`: This specifies which Ubuntu release we want the virtual machine built on
- `--flavour`: This specifies which virtual kernel to use to build the JeOS image
- `--arch`: This specifies the processor architecture (64 bit or 32 bit)
- `-o`: This overwrites the previous version of the virtual machine image
- `--libvirt`: This adds the virtual machine to the list of available virtual machines

Now that we have created a virtual machine, let's look at the next steps.

# JeOS installation

We will examine the settings that are required to get our virtual machine up and running.

# IP address

A good practice for assigning IP address to the virtual machines is to set a fixed IP address, usually from the private pool. Then, include this info as part of the documentation. We will define an IP address with following parameters:

- `--ip` (address): This is the IP address in dotted form
- `--mask` (value): This is the IP mask in dotted form (default is `255.255.255.0`)
- `--net` (value): This is the IP net address (default is `X.X.X.0`)
- `--bcast` (value): This is the IP broadcast (default is `X.X.X.255`)
- `--gw` (address): This is the gateway address (default is `X.X.X.1`)
- `--dns` (address): This is the name server address (default is `X.X.X.1`)

Our command looks like this now:

```
sudo vmbuilder kvm ubuntu --suite trusty --flavour virtual --arch amd64
-o --libvirt qemu:///system --ip 192.168.0.10
```

You may have noticed that we have assigned only the IP, and all others will take the default value.

# Enabling the bridge

We will have to enable the bridge for our virtual machines, as various remote hosts will have to access the applications. We will configure libvirt and modify the vmbuilder template to do so.

First, create the template hierarchy and copy the default template into this folder:

```
mkdir -p VMBuilder/plugins/libvirt/templates
cp /etc/vmbuilder/libvirt/* VMBuilder/plugins/libvirt/templates/
```

Use your favorite editor and modify the following lines in the `VMBuilder/plugins/libvirt/templates/libvirtxml.tmpl` file:

```
<interface type='network'>
  <source network='default'/>
</interface>
```

Replace these lines with the following lines:

```
<interface type='bridge'>
  <source bridge='br0'/>
</interface>
```

# Partitions

You have to allocate partitions to applications for their data storage and working. It is normal to have a separate storage space for each application in /var.

The command provided by vmbuilder for this is --part:

```
--part PATH
```

vmbuilder will read the file from the PATH parameter and consider each line as a separate partition. Each line has two entries, mountpoint and size, where size is defined in MBs and is the maximum limit defined for that mountpoint.

For this particular exercise, we will create a new file with name vmbuilder. partition and enter the following lines for creating partitions:

```
root 6000
swap 4000
---
/var 16000
```

Also, please note that different disks are identified by the delimiter ---.

Now, the command should be like this:

```
sudo vmbuilder kvm ubuntu --suite trusty --flavour virtual \
--arch amd64 -o --libvirt qemu:///system --ip 192.168.0.10 \
--part vmbuilder.partition
```

 Use \ to wrap long text to the next line.

# Setting the user and password

We have to define a user and a password in order for the user to log in to the virtual machine after startup. For now, let's use a generic user identified as user and the password password. We can ask user to change the password after first login.

The following parameters are used to set the username and password:

- --user (username): This sets the username (default is ubuntu)
- --name (fullname): This sets a name for the user (default is ubuntu)
- --pass (password): This sets the password for the user (default is ubuntu)

So, now our command will be as follows:

```
sudo vmbuilder kvm ubuntu --suite trusty --flavour virtual \
--arch amd64 -o --libvirt qemu:///system --ip 192.168.0.10 \
--part vmbuilder.partition --user user --name user --pass password
```

# Final steps in the installation

Our first VM image is almost done. Let's try booting it and see it live in action.

## First boot

There are certain things that will need to be done at the first boot of a machine. We will install openssh-server at first boot. This will ensure that each virtual machine has a key, which is unique. If we had done this earlier in the setup phase, all virtual machines would have been given the same key; this might have posed a security issue.

Let's create a script called first_boot.sh and run it at the first boot of every new virtual machine:

```
# This script will run the first time the virtual machine boots
# It is run as root
apt-get update
apt-get install -qqy --force-yes openssh-server
```

Then, add the following line to the command line:

```
--firstboot first_boot.sh
```

## First login

Remember we had specified a default password for the virtual machine. This means all the machines where this image will be used for installation will have the same password. We will prompt the user to change the password at first login. For this, we will use a shell script named first_login.sh. Add the following lines to the file:

```
# This script is run the first time a user logs in.
echo "Almost at the end of setting up your machine"
echo "As a security precaution, please change your password"
passwd
```

Then, add the parameter to your command line:

```
--firstlogin first_login.sh
```

## Auto updates

You can make your virtual machine update itself at regular intervals. To enable this feature, add a package named `unattended-upgrades` to the command line:

```
--addpkg unattended-upgrades
```

## ACPI handling

ACPI handling will enable your virtual machine to take care of shutdown and restart events that are received from a remote machine. We will install the `acipd` package for the same:

```
--addpkg acipd
```

## The complete command

So, the final command with the parameters that we discussed previously would look like this:

```
sudo vmbuilder kvm ubuntu --suite trusty --flavour virtual \
--arch amd64 -o --libvirt qemu:///system --ip 192.168.0.10 \
--part vmbuilder.partition --user user --name user --pass password \
--firstboot first_boot.sh --firstlogin first_login.sh \
--addpkg unattended-upgrades --addpkg acipd
```

# Summary

In this chapter, we discussed various virtualization techniques. We discussed virtualization as well as the tools and packages that help in creating and running a virtual machine. Also, you learned about the ways we can view, manage, connect to, and make use of the applications running on the virtual machine. Then, we saw the lightweight version of Ubuntu that is fine-tuned to run virtualization and applications on a virtual platform. At the later stages of this chapter, we covered how to build a virtual machine from a command line, how to add packages, how to set up user profiles, and the steps for first boot and first login.

In the next chapter, we will study cloud and OpenStack, how to set up Ubuntu with OpenStack, and more.

# 8
# OpenStack with Ubuntu

In the previous chapters, we discussed topics such as network authentication, monitoring and optimizing your Ubuntu Server, process management, shell management, and user management. Then, we saw the virtualization techniques in Ubuntu. In this chapter, we will study OpenStack, which is the open source solution for cloud computing. First, we will look at the architecture of OpenStack and the different components that make up the complete system. Then, we will look at an example environment that will help in installing the OpenStack components, networking them, and setting up the security. In the later parts of this chapter, we will see how to install the different components that will make up a complete OpenStack system. So let's begin the journey.

## The OpenStack architecture

The following diagram shows the architecture of an OpenStack installation with the components. Let's take a look at what each component does and what the services are called.

We see there are nine blocks with different names, each one for a different component and running different services:

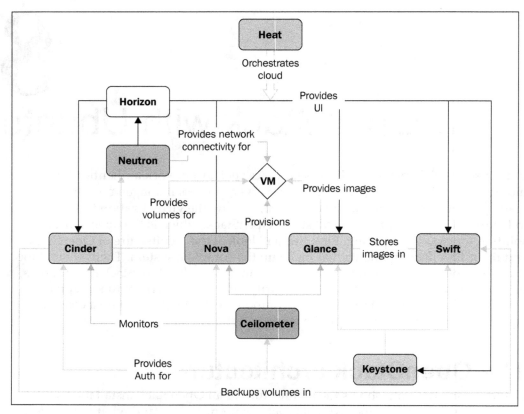

Image source: http://docs.openstack.org/

The following table puts the information of these components together:

| Service | Project | Description |
|---------|---------|-------------|
| Dashboard | Horizon | The Horizon project provides the user with a portal for interacting with the services. Some of the examples are to launch an instance, assign IP addresses, and so on. |

| Service | Project | Description |
| --- | --- | --- |
| Compute | Nova | It is the responsibility of this service to manage the compute instances. They are related to virtual machine spawning, scheduling, and decommissioning. |
| Networking | Neutron | This does the job of enabling network-connectivity-as-a-service for other components in the OpenStack framework. Also, it has an API that can be used for defining networks. |
| Object Storage | Swift | Swift makes use of RESTful for storing and retrieving arbitrary unstructured data objects. Restful is an HTTP-based API. It is fault tolerant owing to its replication and scaling out architecture. It's nothing like a typical file server having mountable directories. |
| Block Storage | Cinder | This provides persistent block storage. Also, the driver is used for creating and managing Block Storage devices. |
| Identity Service | Keystone | Authentication and authorization handling is taken up by Keystone. It also has a catalog of all services. |
| Image Service | Glance | This stores and retrieves the images of virtual machine disks, which will be used during instance provisioning. |
| Telemetry | Ceilometer | Ceilometer does the job of monitoring, metering, billing, benchmarking, and scalability for statistical purposes. |
| Orchestration | Heat | The orchestration of various cloud applications using the HOT template from OpenStack or the AWS CloudFormation template is handled by Heat. |
| Database Service | Trove | This is responsible for providing a scalable functionality for Cloud Database-as-a-Service, and it is for both relational and nonrelational databases. |

# The environment

For a basic setup, let's take a look at the basic environment required. We will need to make sure all our machines are installed with the same version of Ubuntu Server 64 bit version. An example of this architecture is shown the following diagram:

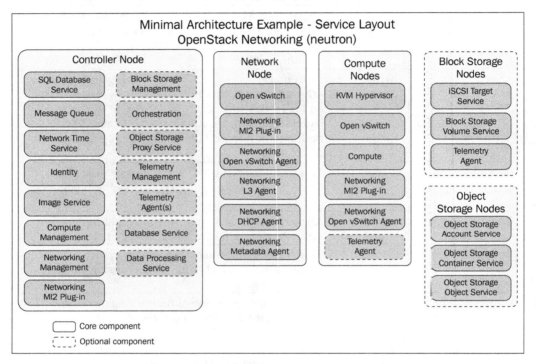

Image source: `http://docs.openstack.org/`

OpenStack will not necessarily need a large amount of resources, and you can refer to the following minimum resource requirements:

- The controller node should have at least one processor, 2 GB memory, and 5GB or more storage

- The network node should have at least one processor, 512 MB memory, and 5 GB or more storage

- The compute node should have at least one processor, 2 GB memory, and 10 GB or more storage

One suggestion would be to go with a minimal installation of Ubuntu and go for a 64 bit Ubuntu version. Alternatively, you can build these on **virtual machines (VMs)**. VMs have the added advantage that one physical server can be used to create multiple nodes with as many network interfaces and they can capture snapshots to roll back, if required.

The three node architecture in the previous diagram manages the components in the following manner. There are a couple of optional nodes in the OpenStack setup, namely, Object Storage and Block Storage:

- The following services are set to run on the controller node: Image, Identity, and Dashboard services, SQL database, plugin for networking, Network Time Protocol, message queue, and Compute and Networking management sections. Additionally, the controller node can run the following services optionally: a portion of Block Storage, Object Storage, Orchestration, Telemetry, Database, and Data Processing.

- The network node is responsible for running the Networking plugin and supporting agents that provision tenant networks that provide switching, routing, and NAT and DHCP services. Also, it handles the Internet connectivity for tenant virtual machines. Tenant virtual machines require Internet connectivity; this is provided by the network node. It runs the services for DHCP, routing, and NAT using the Networking plugin for giving services to the tenant machines.

- The compute node has a running hypervisor, which belongs to the Compute service that operates tenant virtual machines. KVM is the default hypervisor. Some parts of the Networking plugin and firewall services are also run in the compute node. There can be more than one compute node. As an option, even Telemetry services can be run in the compute node for collecting metrics.

- The tenant virtual machines run on instances of stored images. These images are stored on disks, and the Block Storage node is the one that saves these disks. Sometimes, for the purpose of collecting metrics, administrators may also chose to run Telemetry services on the Block Storage node. You can run more than one Block Storage node in an OpenStack setup.

- The Object Storage nodes have the disks that are used by the Object Storage service to store accounts, containers, and objects. You need at least two instances of Object Storage nodes running, but you may run more than that.

# Security

Various security measures such as passwords, policies, and encryption can be implemented for OpenStack services. Also, supporting services support at least password security, for example, the database server and the message broker.

This table has the list of services and the associated password description:

| Password Name | Description |
| --- | --- |
| Database password | Database root password |
| RABBIT_PASS | RabbitMQ user guest password |
| KEYSTONE_DBPASS | Identity service database password |
| DEMO_PASS | User **demo** password |
| ADMIN_PASS | User **admin** password |
| GLANCE_DBPASS | Image service database password |
| GLANCE_PASS | Image service **glance** user password |
| NOVA_DBPASS | Compute service database password |
| NOVA_PASS | Compute service **nova** user password |
| DASH_DBPASS | Dashboard database password |
| CINDER_DBPASS | Block Storage service database password |
| CINDER_PASS | Block Storage service **cinder** user password |
| NEUTRON_DBPASS | Networking service database password |
| NEUTRON_PASS | Networking service **neutron** user password |
| HEAT_DBPASS | Orchestration service database password |
| HEAT_PASS | Orchestration service **heat** user password |
| CEILOMETER_PASS | Telemetry service database password |
| CEILOMETER_PASS | Telemetry service **ceilometer** user password |
| TROVE_DBPASS | Database service database password |
| TROVE_PASS | Database service **trove** user password |

Please note that the services will require admin rights during installation and working.

# Networking

We will have to configure the network interfaces after we have installed the Ubuntu operating system on each of the nodes. It is recommended that you disable any automated network management tools and edit the configuration files manually. Also, all nodes should have access to the Internet for installing OpenStack packages and periodic updates.

# OpenStack networking

Let's consider the three nodes we talked about in the preceding sections: the controller node, network node, and compute note. The controller node has a network interface on the management network. The network node has a network interface on the management network, instance tunnels network, and an external network. The compute node has a network interface on the management network and instance tunnels network. Have a look at the following diagram:

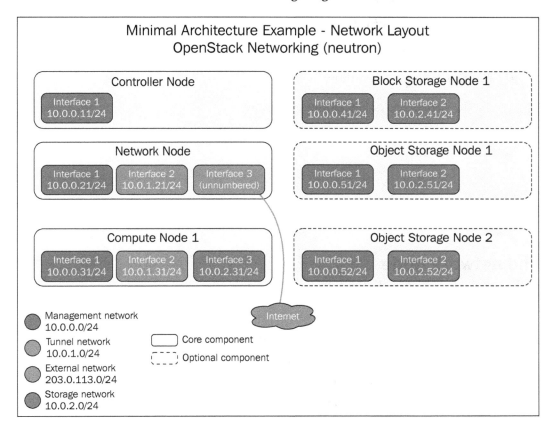

Now, let's configure the different nodes that we saw in the preceding diagram.

# The controller node

In the controller node, we do the following settings:

- Configure the network:

    1. First instance as the management interface:

        ◦ **IP address**: `10.0.0.11`

        ◦ **Network mask**: `255.255.255.0` (or `/24`)

        ◦ **Default gateway**: `10.0.0.1`

    2. Reboot the system for the changes to take effect.

- Configure name resolution:

    1. Set `controller` as the hostname.

    2. Edit the `/etc/hosts` file so that it has the following lines:

```
# controller
10.0.0.11 controller
# network
10.0.0.21 network
# compute1
10.0.0.31 compute1
```

# The network node

In the network node, we do the following settings:

- Configure the network:

    1. First instance as the management interface:

        ◦ **IP address**: `10.0.0.21`

        ◦ **Network mask**: `255.255.255.0` (or `/24`)

        ◦ **Default gateway**: `10.0.0.1`

    2. Second interface as the instance tunnels interface:

        ◦ **IP address**: `10.0.1.21`

        ◦ **Network mask**: `255.255.255.0` (or `/24`)

    3. Third interface as the external interface. You will have to replace `INTERFACE_NAME` with an interface name such as `eth2`.

4. Edit the `/etc/network/interfaces` file to match the following:

```
# The external network interface
auto eth2
iface eth2 inet manual
up ip link set dev $IFACE up
down ip link set dev $IFACE down
```

5. Restart the system to activate the changes.

- Configure name resolution:

   1. Set `network` as the hostname.

   2. Edit the `/etc/hosts` file to have the following content:

```
# network
10.0.0.21 network
# controller
10.0.0.11 controller
# compute1
10.0.0.31 compute1
```

# The compute node

In the compute node, we do the following settings:

- Configure the network:

   1. First instance as the management interface:

      ◦ **IP address**: `10.0.0.31`

      ◦ **Network mask**: `255.255.255.0` (or `/24`)

      ◦ **Default gateway**: `10.0.0.1`

   2. Second interface as the instance tunnels interface:

      ◦ **IP address**: `10.0.1.31`

      ◦ **Network mask**: `255.255.255.0` (or `/24`)

   3. Restart the server for changes to take effect.

- Configure name resolution:

    1. Set `compute1` as the hostname.

    2. Edit the `/etc/hosts` file so that it has the following lines:

    ```
    # compute1
    10.0.0.31 compute1
    # controller
    10.0.0.11 controller
    # network
    10.0.0.21 network
    ```

## Verifying the network connectivity

It is recommended that you check the network connectivity among all nodes and also from all nodes to the Internet. You can use the Ping tool to verify this.

# Network Time Protocol

**Network Time Protocol** (NTP) has to be installed on all nodes so that the services are properly synchronized among all nodes. It is recommended that you configure the controller node to reference the accurate server and all other nodes in the OpenStack system to reference to this controller node.

## Configuring the controller node

To do the configuring, we will follow the steps discussed next.

## Installing the NTP service

Use the following command to install the NTP service on the controller node:

```
apt-get install ntp
```

## Configuring the NTP service

The controller node will synchronize the time by default from public servers. Also, you can optionally edit the `/etc/ntp.conf` file to configure alternate servers:

1. Edit the `/etc/ntp.conf` file and make the necessary modifications to have the contents similar to the following:

    ```
    server NTP_SERVER iburst
    restrict -4 default kod notrap nomodify
    restrict -6 default kod notrap nomodify
    ```

Make sure you replace NTP_SERVER with the hostname or IP address of a suitable and accurate NTP server. Multiple server keys are supported.

2. Restart the NTP service:

```
service ntp restart
```

## Configuring other nodes

To do the configuring, we will follow the steps discussed next.

### Installing the NTP service

Use the following command to install the NTP service on the controller node:

```
apt-get install ntp
```

### Configuring the NTP service

The steps are as follows:

1. Edit the /etc/ntp.conf file and make the following changes. Remove all keys except one server key and change it so that it refers to the controller node:

```
server controller iburst
```

2. Restart the NTP service using the following command:

```
service ntp restart
```

# OpenStack packages

OpenStack packages are a part of the Ubuntu distributions. You may use the ones bundled along with the release or download a package from a different release. Carry out the operations on all nodes in your setup.

## Enabling the OpenStack repository

Run the following command for installing the Ubuntu Cloud archive keyring and repository:

```
apt-get install ubuntu-cloud-keyring
echo "deb http://ubuntu-cloud.archive.canonical.com/ubuntu" \
"trusty-updates/juno main" > /etc/apt/sources.list.d/cloudarchive-juno.
list
```

## Finalizing the installation

You should upgrade the packages on your system using the following command:

```
apt-get update && apt-get dist-upgrade
```

# Database

SQL is used as the default system to store information. This database is usually running on the controller node. We will use MariaDB and MySQL in this chapter. You can also use PostgreSQL.

## Installing and configuring the database server

The steps are as follows:

1.  Use the following command to install the packages:

    ```
    apt-get install mariadb-server python-mysqldb
    ```

2.  Set a password for root during installation.

3.  Modify the /etc/mysql/my.cnf file and make the following changes:

    1.  In the section where you find [mysqld], change the bind address to match the one assigned to the management IP address of the controller node. This will enable access for other nodes through the management network:

        ```
        [mysqld]
        ...
        bind-address = 10.0.0.11
        ```

    2.  Also, in the same section, make the following changes along with setting the UTF-8 character set:

        ```
        [mysqld]
        ...
        default-storage-engine = innodb
        innodb_file_per_table
        collation-server = utf8_general_ci
        init-connect = 'SET NAMES utf8'
        character-set-server = utf8
        ```

# Finalizing the installation

The steps are as follows:

1. Restart the database service using the following command:

   ```
   service mysql restart
   ```

2. Run the following command to secure the database service:

   ```
   mysql_secure_installation
   ```

# The messaging server

Message brokers are the way in which OpenStack coordinates the operations between various services and updates status information. This message broker server is usually run on the controller node. The popular message broker servers supported by OpenStack are RabbitMQ, Qpid, and ZeroMQ. In this chapter, we will discuss RabbitMQ, which is supported by most distributions.

## Installing the RabbitMQ message broker service

Use the following command to install the message broker service:

```
apt-get install rabbitmq-server
```

## Configuring the message broker service

By default, a user called guest is created for the message broker and its username and password are the same: guest. It is recommended that you change the password for the user. The command to do so is as follows:

```
rabbitmqctl change_password guest NEW_PASS
Changing password for user "guest" ...
...done.
```

While executing this, replace the last term NEW_PASS to a password that is suitable for you. For every service that uses message broker in the OpenStack system, you will need to configure the configuration file and set the rabbit_password key.

We are all done with the initial setup and are ready to install the OpenStack services.

# The Identity service

The Identity service is responsible for the following functions in an OpenStack setup:

- Tracking users and their permissions
- Providing a list of services with their API URLs

When we are installing the OpenStack Identity service, we must register all other services in our OpenStack system. It helps the Identity service keep track of all services that are installed and where they are present on the network.

## Installing and configuring the Identity service

We will install the Identity service on the controller node in our setup.

## Configuring the prerequisites

First, we have to create a database and an administrative token. Follow these steps to create a database:

1. We have an access client for the database, so we will connect to the database server as user root:

   ```
   mysql -u root -p
   ```

2. Create a new database called `keystone`:

   ```
   CREATE DATABASE keystone;
   ```

3. Give access to the `keystone` database:

   ```
   GRANT ALL PRIVILEGES ON keystone.* TO 'keystone'@'localhost' \
   IDENTIFIED BY 'PASSWORD';
   GRANT ALL PRIVILEGES ON keystone.* TO 'keystone'@'%' \
   IDENTIFIED BY 'PASSWORD';
   ```

   Make sure you replace PASSWORD with a proper password of your choice.

4. Exit the database client.

5. Now, we need to generate a random token to be used as the administration token for the configuration. The command to do the same is as follows:

   ```
   openssl rand  -hex 10
   ```

   Make sure you note down this token, we will be making use of it soon.

# Installing and configuring the components

Install and configure the components using the following steps:

1. We will install the packages now using the following command:

   ```
   apt-get install keystone python-keystoneclient
   ```

2. Make the following changes in the /etc/keystone/keystone.conf file:

   1. Go to the [DEFAULT] section and assign the admin_token value that we generated in the previous section:

      ```
      [DEFAULT]
      ...
      admin_token = TOKEN
      ```

      Replace TOKEN with the random token generated from the previous section.

   2. In the [database] section, configure the access for database access:

      ```
      [database]
      ...
      connection = mysql://keystone:PASSWORD@controller/keystone
      ```

      Make sure you replace the PASSWORD term with the password you have set for the database.

   3. Set the SQL driver and UUID token in the [token] section:

      ```
      [token]
      ...
      provider = keystone.token.providers.uuid.Provider
      driver = keystone.token.persistence.backends.sql.Token
      ```

3. Populate the database for the Identity service:

   ```
   su -s /bin/sh -c "keystone-manage db_sync" keystone
   ```

# Finalizing the installation

The steps are as follows:

1. We need to restart the Identity service using the following command:

   ```
   service keystone restart
   ```

2. Remove the SQLite database that is embedded by default in the Ubuntu package. We are already using a SQL database server. The command to remove the SQLite database file is as follows:

```
rm -f /var/lib/keystone/keystone.db
```

3. The Identity service does not delete the expired tokens from the database. Over a period of time, these get accumulated and might take up some space in the database. So, it is recommended these expired tokens are deleted to keep your environment clean, especially when there are limited resources.

   The following cron command deletes the expired tokens at an hourly rate:

```
(crontab -l -u keystone 2>&1 | grep -q token_flush) || \
echo '@hourly /usr/bin/keystone-manage token_flush >/var/log/
keystone/
keystone-tokenflush.log 2>&1' \
>> /var/spool/cron/crontabs/keystone
```

# Tenants, users, and roles

We have to create the tenants, users, and roles for the Identity service before we start making use of the service. For this, we will need the administration token that we generated in the previous section, and use this token to manually set the endpoint of the Identity service before running keystone commands

Here, we are setting the temporary environment variable OS_SERVICE_TOKEN to assign the administration token. Next, we set the endpoint to a temporary environment variable named OS_SERVICE_ENDPOINT.

## Configuring prerequisites

The steps are as follows:

1. First, we will configure the administration token:

```
export OS_SERVICE_TOKEN=ADMIN_TOKEN
```

   Make sure you replace the term ADMIN_TOKEN with the actual token value. Pass on the value of the administration token to keystone in the preceding command.

2. Then, we set the endpoint value to a variable:

```
export OS_SERVICE_ENDPOINT=http://controller:35357/v2.0
```

# Creating tenants, users, and roles

The steps are as follows:

1. Let's create an administrative tenant, user, and role. These will be used for all the administration-related operations in the environment.

   1. Create the `admin` tenant using the following command:

      ```
      keystone tenant-create --name admin --description "Admin Tenant"
      ```

   2. Create the `admin` user. Make sure you replace the words ADMIN_PASS with an appropriate password of your choice and EMAIL_ADDRESS with an appropriate e-mail address:

      ```
      keystone user-create --name admin --pass ADMIN_PASS --email EMAIL_ADDRESS
      ```

   3. Create the `admin` role using the following command:

      ```
      keystone role-create --name admin
      ```

   4. Add the `admin` role to the `admin` tenant and user:

      ```
      keystone user-role-add --user admin --tenant admin --role admin
      ```

2. Create a demo tenant and user. These will be used for the normal operations.

   1. Create the `demo` tenant using the following command:

      ```
      keystone tenant-create --name demo --description "Demo Tenant"
      ```

   2. Create the `demo` user under the `demo` tenant:

      ```
      keystone user-create --name demo --tenant demo --pass DEMO_PASS --email EMAIL_ADDRESS
      ```

      Make sure you replace the terms DEMO_PASS with an appropriate password of your choice and EMAIL_ADDRESS with an appropriate e-mail address.

3. OpenStack requires a set of tenants, users, and roles to interact with other services in the setup. Every service needs to have at least one user with at least one admin role user which comes under the `service` tenant.

4. Create the `service` tenant using the following command:

   ```
   keystone tenant-create --name service --description "Service Tenant"
   ```

## The service entity and API endpoint

We have already created the tenants, users, and roles. Next, we should create the service entity and API endpoint for the Identity service.

### Configuring the prerequisites

We have to set the environment variables `OS_SERVICE_TOKEN` and `OS_SERVICE_ENDPOINT`. We have already done it in the previous sections, but repeat the same.

### Creating the service entity and API endpoint

The steps are as follows:

1.  The Identity service in your OpenStack environment has a list of all the available services. All services use this list to locate other services in your system:

    ```
    keystone service-create --name keystone --type identity \
    --description "OpenStack Identity"
    ```

2.  For each service that is present in the list maintained by the Identity service, there is a corresponding list of API endpoints associated. These help other services with possible means of communication. Use the following command to create the service API endpoints:

    ```
    keystone endpoint-create \
    --service-id $(keystone service-list | awk '/ identity / {print $2}') \
    --publicurl http://controller:5000/v2.0 \
    --internalurl http://controller:5000/v2.0 \
    --adminurl http://controller:35357/v2.0 \
    --region regionOne
    ```

# The Image service

The Image service in the OpenStack environment is responsible for helping users discover, register, and retrieve images of virtual machines. A REST API is provided for users to query the metadata of virtual machines so as to retrieve the actual image. Virtual machine images can be stored in various locations, from filesystems to the Object Storage service offered by OpenStack.

# Installing and configuring the Image service

We will discuss how to install and configure the Image service on the controller node. As part of this exercise, we will store the images of the virtual machine on local filesystem storage.

## Configuring the prerequisites

We need to create database, credentials, and API endpoints so that we can install and configure the Image service.

1. Here are the steps to create a database:

    1. Connect to the database server as root user:

       ```
       mysql -u root -p
       ```

    2. Create a new database named `glance` using the following command:

       ```
       CREATE DATABASE glance;
       ```

    3. Grant all the required access to the newly created database `glance` using the following command:

       ```
       GRANT ALL PRIVILEGES ON glance.* TO 'glance'@'localhost' \
       IDENTIFIED BY 'GLANCE_DBPASS';
       GRANT ALL PRIVILEGES ON glance.* TO 'glance'@'%' \
       IDENTIFIED BY 'GLANCE_DBPASS';
       ```

       Make sure you replace the term GLANCE_DBPASS with an appropriate password of your choice.

    4. Exit the database client connection.

2. Next, for gaining access to the admin-only CLI commands, source the admin credentials:

   ```
   source admin-openrc.sh
   ```

3. Carry on the following steps to create service credentials:

    1. Create new user `glance` using the following command:

       ```
       keystone user-create --name glance --pass GLANCE_PASS
       ```

       Make sure you replace the term GLANCE_PASS with an appropriate password of your choice.

2. Add admin role to user `glance` using the following command:

```
keystone user-role-add --user glance --tenant service --role
admin
```

3. Create a new service entry for `glance` using the following command:

```
keystone service-create --name glance --type image \
--description "OpenStack Image Service"
```

4. Create an API endpoint for the Image service using the following commands:

```
keystone endpoint-create \
--service-id $(keystone service-list | awk '/ image / {print $2}')
\
--publicurl http://controller:9292 \
--internalurl http://controller:9292 \
--adminurl http://controller:9292 \
--region regionOne
```

## Installing and configuring the Image service components

The steps are as follows:

1. Install the packages using the following command:

```
apt-get install glance python-glanceclient
```

2. Make the following changes in the `/etc/glance/glance-api.conf` file:

1. Go to the `[database]` section and configure the database access:

```
[database]
...
connection = mysql://glance:GLANCE_DBPASS@controller/glance
```

Make sure you replace the term GLANCE_DBPASS with an appropriate password of your choice.

2. Configure the Identity service access in the sections `[keystone_authtoken]` and `[paste_deploy]`:

```
[keystone_authtoken]
...
auth_uri = http://controller:5000/v2.0
```

```
identity_uri = http://controller:35357
admin_tenant_name = service
admin_user = glance
admin_password = GLANCE_PASS
[paste_deploy]
. . .
flavor = keystone
```

Make sure you replace the term GLANCE_PASS with an appropriate password of your choice.

3.  In the [glance_store] section, make the configuration changes for local filesystem storage and the location of image files:

```
[glance_store]
. . .
default_store = file
filesystem_store_datadir = /var/lib/glance/images/
```

3.  Then, edit the /etc/glance/glance-registry.conf file and make the following changes:

    1.  Configure database access in the [database] section:

    ```
    [database]
    . . .
    connection = mysql://glance:GLANCE_DBPASS@controller/glance
    ```

    Make sure you replace the term GLANCE_DBPASS with an appropriate password of your choice.

    2.  Go to the sections [keystone_authtoken] and [paste_deploy], and configure the Identity service access:

    ```
    [keystone_authtoken]
    . . .
    auth_uri = http://controller:5000/v2.0
    identity_uri = http://controller:35357
    admin_tenant_name = service
    admin_user = glance
    admin_password = GLANCE_PASS
    [paste_deploy]
    . . .
    flavor = keystone
    ```

    Make sure you replace the term GLANCE_PASS with an appropriate password of your choice.

4. Populate the Image service database using the following command:

```
su -s /bin/sh -c "glance-manage db_sync" glance
```

## Finalizing the installation

The steps are as follows:

1. Restart the service using the following command:

```
service glance-registry restart
service glance-api restart
```

2. Next, as we did in the previous section, remove the SQLite database file using the following command:

```
rm -f /var/lib/glance/glance.sqlite
```

# The Compute service

The cloud computing systems in OpenStack are hosted and managed by the Compute service. This service is one of the dominant parts of the **Infrastructure-as-a-Service (IaaS)** system. The Compute service refers to the Identity service for authentication, the Image service for disk and server images, and the dashboard for the user and administrative interface. The Compute service can scale horizontally and it launches instances from the downloaded images.

# Installing and configuring the Compute service

We will look at installing and configuring the Compute service on the controller node.

## Configuring the prerequisites

We need to create database, credentials, and API endpoints so that we can install and configure the Compute service. The steps are as follows:

1. Here are the steps to create a database:

    1. Connect to the database server as root user using the following command:

```
mysql -u root -p
```

2. Create a new database named nova using the following command:

```
CREATE DATABASE nova;
```

3. Grant all the required access to the newly created database nova using the following command:

```
GRANT ALL PRIVILEGES ON nova.* TO 'nova'@'localhost' \
IDENTIFIED BY 'NOVA_DBPASS';
GRANT ALL PRIVILEGES ON nova.* TO 'nova'@'%' \
IDENTIFIED BY 'NOVA_DBPASS';
```

Make sure you replace the term NOVA_DBPASS with an appropriate password of your choice.

4. Exit the database client connection.

2. To gain access to the admin-only CLI commands, source the admin credentials using the following command:

```
source admin-openrc.sh
```

3. Carry on the following steps to create the service credentials:

1. Create new user nova using the following command:

```
keystone user-create --name nova --pass NOVA_PASS
```

Make sure you replace the term NOVA_PASS with an appropriate password of your choice.

2. Add admin role to user nova using the following command:

```
keystone user-role-add --user nova --tenant service --role admin
```

3. Create a new service entry for nova using the following command:

```
keystone service-create --name nova --type compute \
--description "OpenStack Compute"
```

4. Create an API endpoint for the Compute service using the following command:

```
keystone endpoint-create \
--service-id $(keystone service-list | awk '/ compute / {print $2}') \
```

```
--publicurl http://controller:8774/v2/%\(tenant_id\)s \
--internalurl http://controller:8774/v2/%\(tenant_id\)s \
--adminurl http://controller:8774/v2/%\(tenant_id\)s \
--region regionOne
```

# Installing and configuring the Compute service components

We will now install and configure the components for the Compute service. Complete the following steps:

1.  Install the packages using the following command:

    ```
    apt-get install glance nova-api nova-cert nova-conductor nova-consoleauth \
    nova-novncproxy nova-scheduler python-novaclient
    ```

2.  Make the following changes in the /etc/nova/nova.conf file:

    1.  Go to the [database] section and configure the database access:

        ```
        [database]
        ...
        connection = mysql://nova:NOVA_DBPASS@controller/nova
        ```

        Make sure you replace the term NOVA_DBPASS with an appropriate password of your choice.

    2.  Next, go to the [DEFAULT] section and configure the RabbitMQ broker access:

        ```
        [DEFAULT]
        ...
        rpc_backend = rabbit
        rabbit_host = controller
        rabbit_password = RABBIT_PASS
        ```

        Make sure you replace the term RABBIT_DBPASS with an appropriate password of your choice.

3. Next, go to the `[keystone_authtoken]` and `[DEFAULT]` sections, and configure the Identity service access:

```
[DEFAULT]
...
auth_strategy = keystone
[keystone_authtoken]
...
auth_uri = http://controller:5000/v2.0
identity_uri = http://controller:35357
admin_tenant_name = service
admin_user = nova
admin_password = NOVA_PASS
```

Make sure you replace the term NOVA_PASS with an appropriate password of your choice.

4. Set the `my_ip` option in the `[DEFAULT]` section so that the management interface IP address is used on the controller node:

```
[DEFAULT]
...
my_ip = 10.0.0.11
```

5. Now we will configure the VNC proxy so that it uses the IP address of the management interface on the controller node in the same `[DEFAULT]` section:

```
[DEFAULT]
...
vncserver_listen = 10.0.0.11
vncserver_proxyclient_address = 10.0.0.11
```

6. Next, configure the location of the Image service in the `[glance]` section:

```
[glance]
...
host = controller
```

3. Populate the Compute service database using the following command:

```
su -s /bin/sh -c "nova-manage db sync" nova
```

# Finalizing the installation

The final steps for finishing the installation of the Compute service components are as follows:

1. First, we will restart the service using the following commands:

```
service nova-api restart
service nova-cert restart
service nova-consoleauth restart
service nova-scheduler restart
service nova-conductor restart
service nova-novncproxy restart
```

2. Next, as we did in the previous section, remove the SQLite database file using the following command:

```
rm -f /var/lib/nova/nova.sqlite
```

# Installing and configuring the compute node

Now, we will discuss installing and configuring the Compute service on the compute node. The compute node has built-in support for hypervisors for deploying instances and virtual machines. In this section, we will use the Qemu hypervisor that we discussed in the previous chapter.

## Installing and configuring the compute hypervisor components

We will now install and configure the hypervisor components. Complete the following steps:

1. Install the packages using the following command:

```
apt-get install nova-compute sysfsutils
```

2. Make the following changes in the /etc/nova/nova.conf file:

   1. Go to the [DEFAULT] section and configure the RabbitMQ message broker:

```
[DEFAULT]
...
rpc_backend = rabbit
rabbit_host = controller
rabbit_password = RABBIT_PASS
```

Make sure you replace the term RABBIT_PASS with an appropriate password of your choice.

2. Next, go to the sections [keystone_authtoken] and [DEFAULT] and configure the Identity service access:

```
[DEFAULT]
...
auth_strategy = keystone
[keystone_authtoken]
...
auth_uri = http://controller:5000/v2.0
identity_uri = http://controller:35357
admin_tenant_name = service
admin_user = nova
admin_password = NOVA_PASS
```

Make sure you replace the term NOVA_PASS with an appropriate password of your choice.

3. Set the my_ip option in the [DEFAULT] section so that the management interface IP address is used on the compute node:

```
[DEFAULT]
...
my_ip = MANAGEMENT_INTERFACE_IP_ADDRESS
```

Make sure you replace the term MANAGEMENT_INTERFACE_IP_ADDRESS with the appropriate IP address on the management network interface on the compute node.

4. Now, we will enable and configure remote console access in the same [DEFAULT] section:

```
[DEFAULT]
...
vnc_enabled = True
vncserver_listen = 0.0.0.0
vncserver_proxyclient_address = MANAGEMENT_INTERFACE_IP_
ADDRESS
novncproxy_base_url = http://controller:6080/vnc_auto.html
```

Make sure you replace the term MANAGEMENT_INTERFACE_IP_ADDRESS with the appropriate IP address on the management network interface on the compute node.

5. Next, configure the location of the Image service in the `[glance]` section using the following commands:

```
[glance]
...
host = controller
```

## Finalizing the installation

The final steps for finishing the installation of the Compute service components are as follows:

1. Check whether the compute node supports the virtual machines' hardware acceleration:

```
egrep -c '(vmx|svm)' /proc/cpuinfo
```

If the preceding command returns any non-zero value, then the compute node supports hardware acceleration. If it returns a zero value, then you might have to do some additional settings. To configure libvirt to use Qemu, make the following changes in the `/etc/nova/nova-compute.conf` file in the `[libvirt]` section:

```
[libvirt]
...
virt_type = qemu
```

2. Restart the compute service using the following command:

```
service nova-compute restart
```

3. Next, as we did in the previous section, remove the SQLite database file using the following command:

```
rm -f /var/lib/nova/nova.sqlite
```

# OpenStack networking

Networking in OpenStack lets users create and attach devices that are managed by other services to networks. Also, users can implement plugins in order to get different types of networking equipment. OpenStack networking is responsible for managing the **virtual network infrastructure** (**VNI**) and access layers of **physical network infrastructure** (**PNI**). Tenants in OpenStack Networking can create various topologies, such as firewalls, load balancers, and VPNs in the virtual network.

# Installing and configuring the controller node

In this section, we will discuss installing and configuring the Compute service on the controller node.

## Configuring the prerequisites

We need to create database, credentials, and API endpoints so that we can install and configure the OpenStack Networking service. The steps are as follows:

1. Here are the steps to create a database.

    1. Connect to the database server as root user using the following command:

       ```
       mysql -u root -p
       ```

    2. Create a new database named neutron using the following command:

       ```
       CREATE DATABASE neutron;
       ```

    3. Grant all the required access to the newly created database neutron using the following commands:

       ```
       GRANT ALL PRIVILEGES ON neutron.* TO 'neutron'@'localhost' \
       IDENTIFIED BY 'NEUTRON_DBPASS';
       GRANT ALL PRIVILEGES ON neutron.* TO 'neutron'@'%' \
       IDENTIFIED BY 'NEUTRON_DBPASS';
       ```

       Make sure you replace the term NEUTRON_DBPASS with an appropriate password of your choice.

    4. Exit the database client connection.

2. For gaining access to the admin-only CLI commands, source the admin credentials using the following command:

   ```
   source admin-openrc.sh
   ```

3. Carry out the following steps to create the service credentials:

    1. Create a new user neutron using the following command:

       ```
       keystone user-create --name neutron --pass NEUTRON _PASS
       ```

       Make sure you replace the term NEUTRON_PASS with an appropriate password of your choice.

2. Add the admin role to user neutron using the following command:

```
keystone user-role-add --user neutron --tenant service
--role admin
```

3. Create a new service entry for neutron using the following command:

```
keystone service-create --name neutron --type network \
--description "OpenStack Networking"
```

4. Create an API endpoint for the Compute service using the following commands:

```
keystone endpoint-create \
--service-id $(keystone service-list | awk '/ network / {print
$2}') \
--publicurl http://controller:9696 \
--adminurl http://controller:9696 \
--internalurl http://controller:9696 \
--region regionOne
```

# Installing the Networking components

Use the following command to install the Networking components:

```
apt-get install neutron-server neutron-plugin-ml2 python-neutronclient
```

# Configuring the server components of Networking

Networking server components consists of the following: database, authentication, message broker, notification about topology change, and plugins.

1. Make the following changes in the /etc/neutron/neutron.conf file:

   1. Go to the [database] section and configure the database access:

      ```
      [database]
      ...
      connection = mysql://neutron:NEUTRON_DBPASS@controller/
      neutron
      ```

      Make sure you replace the term NEUTRON_DBPASS with an appropriate password of your choice.

2. Next, go to the [DEFAULT] section and configure the RabbitMQ broker access:

```
[DEFAULT]
...
rpc_backend = rabbit
rabbit_host = controller
rabbit_password = RABBIT_PASS
```

Make sure you replace the term RABBIT_PASS with an appropriate password of your choice.

3. Go to the sections [keystone_authtoken] and [DEFAULT], and configure the Identity service access:

```
[DEFAULT]
...
auth_strategy = keystone
[keystone_authtoken]
...
auth_uri = http://controller:5000/v2.0
identity_uri = http://controller:35357
admin_tenant_name = service
admin_user = neutron
admin_password = NEUTRON_PASS
```

Make sure you replace the term NEUTRON_PASS with an appropriate password of your choice.

4. Enable the ML2 plugin in the [DEFAULT] section, and enable the router service and overlapping IP address:

```
[DEFAULT]
...
core_plugin = ml2
service_plugins = router
allow_overlapping_ips = True
```

5. Now, configure Networking so that it notifies the compute node of any change in network topology in the same [DEFAULT] section:

```
[DEFAULT]
...
notify_nova_on_port_status_changes = True
```

```
notify_nova_on_port_data_changes = True
nova_url = http://controller:8774/v2
nova_admin_auth_url = http://controller:35357/v2.0
nova_region_name = regionOne
nova_admin_username = nova
nova_admin_tenant_id = SERVICE_TENANT_ID
nova_admin_password = NOVA_PASS
```

Here, you will have to replace SERVICE_TENANT_ID with the value the service tenant identifies from the Identity service, and replace the term NOVA_PASS with password you had chosen earlier for the nova user.

2. Next, get the service tenant ID:

```
source admin-openrc.sh
keystone tenant-get service
```

# Configuring the Modular Layer 2 plugin

Make the following changes in the /etc/neutron/plugins/ml2/ml2_conf.ini file:

1. Go to the [ml2] section and configure the following: the **generic network encapsulation (GRE)** driver, tenant networks for GRE, and the driver for **Open vSwitch (OVS)** mechanism. The code is as follows:

```
[ml2]
...
type_drivers = flat,gre
tenant_network_types = gre
mechanism_drivers = openvswitch
```

2. Next, go to the [securitygroup] section, configure the OVS iptables firewall, and enable security group ipset:

```
[securitygroup]
...
enable_security_group = True
enable_ipset = True
firewall_driver = neutron.agent.linux.iptables_firewall.
OVSHybridIptablesFirewallDriver
```

# Configuring Networking on the compute node

Make the following changes in the /etc/nova/nova.conf file:

1. Go to the [database] section and configure the database access:

```
[DEFAULT]
...
network_api_class = nova.network.neutronv2.api.API
security_group_api = neutron
linuxnet_interface_driver = nova.network.linux_net.
LinuxOVSInterfaceDriver
firewall_driver = nova.virt.firewall.NoopFirewallDriver
```

2. Next, go to the [neutron] section and configure the access parameters:

```
[neutron]
...
url = http://controller:9696
auth_strategy = keystone
admin_auth_url = http://controller:35357/v2.0
admin_tenant_name = service
admin_username = neutron
admin_password = NEUTRON_PASS
```

Make sure you replace the term NEUTRON_PASS with an appropriate password of your choice.

# Finalizing the installation

The steps are as follows:

1. First, populate the database using the following commands:

```
su -s /bin/sh -c "neutron-db-manage --config-file /etc/neutron/
neutron.
conf \
--config-file /etc/neutron/plugins/ml2/ml2_conf.ini upgrade juno"
neutron
```

2. Restart the Compute service using the following commands:

```
service nova-api restart
service nova-scheduler restart
service nova-conductor restart
```

3. Restart the Networking service using the following command:

```
service neutron-server restart
```

# Installing and configuring the network node

There are some prerequisites that we will need to take care of before we can start installing and configuring the network node.

## Configuring the prerequisites

We have to configure some kernel network parameters before installing and configuring OpenStack Networking. The steps are as follows:

1. First, edit the /etc/sysctl.conf file and make the following changes:

```
net.ipv4.ip_forward=1
net.ipv4.conf.all.rp_filter=0
net.ipv4.conf.default.rp_filter=0
```

2. Run the following command:

```
sysctl -p
```

## Installing the Networking components

Run the following command:

```
apt-get install neutron-plugin-ml2 neutron-plugin-openvswitch-agent \
neutron-13-agent neutron-dhcp-agent
```

## Configuring the Networking components

The Networking component configuration has the following: an authentication mechanism, message broker, and plugin. Make the following changes in the /etc/neutron/neutron.conf file:

1. Go to the [database] section and comment the lines for the connection option, as network nodes will not be accessing the database directly.

2. Next, go to section [DEFAULT] and configure RabbitMQ broker access:

```
[DEFAULT]
...
rpc_backend = rabbit
```

```
rabbit_host = controller
rabbit_password = RABBIT_PASS
```

Make sure you replace the term RABBIT_PASS with an appropriate password of your choice.

3. Next, go to sections [keystone_authtoken] and [DEFAULT], and configure the Identity service access:

```
[DEFAULT]
...
auth_strategy = keystone
[keystone_authtoken]
...
auth_uri = http://controller:5000/v2.0
identity_uri = http://controller:35357
admin_tenant_name = service
admin_user = neutron
admin_password = NEUTRON_PASS
```

Make sure you replace the term NEUTRON_PASS with an appropriate password of your choice.

4. Enable the ML2 plugin, router service, and overlapping IP address in the [DEFAULT] section:

```
[DEFAULT]
...
core_plugin = ml2
service_plugins = router
allow_overlapping_ips = True
```

# Configuring the Modular Layer 2 plugin

The **Modular Layer 2 (ML2)** plugin makes use of the OVS agent for building a virtual networking framework for instances. We have to make the following changes in the /etc/neutron/plugins/ml2/ml2_conf.ini file:

1. Go to the [ml2] section and configure the following: the GRE driver, tenant networks for GRE, and driver for the OVS mechanism. The code is as follows:

```
[ml2]
...
type_drivers = flat,gre
tenant_network_types = gre
mechanism_drivers = openvswitch
```

2. Go to the `[ml2_type_flat]` section and set the external flat provider network:

```
[ml2_type_flat]
...
flat_networks = external
```

3. In the `[ml2_type_gre]` section, set the tunnel ID range:

```
[ml2_type_gre]
...
tunnel_id_ranges = 1:1000
```

4. Now, enable groups, enable `ipset`, and configure the OVS `iptables` firewall driver. This is done in the `[securitygroup]` section:

```
[securitygroup]
...
enable_security_group = True
enable_ipset = True
firewall_driver = neutron.agent.linux.iptables_firewall.
OVSHybridIptablesFirewallDriver
```

5. Go to the `[ovs]` section and set the tunnels, local tunnel endpoint, and external flat provider network:

```
[ovs]
...
local_ip = INSTANCE_TUNNELS_INTERFACE_IP_ADDRESS
enable_tunneling = True
bridge_mappings = external:br-ex
```

Make sure you replace the term `INSTANCE_TUNNELS_INTERFACE_IP_ADDRESS` with the appropriate IP address in the instance tunnel network in your network node.

6. Enable GRE tunnels in the `[agent]` section:

```
[agent]
...
tunnel_types = gre
```

# Configuring the Layer 3 agent

The **Layer 3 (L3)** layer is responsible for routing services for virtual networks. Let's make the changes in the `/etc/neutron.l3_agent.ini` file.

Go to the [DEFAULT] section and set the driver, network namespace, and external network bridge:

```
[DEFAULT]
...
interface_driver = neutron.agent.linux.interface.OVSInterfaceDriver
use_namespaces = True
external_network_bridge = br-ex
```

## Configuring the DHCP agent

The DHCP agent is responsible for the DHCP services for virtual networks. Let's edit the /etc/neutron/dhcp_agent.ini file to make some changes.

Go to the [DEFAULT] section, set the drivers, and turn on namespaces:

```
[DEFAULT]
...
interface_driver = neutron.agent.linux.interface.OVSInterfaceDriver
dhcp_driver = neutron.agent.linux.dhcp.Dnsmasq
use_namespaces = True
```

## Configuring the metadata agent

The metadata agent provides information to instances, for example, credentials. The steps to configure the metadata agent are as follows:

1. Make the following changes in the /etc/neutron/metadata_agent.ini file:

   1. Go to the [DEFAULT] section and configure the parameters for access:
      ```
      [DEFAULT]
      ...
      auth_url = http://controller:5000/v2.0
      auth_region = regionOne
      admin_tenant_name = service
      admin_user = neutron
      admin_password = NEUTRON_PASS
      ```

      Make sure you replace the term NEUTRON_PASS with an appropriate password of your choice.

2. In the same `[DEFAULT]` section, set the metadata host using the following code:

```
[DEFAULT]
...
nova_metadata_ip = controller
```

3. Next, configure the metadata proxy shared secret using the following code:

```
[DEFAULT]
...
metadata_proxy_shared_secret = METADATA_SECRET
```

Make sure you replace the term METADATA_SECRET with an appropriate password of your choice.

2. Go to the controller node and make the following changes in the `/etc/nova/nova.conf` file. Navigate to the `[neutron]` section and set metadata proxy and secret:

```
[neutron]
...
service_metadata_proxy = True
metadata_proxy_shared_secret = METADATA_SECRET
```

Make sure you replace the term METADATA_SECRET with an appropriate password of your choice.

3. From the controller node, restart the Compute API service using the following command:

```
service nova-api restart
```

## Configuring the OVS service

The OVS is responsible for providing the virtual networking framework for the instances. `br-int` is for the internal traffic in OVS and `br-ext` is for the external traffic. There should be a port that connects the virtual and physical networks. The steps to configure the OVS service are as follows:

1. First, let's restart the OVS service using the following command:

```
service openvswitch-switch restart
```

2. Next, add the external bridge using the following command:

```
ovs-vsctl add-br br-ex
```

3. Now, add a port to the external bridge for connecting to the physical network:

```
ovs-vsctl add-port br-ex INTERFACE_NAME
```

Make sure you replace the term INTERFACE_NAME with an appropriate port.

## Finalizing the installation

We will restart all the networking services using the following commands:

```
service neutron-plugin-openvswitch-agent restart
service neutron-l3-agent restart
service neutron-dhcp-agent restart
service neutron-metadata-agent restart
```

# Installing and configuring the compute node

The compute node is responsible for the connectivity and security groups for instances.

## Configuring the prerequisites

It is necessary to set some kernel networking parameters before we install and configure OpenStack Networking:

1. Edit the /etc/sysctl.conf file and make the following changes:
   ```
   net.ipv4.conf.all.rp_filter=0
   net.ipv4.conf.default.rp_filter=0
   ```

2. Run the following command so that the changes take effect:
   ```
   sysctl -p
   ```

## Installing the Networking components

Run the following command to install the packages for the Networking components:

```
apt-get install neutron-plugin-ml2 neutron-plugin-openvswitch-agent
```

# Configuring the Networking common components

The Networking component configuration has the following: an authentication mechanism, message broker, and plugin. Make the following changes in the `/etc/neutron/neutron.conf` file:

1. Go to the `[database]` section and comment the lines for the connection option, as network nodes will not be accessing the database directly.

2. Next, go to the `[DEFAULT]` section and configure RabbitMQ broker access:

   ```
   [DEFAULT]
   ...
   rpc_backend = rabbit
   rabbit_host = controller
   rabbit_password = RABBIT_PASS
   ```

   Make sure you replace the term `RABBIT_PASS` with an appropriate password of your choice.

3. Go to the `[keystone_authtoken]` and `[DEFAULT]` sections, and configure the Identity service access using the following code:

   ```
   [DEFAULT]
   ...
   auth_strategy = keystone
   [keystone_authtoken]
   ...
   auth_uri = http://controller:5000/v2.0
   identity_uri = http://controller:35357
   admin_tenant_name = service
   admin_user = neutron
   admin_password = NEUTRON_PASS
   ```

   Make sure you replace the term `NEUTRON_PASS` with an appropriate password of your choice.

4. Enable the ML2 plugin in the `[DEFAULT]` section, and also the router service and overlapping IP address:

   ```
   [DEFAULT]
   ...
   core_plugin = ml2
   service_plugins = router
   allow_overlapping_ips = True
   ```

# Configuring the ML2 plugin

The ML2 plugin makes use of the OVS agent for building virtual networking framework for instances. We will have to make the following changes in the `/etc/neutron/plugins/ml2/ml2_conf.ini` file:

1. Go to the `[ml2]` section and configure the following: the GRE driver, tenant networks for GRE, and the driver for the OVS mechanism. The code is as follows:

   ```
   [ml2]
   ...
   type_drivers = flat,gre
   tenant_network_types = gre
   mechanism_drivers = openvswitch
   ```

2. In the `[ml2_type_gre]` section, set the tunnel ID range:

   ```
   [ml2_type_gre]
   ...
   tunnel_id_ranges = 1:1000
   ```

3. Now, let's enable groups, enable `ipset`, and configure the OVS `iptables` firewall driver. This is done in the `[securitygroup]` section:

   ```
   [securitygroup]
   ...
   enable_security_group = True
   enable_ipset = True
   firewall_driver = neutron.agent.linux.iptables_firewall.
   OVSHybridIptablesFirewallDriver
   ```

4. Go to the `[ovs]` section and set the tunnels, local tunnel endpoint, and the external flat provider network:

   ```
   [ovs]
   ...
   local_ip = INSTANCE_TUNNELS_INTERFACE_IP_ADDRESS
   enable_tunneling = True
   bridge_mappings = external:br-ex
   ```

   Make sure you replace the term INSTANCE_TUNNELS_INTERFACE_IP_ADDRESS with the appropriate IP address in the instance tunnel network in your network node.

5.  Lastly, enable the GRE tunnels in the `[agent]` section:

```
[agent]
...
tunnel_types = gre
```

# Configuring the OVS service

OVS is responsible for providing the virtual networking framework for the instances.

Let's restart the OVS service using the following command:

```
service openvswitch-switch restart
```

# Configuring Compute to use Networking

It is necessary to reconfigure Compute to use Networking. Make the following changes in the `/etc/nova/nova.conf` file:

1.  First, set the APIs and drivers in the `[DEFAULT]` section:

```
[DEFAULT]
...
network_api_class = nova.network.neutronv2.api.API
security_group_api = neutron
linuxnet_interface_driver = nova.network.linux_net.
LinuxOVSInterfaceDriver
firewall_driver = nova.virt.firewall.NoopFirewallDriver
```

2.  Go to the `[neutron]` section and set access parameters:

```
[neutron]
...
url = http://controller:9696
auth_strategy = keystone
admin_auth_url = http://controller:35357/v2.0
admin_tenant_name = service
admin_username = neutron
admin_password = NEUTRON_PASS
```

Make sure you replace the term NEUTRON_PASS with an appropriate password of your choice for the neutron user from the Identity service.

# Finalizing the installation

The steps are as follows:

1. We will restart the Compute service using the following command:

   ```
   service nova-compute restart
   ```

2. Next, restart the OVS agent using the following command:

   ```
   service nova-compute restart
   ```

# Creating initial networks

There are some final steps to be taken care of before launching the first instance. We should create the required virtual network infrastructure for instances to connect to, along with the external network and the tenant network. Have a look at the following diagram:

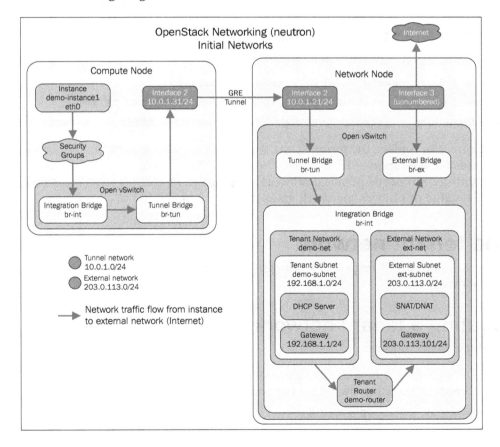

# External networks

The purpose of external networks is to provide access to the Internet for the instances. It uses **network address translation (NAT)** underneath for Internet access to the instances.

## Creating an external network

The steps are as follows:

1.  For gaining access to the admin-only CLI commands, source the admin credentials using the following command:

    ```
    source admin-openrc.sh
    ```

2.  Use the following command to create the network:

    ```
    neutron net-create ext-net --router:external True \
    --provider:physical_network external --provider:network_type flat
    ```

### Creating the subnet for the external network

Run the following command to create the subnet:

```
neutron subnet-create ext-net --name ext-subnet \
--allocation-pool start=FLOATING_IP_START,end=FLOATING_IP_END \
--disable-dhcp --gateway EXTERNAL_NETWORK_GATEWAY EXTERNAL_NETWORK_CIDR
```

Make sure you replace the terms FLOATING_IP_START and FLOATING_IP_END with IP addresses for the range of IP addresses you want. Also, replace EXTERNAL_NETWORK_ CIDR with the subnet of physical network. Replace EXTERNAL_NETWORK_GATEWAY with the value of physical network gateway.

# The tenant network

The tenant network is responsible for providing internal network access to the instances.

## Creating a tenant network

The steps are as follows:

1.  For gaining access to the admin-only CLI commands, source the admin credentials using the following command:

    ```
    source admin-openrc.sh
    ```

2. Use the following command to create the network:

```
neutron net-create demo-net
```

## Creating the subnet for the tenant network

Run the following command to create the subnet:

```
neutron subnet-create demo-net --name demo-subnet \
--gateway TENANT_NETWORK_GATEWAY TENANT_NETWORK_CIDR
```

Make sure you replace the term EXTERNAL_NETWORK_CIDR with the subnet of the physical network. Also, replace EXTERNAL_NETWORK_GATEWAY with value of the physical network gateway.

# Creating the router to attach the external and tenant networks

The steps are as follows:

1. Run the following command to create the router:

```
neutron router-create demo-router
```

2. Next, use the following command for attaching the router to the tenant subnet. The name of the subnet here is demo:

```
neutron router-interface-add demo-router demo-subnet
```

3. Lastly, let's attach the router to the external network by setting the gateway:

```
neutron router-gateway-set demo-router ext-net
```

# Dashboard

Dashboard is a web interface that helps administrators and users manage and access OpenStack services. It uses the OpenStack API for providing these services. In this chapter, we will use the Apache server for deployment.

# Prerequisites

We need to take care of some prerequisites before installing the dashboard as part of our OpenStack setup. Make sure the following requirements are met:

- OpenStack Compute is already installed and the Identity service is enabled
- The user for Identity service has sudo access enabled
- Python version 2.6 or 2.7 is installed, and it should support Django

# Installing and configuring the dashboard

Now, we will install and configure the packages for the dashboard component.

## Installing the packages

The command to install the packages is as follows:

```
apt-get install openstack-dashboard apache2 libapache2-mod-wsgi
memcached python-memcache
```

## Configuring the dashboard

Edit the `/etc/openstack-dashboard/local_settings.py` file and make the following changes:

1. Set the dashboard to run on the controller node using the following code:
   ```
   OPENSTACK_HOST = "controller"
   ```

2. Allow all hosts access to the dashboard using the following code:
   ```
   ALLOWED_HOSTS = ['*']
   ```

3. Lastly, configure the memcached session storage:
   ```
   CACHES = {
   'default': {
   'BACKEND': 'django.core.cache.backends.memcached.
   MemcachedCache',
   'LOCATION': '127.0.0.1:11211',
     }
   }
   ```

## Finalizing the installation

Restart the web server and session storage using the following commands:

```
service apache2 restart
service memcached restart
```

# The Block Storage service

The Block Storage service is responsible for providing block storage devices to various instances. The API and scheduler services run on the controller node, whereas the services for storing volumes run on the storage node.

Block Storage helps with adding persistent storage to virtual machines, and also manages volume snapshots and volume types.

# Installing and configuring the controller node

In this section, we will discuss installing the Block Storage service on the controller node. The Block Storage service needs an additional storage node running, which helps with volumes for the instances.

## Configuring the prerequisites

We need to create database, credentials, and the API endpoints so that we can install and configure the Block Storage service. The steps are as follows:

1. Here are the steps to create a database:

    1. Connect to the database server as root user using the following command:

       ```
       mysql -u root -p
       ```

    2. Create a new database named cinder using the following command:

       ```
       CREATE DATABASE cinder;
       ```

    3. Grant all the required access to the newly created database cinder using the following commands:

       ```
       GRANT ALL PRIVILEGES ON cinder.* TO 'cinder'@'localhost' \
       IDENTIFIED BY 'CINDER_DBPASS';
       ```

```
GRANT ALL PRIVILEGES ON cinder.* TO 'cinder'@'%' \
IDENTIFIED BY 'CINDER_DBPASS';
```

Make sure you replace the term CINDER_DBPASS with an appropriate password of your choice.

4. Exit the database client connection.

2. For gaining access to the admin-only CLI commands, source the admin credentials:

```
source admin-openrc.sh
```

3. Carry on the following steps for creating the service credentials:

1. Create a new user cinder using the following command:

```
keystone user-create --name cinder --pass CINDER_PASS
```

Make sure you replace the term CINDER_PASS with an appropriate password of your choice.

2. Add the admin role to the user cinder using the following command:

```
keystone user-role-add --user cinder --tenant service --role admin
```

3. Create a new service entry for cinder using the following command:

```
keystone service-create --name cinder --type image \
--description "OpenStack Block Service"
```

4. Create an API endpoint for the Image service using the following commands:

```
keystone endpoint-create \
--service-id $(keystone service-list | awk '/ volume / {print $2}') \
--publicurl http://controller:8776/v1/%\(tenant_id\)s \
--internalurl http://controller:8776/v1/%\(tenant_id\)s \
--adminurl http://controller:8776/v1/%\(tenant_id\)s \
--region regionOne
```

# Installing and configuring the Block Storage service components

The steps are as follows:

1.  Install the packages using the following command:

    ```
    apt-get install cinder-api cinder-scheduler python-cinderclient
    ```

2.  Make the following changes in the /etc/cinder/cinder.conf file:

    1.  Go to the [database] section and configure the database access:

        ```
        [database]
        ...
        connection = mysql://cinder:CINDER_DBPASS@controller/cinder
        ```

        Make sure you replace the term CINDER_DBPASS with an appropriate password of your choice.

    2.  Next, go to the [DEFAULT] section and configure the RabbitMQ broker access:

        ```
        [DEFAULT]
        ...
        rpc_backend = rabbit
        rabbit_host = controller
        rabbit_password = RABBIT_PASS
        ```

        Make sure you replace the term RABBIT_PASS with an appropriate password of your choice.

    3.  Next, go to the sections [keystone_authtoken] and [DEFAULT], and configure the Identity service access:

        ```
        [DEFAULT]
        ...
        auth_strategy = keystone
        [keystone_authtoken]
        ...
        auth_uri = http://controller:5000/v2.0
        identity_uri = http://controller:35357
        admin_tenant_name = service
        admin_user = cinder
        admin_password = CINDER_PASS
        ```

        Make sure you replace the term CINDER_PASS with an appropriate password of your choice.

4. Set the `my_ip` option in the `[DEFAULT]` section so that the management interface IP address is used on the controller node:

```
[DEFAULT]
...
my_ip = 10.0.0.11
```

3. Lastly, populate the Block Storage database using the following command:

```
su -s /bin/sh -c "cinder-manage db sync" cinder
```

## Finalizing the installation

The steps are as follows:

1. Restart the Block Storage service using the following command:

```
service cinder-scheduler restart
service cinder-api restart
```

2. Next, as we did in the previous section, remove the SQLite database file:

```
rm -f /var/lib/cinder/cinder.sqlite
```

# Installing and configuring the storage node

Before we start with the installation of the Storage node, we need to take care of some prerequisites.

## Configuring the prerequisites

Before we can start to configure the storage node, we must install and configure the volume service. Create an interface for the storage node on the management network. Also, the storage node will require an empty block storage device. The steps are as follows:

1. Set the following values while configuring the management interface:

    ° **IP address**: `10.0.0.41`
    ° **Network mask**: `255.255.255.0` (or `/24`)
    ° **Default gateway**: `10.0.0.1`

2. Change the hostname to `block1`:

3. Copy the file contents of `/etc/hosts` from the controller node to the storage node and append the following:

```
# block1
10.0.0.41 block1
```

4. We have installed NTP in a previous section. Follow the same steps and install it in here.

5. Next, install the LVM package using the following command:

```
apt-get install lvm2
```

6. Create a new physical volume in LVM named `/dev/sdb1` using the following command:

```
pvcreate /dev/sdb1
```

7. Create a new volume group named `cinder-volumes` using the following command:

```
vgcreate cinder-volumes /dev/sdb1
```

8. Restrict the LVM for the Block Storage service to access and cache only the `cinder-volume` volume group by editing the `/etc/lvm/lvm.conf` file and making the following changes:

```
devices {
...
filter = [ "a/sdb/", "r/.*/"]
}
```

# Installing and configuring the Block Storage volume components

The steps are as follows:

1. Install the packages using the following command:

```
apt-get install cinder-volume python-mysqldb
```

2. Make the following changes in the `/etc/cinder/cinder.conf` file:

  1. Go to the `[database]` section and configure the database access:

```
[database]
...
connection = mysql://cinder:CINDER_DBPASS@controller/cinder
```

     Make sure you replace the term `CINDER_DBPASS` with an appropriate password of your choice.

2. Next, go to the [DEFAULT] section and configure the RabbitMQ broker access:

```
[DEFAULT]
...
rpc_backend = rabbit
rabbit_host = controller
rabbit_password = RABBIT_PASS
```

Make sure you replace the term RABBIT_PASS with an appropriate password of your choice.

3. Next, go to the [keystone_authtoken] and [DEFAULT] sections, and configure the Identity service access:

```
[DEFAULT]
...
auth_strategy = keystone
[keystone_authtoken]
...
auth_uri = http://controller:5000/v2.0
identity_uri = http://controller:35357
admin_tenant_name = service
admin_user = cinder
admin_password = CINDER_PASS
```

Make sure you replace the term CINDER_PASS with an appropriate password of your choice.

4. Set the my_ip option in the [DEFAULT] section so that the management interface IP address is used on the controller node:

```
[DEFAULT]
...
my_ip = MANAGEMENT_INTERFACE_IP_ADDRESS
```

Make sure you replace the term MANAGEMENT_INTERFACE_IP_ADDRESS with the appropriate IP address on the management network interface on the storage node.

5. In the [DEFAULT] section, set the location of the Image service:

```
[DEFAULT]
...
glance_host = controller
```

# Finalizing the installation

The steps are as follows:

1. Restart the Block Storage volume service using the following commands:

```
service tgt restart
service cinder-volume restart
```

2. Next, as we did in the previous section, remove the SQLite database file:

```
rm -f /var/lib/cinder/cinder.sqlite
```

# The Object Storage service

The Object Storage service makes use of the REST API for providing object storage and retrieval. The minimum requirement is the Identity service. It can be scaled to handle a vast amount of unstructured data.

# Installing and configuring the controller node

In this chapter, we will install the Object Service storage on the controller node. However, you can install the service on any node.

## Configuring the prerequisites

The steps are as follows:

1. Create the Identity service credentials as follows:

   1. Using the following command, create a user named `swift`:

   ```
   keystone user-create --name swift --pass SWIFT_PASS
   ```

   Make sure you replace the term SWIFT_PASS with an appropriate password of your choice.

   2. Next, add the admin role to the `swift` user using the following command:

   ```
   keystone user-role-add --user swift --tenant service --role admin
   ```

   3. Lastly, create a `swift` entity using the following command:

   ```
   keystone service-create --name swift --type object-store \
   --description "OpenStack Object Storage"
   ```

2. Create an API endpoint for the Object Storage service using the following commands:

```
keystone endpoint-create \
--service-id $(keystone service-list | awk '/ object-store /
{print
$2}') \
--publicurl 'http://controller:8080/v1/AUTH_%(tenant_id)s' \
--internalurl 'http://controller:8080/v1/AUTH_%(tenant_id)s' \
--adminurl http://controller:8080 \
--region regionOne
```

# Installing and configuring the controller node components

The steps are as follows:

1. Install the packages using the following command:
   ```
   apt-get install swift swift-proxy python-swiftclient
   pythonkeystoneclient

   \ python-keystonemiddleware memcached
   ```

2. Create a new directory /etc/swift using the following command:
   ```
   mkdir /etc/swift
   ```

3. Get the configuration file for the proxy service from the Object Storage repository:
   ```
   curl -o /etc/swift/proxy-server.conf \

   https://raw.githubusercontent.com/openstack/swift/stable/juno/etc/
   proxyserver.

   conf-sample
   ```

4. Make the following changes in the /etc/swift/proxy-server/conf file:

   1. Go to the [DEFAULT] section and get the bind port, user, and configuration directory:
      ```
      [DEFAULT]
      ...
      bind_port = 8080
      user = swift
      swift_dir = /etc/swift
      ```

2. In the `[pipeline:mail]` section, turn on the required modules:

```
[pipeline:main]
pipeline = authtoken cache healthcheck keystoneauth proxy-
logging
proxy-server
```

3. Enable account management in the `[app:proxy-server]` section:

```
[app:proxy-server]
...
allow_account_management = true
account_autocreate = true
```

4. Next, set the operator rules in the `[filter:keystoneauth]` section:

```
[filter:keystoneauth]
use = egg:swift#keystoneauth
...
operator_roles = admin,_member_
```

5. Configure the Identity service access in the `[filter:authtoken]` section:

```
[filter:authtoken]
paste.filter_factory = keystonemiddleware.auth_token:filter_
factory
...
auth_uri = http://controller:5000/v2.0
identity_uri = http://controller:35357
admin_tenant_name = service
admin_user = swift
admin_password = SWIFT_PASS
delay_auth_decision = true
```

Make sure you replace the term SWIFT_PASS with the password you had previously set for the swift user in the Identity service.

6. Lastly, set the memcached location in the `[filter:cache]` section:

```
[filter:cache]
...
memcache_servers = 127.0.0.1:11211
```

# Installing and configuring the storage node

We will first configure some prerequisites and then install the storage node.

## Configuring the prerequisites

It is necessary to configure the storage nodes before we can go ahead and install the OpenStack Object Storage service on it. Also, they should contain the network interface on the management network. We will configure two storage nodes as part of this exercise:

1.  Configure the first storage node as follows:

    1.  Configure the management network:

        °  **IP address**: 10.0.0.51

        °  **Network mask**: 255.255.255.0 (or /24)

        °  **Default gateway**: 10.0.0.1

    2.  Change the hostname to object1.

2.  Configure the second storage node as follows:

    1.  Configure the management network:

        °  **IP address**: 10.0.0.52

        °  **Network mask**: 255.255.255.0 (or /24)

        °  **Default gateway**: 10.0.0.1

    2.  Change the hostname to object2.

3.  Configure the items shared between both storage nodes as follows:

    1.  Copy the file contents of /etc/hosts from the controller node to the storage node and append the following:

        ```
        # object1
        10.0.0.51 object1
        # object2
        10.0.0.52 object2
        ```

        Add the same contents to file /etc/hosts in all nodes.

2. We have installed NTP in a previous section, follow the same steps and install it here.

3. Install the utility packages using the following command:

```
apt-get install xfsprogs rsync
```

4. Prepare new partitions with XFS partition using the following commands:

```
mkfs.xfs /dev/sdb1
mkfs.xfs /dev/sdc1
```

5. Create a mount point for these partitions using the following commands:

```
mkdir -p /srv/node/sdb1
mkdir -p /srv/node/sdc1
```

6. Edit the /etc/fstabd file and make the following changes:

```
/dev/sdb1 /srv/node/sdb1 xfs noatime,nodiratime,nobarrier,l
ogbufs=8 0 2
/dev/sdc1 /srv/node/sdc1 xfs noatime,nodiratime,nobarrier,l
ogbufs=8 0 2
```

7. Lastly, mount the devices using the following commands:

```
mount /srv/node/sdb1
mount /srv/node/sdc1
```

4. Edit the /etc/rsyncd.conf file and make the following changes:

```
uid = swift
gid = swift
log file = /var/log/rsyncd.log
pid file = /var/run/rsyncd.pid
address = MANAGEMENT_INTERFACE_IP_ADDRESS
[account]
max connections = 2
path = /srv/node/
read only = false
lock file = /var/lock/account.lock
[container]
max connections = 2
path = /srv/node/
read only = false
```

```
lock file = /var/lock/container.lock
[object]
max connections = 2
path = /srv/node/
read only = false
lock file = /var/lock/object.lock
```

Make sure you replace the term MANAGEMENT_INTERFACE_IP_ADDRESS with the IP address of the storage node management network.

5.  Turn on rsync in the /etc/default/rsync file using the following code:

    RSYNC_ENABLE=true

6.  Start the rsync service using the following command:

    ```
    service rsync start
    ```

# Installing and configuring the storage node components

We have to do the following operations on all storage nodes:

1.  Install the packages using the following command:

    ```
    apt-get install swift swift-account swift-container swift-object
    ```

2.  Get the accounting, container, and object service configuration files from the Object Storage source repository:

    ```
    curl -o /etc/swift/account-server.conf \
    ```

    ```
    https://raw.githubusercontent.com/openstack/swift/stable/juno/etc/
    account-server.conf-sample
    ```

    ```
    curl -o /etc/swift/container-server.conf \
    ```

    ```
    https://raw.githubusercontent.com/openstack/swift/stable/juno/etc/
    container-server.conf-sample
    ```

    ```
    curl -o /etc/swift/object-server.conf \
    ```

    ```
    https://raw.githubusercontent.com/openstack/swift/stable/juno/etc/
    object-server.conf-sample
    ```

3. Edit the `/etc/swift/account-server.conf` file and make the following changes:

   1. Go to the `[DEFAULT]` section and get the bind port, user, and configuration directory:

      ```
      [DEFAULT]
      ...
      bind_ip = MANAGEMENT_INTERFACE_IP_ADDRESS
      bind_port = 6002
      user = swift
      swift_dir = /etc/swift
      devices = /srv/node
      ```

      Make sure you replace the term MANAGEMENT_INTERFACE_IP_ADDRESS with the IP address of the storage node management network.

   2. In the `[pipeline:mail]` section, turn on the required modules using the following code:

      ```
      [[pipeline:main]
      pipeline = healthcheck recon account-server
      ```

   3. Enable the `recon` cache directory in the `[filter:recon]` section using the following code:

      ```
      [filter:recon]
      ...
      recon_cache_path = /var/cache/swift
      ```

4. Edit the `/etc/swift/container-server.conf` file and make the following changes:

   1. Go to the `[DEFAULT]` section and get the bind port, user, and configuration directory:

      ```
      [DEFAULT]
      ...
      bind_ip = MANAGEMENT_INTERFACE_IP_ADDRESS
      bind_port = 6001
      user = swift
      swift_dir = /etc/swift
      devices = /srv/node
      ```

      Make sure you replace the term MANAGEMENT_INTERFACE_IP_ADDRESS with the IP address of the storage node management network.

2. In the `[pipeline:mail]` section, turn on the required modules using the following code:

```
[[pipeline:main]
pipeline = healthcheck recon container-server
```

3. Enable the `recon` cache directory in the `[filter:recon]` section using the following command:

```
[filter:recon]
...
recon_cache_path = /var/cache/swift
```

5. Edit the `/etc/swift/object-server.conf` file and make the following changes:

1. Go to the `[DEFAULT]` section and get the bind port, user, and configuration directory:

```
[DEFAULT]
...
bind_ip = MANAGEMENT_INTERFACE_IP_ADDRESS
bind_port = 6000
user = swift
swift_dir = /etc/swift
devices = /srv/node
```

Make sure you replace the term MANAGEMENT_INTERFACE_IP_ADDRESS with the IP address of the storage node management network.

2. In the `[pipeline:mail]` section, turn on the required modules:

```
[[pipeline:main]
pipeline = healthcheck recon object-server
```

3. Enable the `recon` cache directory in the `[filter:recon]` section using the following code:

```
[filter:recon]
...
recon_cache_path = /var/cache/swift
```

6. Change the owner of the mount point directory using the following command:

```
chown -R swift:swift /srv/node
```

7. Create a new directory `recon` and change the owner for it:

```
mkdir -p /var/cache/swift
chown -R swift:swift /var/cache/swift
```

# Summary

So far, we have discussed so many components of the OpenStack system. In the next chapter, we will look at the remaining components, such as creating rings and launching an instance. Also, we will study some of the best practices of the Ubuntu Server OS. The topics we will study in the next chapter will be creating the initial rings, the Orchestration module, the Telemetry module, the Database service and lastly, the Data Processing service. The next chapter will be the concluding chapter of this book.

# OpenStack and Ubuntu Best Practices

In the previous chapter, we started with OpenStack with Ubuntu and we saw the architecture, environment, and various components of the OpenStack setup. We talked about services such as Identity service, Image service, Compute service, Dashboard, Networking, Block Storage, and Object Storage. In this chapter, we will cover the remaining components, namely, Orchestration, Telemetry, Database, and Data Processing services. Also, we will look at some of the best practices for the Ubuntu OS.

## Creating rings for Object Storage

Object Storage requires three types of rings set to start functioning. These rings are named account, container, and object rings. The configurations created for the rings are used by the nodes for setting up the storage architecture. Let's create these rings now.

## Creating an account ring

Complete the following steps to install the account ring. The commands are to be run on the controller node:

1. Navigate to the /etc/swift folder:

   ```
   cd /etc/swift
   ```

2. With the following command, create a new file base account.builder:

   ```
   swift-ring-builder account.builder create 10 3 1
   ```

3. Add storage nodes to the ring:

```
swift-ring-builder account.builder add

r1z1-STORAGE_NODE_MANAGEMENT_INTERFACE_IP_ADDRESS:6002/DEVICE_NAME
DEVICE_WEIGT
```

Make sure that you replace STORAGE_NODE_MANAGEMENT_INTERFACE_
IP_ADDRESS with the IP address of storage node's management network.
DEVICE_NAME should be replaced with a storage name (for example, sda1) in
the preceding command. We should run the same command on all the storage
nodes and for every storage device on each node. DEVICE_WEIGHT should be
replaced with the number of partitions assigned in this storage. This weight is
relative to the other storage nodes and partitions assigned in them.

4. Run the following command to check whether the previous commands
were successful:

```
swift-ring-builder account.builder
```

5. Run the following command to rebalance the ring:

```
swift-ring-builder account.builder rebalance
```

# Creating a container ring

The container server has to maintain a list of objects. For this purpose, it makes
use of the container ring. Run the following commands on the controller node to
create the container ring:

1. Navigate to the /etc/swift folder:

```
cd /etc/swift
```

2. With the following command, create a new file base container.builder:

```
swift-ring-builder container.builder create 10 3 1
```

3. Add storage nodes to the ring:

```
swift-ring-builder container.builder add

r1z1-STORAGE_NODE_MANAGEMENT_INTERFACE_IP_ADDRESS:6001/DEVICE_NAME
DEVICE_WEIGT
```

Make sure that you replace STORAGE_NODE_MANAGEMENT_INTERFACE_
IP_ADDRESS with the IP address of storage node's management network.
DEVICE_NAME should be replaced with a storage name (for example, sda1) in
the preceding command. We should run the same command on the storage
node and for every storage device on each node.

4. Run the following command to check if the previous commands were successful:

```
swift-ring-builder container.builder
```

5. Run the following command to rebalance the ring:

```
swift-ring-builder container.builder rebalance
```

# Creating an object ring

The object server has the responsibility of maintaining a list of object locations present on the local device. For this, the object server makes use of the object ring. Follow these steps to create the object ring:

1. Navigate to the /etc/swift folder:

```
cd /etc/swift
```

2. With the following command, create a new file base object.builder:

```
swift-ring-builder object.builder create 10 3 1
```

3. Add storage nodes to the ring:

```
swift-ring-builder object.builder add

r1z1-STORAGE_NODE_MANAGEMENT_INTERFACE_IP_ADDRESS:6000/DEVICE_NAME
DEVICE_WEIGT
```

Make sure that you replace STORAGE_NODE_MANAGEMENT_INTERFACE_ IP_ADDRESS with the IP address of storage node's management network. DEVICE_NAME should be replaced with a storage name (for example, sda1) in the preceding command. We should run the same command on the storage node and for every storage device on each node.

4. Run the following command to check if the previous commands were successful:

```
swift-ring-builder object.builder
```

5. Run the following command to rebalance the ring.

```
swift-ring-builder object.builder rebalance
```

# Copying the configuration files for rings

After completing the previous steps, we will have to copy the three files, namely, `account.ring.gz`, `container.ring.gz`, and `object.ring.gz` on all the storage nodes in the OpenStack setup. The folder to copy these files to is `/etc/swift`.

# Finalizing the installation

The final stage of ring installation involves configuring hash and setting the default storage policy. The steps are as follows:

1.  Get the `/etc/swift/swift.conf` file from the repository for Object Storage:

    ```
    curl -o /etc/swift/swift.conf \
    https://raw.githubusercontent.com/openstack/swift/stable/juno/etc/
    swift.
    conf-sample
    ```

2.  Edit the same file `/etc/swift/swift.conf` and make the following changes:

    1.  Go to the `[swift-hash]` section and set the prefix and suffix for the hash path:

        ```
        [swift-hash]
        ...
        swift_hash_path_suffix = HASH_PATH_PREFIX
        swift_hash_path_prefix = HASH_PATH_SUFFIX
        ```

        Make sure that you assign some secret values to both `HASH_PATH_PREFIX` and `HASH_PATH_SUFFIX` and keep them safe like a password.

    2.  Next, go to the `[storage-policy:0]` section and set the storage policy default value:

        ```
        [storage-policy:0]
        ...
        name = Policy-0
        default = yes
        ```

3.  Now, get the `swift.conf` file and copy this to all storage nodes in the `/etc/swift/` folder.

4.  Change the ownership of these files on all storage nodes and set to the `swift` user and the `swift` group:

    ```
    chown -R swift:swift /etc/swift
    ```

5. Then, on all the nodes where proxy services are running, restart the Object Storage service:

```
service memcached restart
service swift-proxy restart
```

6. Lastly, start the Object Storage service on storage node:

```
swift-init all start
```

# The Orchestration module

The Orchestration module can be termed as the one most useful for developers. It provides a template to the users, so that user can describe the application. This module makes use of the OpenStack API calls to generate the running cloud applications. The user is given a one-file template, which can be used to create instances, security groups and users, and IP addresses. This template is then used by deployers to deploy an application in OpenStack.

# Installing and configuring

We will install and configure the Orchestration module on the controller node.

# Configuring the prerequisites

We need to create database, credentials, and API endpoints so that we can install and configure the Orchestration module. The steps are as follows:

1. The following are the steps to create a database:

    1. Connect to the database server as root user:

    ```
    mysql -u root -p
    ```

    2. Create a new database named heat:

    ```
    CREATE DATABASE heat;
    ```

    3. Grant all the required access to the newly created database heat:

    ```
    GRANT ALL PRIVILEGES ON glance.* TO heat@'localhost' \
    IDENTIFIED BY 'HEAT_DBPASS';
    GRANT ALL PRIVILEGES ON glance.* TO heat@'%' \
    IDENTIFIED BY 'HEAT_DBPASS';
    ```

    Make sure that you replace the term HEAT_DBPASS with an appropriate password of your choice.

    4. Exit the database client connection.

2. To gain access to admin-only CLI commands, source the admin credentials:

```
source admin-openrc.sh
```

3. Carry on the following steps to create the service credentials:

    1. Create new user heat:

    ```
    keystone user-create --name heat --pass HEAT_PASS
    ```

    Make sure that you replace the term HEAT_PASS with an appropriate password of your choice.

    2. Add admin role to the user heat:

    ```
    keystone user-role-add --user heat --tenant service --role
    admin
    ```

    3. Create a new role named heat_stack_owner:

    ```
    keystone role-create --name heat_stack_owner
    ```

    4. Next, we will add this new role heat_stack_owner to the demo tenant and user:

    ```
    keystone user-role-add --user demo --tenant demo --role \
    heat_stack_owner
    ```

    5. Create a new role named heat_stack_user:

    ```
    keystone role-create --name heat_stack_user
    ```

    6. Next, create service entities heat and heat-cfn:

    ```
    keystone service-create --name heat --type orchestration \
    --description "Orchestration"
    keystone service-create --name heat-cfn --type
    cloudformation --description "Orchestration"
    ```

4. Create an API endpoint for the Image service:

```
keystone endpoint-create \
--service-id $(keystone service-list | awk '/ orchestration /
{print
$2}') \
--publicurl http://controller:8004/v1/%\(tenant_id\)s \
--internalurl http://controller:8004/v1/%\(tenant_id\)s \
--adminurl http://controller:8004/v1/%\(tenant_id\)s \
--region regionOne
```

# Installing and configuring the Orchestration components

The steps to install and configure the Orchestration components are as follows:

1.  Install the packages:

    ```
    apt-get install heat-api heat-api-cfn heat-engine python-
    heatclient
    ```

2.  Make the following changes in the `/etc/heat/heat.conf` file:

    1.  Go to the `[database]` section and configure the database access:

        ```
        [database]
        ...
        connection = mysql://glance:HEAT_DBPASS@controller/glance
        ```

        Make sure that you replace the term HEAT_DBPASS with an appropriate password of your choice.

    2.  Next, go to the `[DEFAULT]` section and configure the RabbitMQ broker access:

        ```
        [DEFAULT]
        ...
        rpc_backend = rabbit
        rabbit_host = controller
        rabbit_password = RABBIT_PASS
        ```

        Make sure that you replace the term RABBIT_PASS with an appropriate password of your choice.

    3.  Next, go to the `[keystone_authtoken]` and `[ec2authtoken]` sections and configure the Identity service access:

        ```
        [keystone_authtoken]
        ...
        auth_uri = http://controller:5000/v2.0
        identity_uri = http://controller:35357
        admin_tenant_name = service
        admin_user = heat
        admin_password = HEAT_PASS
        [ec2authtoken]
        ...
        auth_uri = http://controller:5000/v2.0
        ```

        Make sure that you replace the term HEAT_PASS with password set in the Identity service for the heat user.

4.  Next, configure the metadata and URLs for the wait condition in the
    [DEFAULT] section:

```
[DEFAULT]
...
heat_metadata_server_url = http://controller:8000
heat_waitcondition_server_url = http://controller:8000/v1/
waitcondition
```

## Finalizing the installation

The following are the final steps for finishing the installation of the Image
service components:

1.  First, we will restart the services:

    ```
    service heat-api restart
    service heat-api-cfn restart
    service heat-engine restart
    ```

2.  Next, as we did in the previous section, we will remove the SQLite
    database file:

    ```
    rm -f /var/lib/heat/heat.sqlite
    ```

# The Telemetry module

The Telemetry module is similar to a stats collector. It collects various types of data
from different components and systems. The Telemetry module gets data about
CPU and network utilization, which in turn is helpful for fine-tuning the operating
circumstances. It makes use of the REST API for reading or writing these stats. Users
can also create plugins for custom collection of metered data.

# Installing and configuring the controller node

In this section, we will see how to install the Telemetry module, known as
**ceilometer**, on the controller node.

# Configuring the prerequisites

We will install MongoDB and create a database, and then we will create the service credentials for it and the API endpoints, so that we can install the Telemetry module. The steps are as follows:

1. Install the MongoDB package:

   ```
   apt-get install mongodb-server
   ```

2. Edit the `/etc/mongodb.conf` file and make the following changes:

   1. Set the `bind_ip` key to the IP address of the controller node management network:

      ```
      bind_ip = 10.0.0.11
      ```

   2. We can also reduce the size of journal files from the default 1 GB. To do so, we have to set a flag in the configuration file as follows:

      ```
      smallfiles = true
      ```

      After this, we will need to stop MongoDB, remove the journal files that are already present, and start the service again:

      ```
      service mongodb stop
      rm /var/lib/mongodb/journal/prealloc.*
      service mongodb start
      ```

   3. Next, we restart the MongoDB service:

      ```
      service mongodb restart
      ```

3. Create a database named `ceilometer` in MongoDB:

   ```
   mongo --host controller --eval '
   db = db.getSiblingDB("ceilometer");
   db.addUser({user: "ceilometer",
   pwd: "CEILOMETER_DBPASS",
   roles: [ "readWrite", "dbAdmin" ]})'
   ```

   Make sure that you replace the term `CEILOMETER_DBPASS` with an appropriate password of your choice.

4. Next, to gain access to the admin-only CLI commands, source the admin credentials:

   ```
   source admin-openrc.sh
   ```

5. Carry on following these steps to create the service credentials:

   1. Create new user `ceilometer`:

      ```
      keystone user-create --name ceilometer --pass CEILOMETER_
      PASS
      ```

      Make sure that you replace the term CEILOMETER_PASS with an appropriate password of your choice.

   2. Add admin role to the user `ceilometer`:

      ```
      keystone user-role-add --user ceilometer -tenant service
      --role admin
      ```

   3. Create a new service entry for `ceilometer`:

      ```
      keystone service-create --name ceilometer -type metering
      --description "Telemetry"
      ```

6. Create an API endpoint for the Telemetry service:

   ```
   keystone endpoint-create \
   --service-id $(keystone service-list | awk '/ metering / {print
   $2}') \
   --publicurl http://controller:8777 \
   --internalurl http://controller:8777 \
   --adminurl http://controller:8777 \
   --region regionOne
   ```

# Installing and configuring the Telemetry components

The steps to install and configure the Telemetry components are as follows:

1. Install the packages:

   ```
   apt-get install ceilometer-api ceilometer-collector ceilometer-
   agentcentral
   \
   ceilometer-agent-notification ceilometer-alarm-evaluator
   ceilometeralarm-
   notifier \
   python-ceilometerclient
   ```

2. Next, we need a secret value. Let's generate one using the following command:

```
openssl rand -hex 10
```

3. Make the following changes in the `/etc/ceilometer/ceilometer.conf` file:

   1. Go to the `[database]` section and configure the database access:

      ```
      [database]
      ...
      connection = mongodb://ceilometer:CEILOMETER_DBPASS@
      controller:27017/
      ceilometer
      ```

      Make sure that you replace the term `CEILOMETER_DBPASS` with an appropriate password of your choice.

   2. Next, go to the `[DEFAULT]` section and configure the RabbitMQ broker access:

      ```
      [DEFAULT]
      ...
      rpc_backend = rabbit
      rabbit_host = controller
      rabbit_password = RABBIT_PASS
      ```

      Make sure that you replace the term `RABBIT_PASS` with the password set previously for RabbitMQ.

   3. Next, go to the `[keystone_authtoken]` and `[DEFAULT]` sections and configure the Identity service access:

      ```
      [DEFAULT]
      ...
      auth_strategy = keystone
      [keystone_authtoken]
      ...
      auth_uri = http://controller:5000/v2.0
      identity_uri = http://controller:35357
      admin_tenant_name = service
      admin_user = ceilometer
      admin_password = CEILOMETER_PASS
      ```

      Make sure that you replace the term `CEILOMETER _PASS` with the password you set for `ceilometer` in Identity service.

4. Set the service credentials in the `[service-credentials]` section:

```
[service_credentials]
...
os_auth_url = http://controller:5000/v2.0
os_username = ceilometer
os_tenant_name = service
os_password = CEILOMETER_PASS
```

Make sure that you replace the term `CEILOMETER _PASS` with the password you set for `ceilometer` in Identity service.

5. Set the metering secret value in the `[publisher]` section (we had generated this secret in the previous section):

```
[publisher]
...
metering_secret = METERING_SECRET
```

6. Lastly, we configure the logging in the `[DEFAULT]` section:

```
[DEFAULT]
...
log_dir = /var/log/ceilometer
```

## Finalizing the installation

Run the following commands to restart the services for Telemetry:

```
service ceilometer-agent-central restart
service ceilometer-agent-notification restart
service ceilometer-api restart
service ceilometer-collector restart
service ceilometer-alarm-evaluator restart
service ceilometer-alarm-notifier restart
```

# Installing and configuring the Compute agent

In this section, we will cover how to install and configure the Telemetry agent on the Compute node.

# Configuring the prerequisites

The steps to configure the prerequisites are as follows:

1.  Installing the package:

    ```
    apt-get install ceilometer-agent-compute
    ```

2.  Add the following in the [DEFAULT] section of the /etc/nova/nova.conf file:

    ```
    [DEFAULT]
    ...
    instance_usage_audit = True
    instance_usage_audit_period = hour
    notify_on_state_change = vm_and_task_state
    notification_driver = nova.openstack.common.notifier.rpc_notifier
    notification_driver = ceilometer.compute.nova_notifier
    ```

3.  Lastly, restart the Compute service:

    ```
    service nova-compute restart
    ```

# Configuring the Compute agent for the Telemetry module

Edit the /etc/ceilometer/ceilometer.conf file and make the following changes:

1.  Go to the [publisher] section, and set the secret token we created in the previous section. The secret token comes in the place of the CEILOMETER_ TOKEN term:

    ```
    [publisher]
    # Secret value for signing metering messages (string value)
    metering_secret = CEILOMETER_TOKEN
    ```

2.  Next, go to the [DEFAULT] section and configure the RabbitMQ broker access:

    ```
    [DEFAULT]
    ...
    rpc_backend = rabbit
    rabbit_host = controller
    rabbit_password = RABBIT_PASS
    ```

    Make sure that you replace the term RABBIT_PASS with the password set for RabbitMQ previously.

3. Next, go to the [keystone_authtoken] and [DEFAULT] sections and configure Identity service access:

```
[keystone_authtoken]
auth_uri = http://controller:5000/v2.0
identity_uri = http://controller:35357
admin_tenant_name = service
admin_user = ceilometer
admin_password = CEILOMETER_PASSS
```

Make sure that you replace the term CEILOMETER _PASS with the password you set for the Telemetry module service.

4. Set the service credentials in the [service-credentials] section:

```
[service_credentials]
os_auth_url = http://controller:5000/v2.0
os_username = ceilometer
os_tenant_name = service
os_password = CEILOMETER_PASS
os_endpoint_type = internalURL
```

Make sure that you replace the term CEILOMETER _PASS with the password you set for the ceilometer in Identity service.

5. Lastly, we configure the logging in the [DEFAULT] section:

```
[DEFAULT]
...
log_dir = /var/log/ceilometer
```

## Finalizing the installation

Restart the service in order for the changes to take effect:

```
service ceilometer-agent-compute restart
```

## Configuring the Image service

Edit the /etc/glance/glance-api.conf file and make the following changes in the [DEFAULT] section:

```
notification_driver = messaging
rpc_backend = rabbit
rabbit_host = controller
rabbit_password = RABBIT_PASS
```

Next, we will restart the Image services in order for the settings to take effect:

```
service glance-registry restart
service glance-api restart
```

# Adding the Block Storage agent for Telemetry

The steps to add the Block Storage agent for Telemetry are as follows:

1.  Make the following edits to the /etc/cinder/cinder.conf file in the [DEFAULT] section:

    ```
    control_exchange = cinder
    notification_driver = cinder.openstack.common.notifier.rpc_
    notifier
    ```

2.  Next, restart the Image services in order for the settings to take effect:

    1.  Run the following commands on the controller node:

        ```
        service cinder-api restart
        service cinder-scheduler restart
        ```

    2.  Run the following command on the storage node:

        ```
        service cinder-volume restart
        ```

# Configuring Object Storage for Telemetry

The steps to configure Object Storage for Telemetry are as follows:

1.  Run the following command on the Object Storage server:

    ```
    apt-get install python-ceilometerclient
    ```

2.  Add permissions to the roles for sufficient access to the Telemetry module:

    ```
    keystone role-create --name ResellerAdmin
    keystone user-role-add --tenant service --user ceilometer \
    --role ID_VALUE
    ```

    Make sure that you replace the term ID_VALUE with the ID value generated in the preceding command.

3. Next, edit the /etc/swift/proxy-server.conf file and make the following changes:

```
[filter:ceilometer]
use = egg:ceilometer#swift
```

4. Go to the [pipeline:main] section and add the following lines:

```
[pipeline:main]
pipeline = healthcheck cache authtoken keystoneauth ceilometer
proxy-server
```

5. Next, add the swift user to the ceilometer group:

```
usermod -a -G ceilometer swift
```

6. In the operator_roles section, add the following line:

```
operator_roles = Member,admin,swiftoperator,_member_,ResellerAdmin
```

7. Restart the service for the changes to take effect:

```
service swift-proxy restart
```

# The Database service

Database service is a component of the OpenStack system that helps users with scalability and provisioning of databases. Users can automate the administrative tasks related to cloud configuration, deployment, monitoring, backup, restore and patching.

# Installing the Database service

Complete the following steps to install Database service on the controller node.

## Taking care of the prerequisites

The Compute, Image, and Identity services should be running. Object Storage and Block Storage services are optional.

# Installing the Database module

The steps to install the Database module are as follows:

1. Install the package:

```
apt-get install python-trove python-troveclient python-
glanceclient \
trove-common trove-api trove-taskmanager
```

2. Prepare OpenStack:

   1. Source the admin credentials:

   ```
   source admin-openrc.sh
   ```

   2. Create a user `trove` and give the user administrative rights:

   ```
   keystone user-create --name trove --pass TROVE_PASS
   keystone user-role-add --user trove --tenant service --role
   admin
   ```

   Make sure that you replace the term TROVE_PASS with an appropriate password of your choice.

3. Edit the following files and make the changes listed in each of the file:

   ° `trove.conf`
   ° `trove-taskmanager.conf`
   ° `trove-conductor.conf`

   The following are the changes:

   1. Go to the [DEFAULT] section and set SQL connection, logging, and messaging URLS for OpenStack services:

   ```
   [DEFAULT]
   log_dir = /var/log/trove
   trove_auth_url = http://controller:5000/v2.0
   nova_compute_url = http://controller:8774/v2
   cinder_url = http://controller:8776/v1
   swift_url = http://controller:8080/v1/AUTH_
   sql_connection = mysql://trove:TROVE_DBPASS@controller/trove
   notifier_queue_hostname = controller
   ```

2.  Next, go to the `[DEFAULT]` section and configure the RabbitMQ broker access:

```
[DEFAULT]
...
rpc_backend = rabbit
rabbit_host = controller
rabbit_password = RABBIT_PASS
```

4.  Edit the `api-paste.ini` file and make the following changes in the `[filter:authtoken]` section:

```
[filter:authtoken]
auth_uri = http://controller:5000/v2.0
identity_uri = http://controller:35357
admin_user = trove
admin_password = ADMIN_PASS
admin_tenant_name = service
signing_dir = /var/cache/trove
```

5.  Make the following changes in the `trove.conf` file:

```
[DEFAULT]
default_datastore = mysql
....
# Config option for showing the IP address that nova doles out
add_addresses = True
network_label_regex = ^NETWORK_LABEL$
....
api_paste_config = /etc/trove/api-paste.ini
```

6.  Edit the `trove-taskmanager.conf` file and make the following changes:

```
[DEFAULT]
....
# Configuration options for talking to nova via the novaclient.
# These options are for an admin user in your keystone config.
# It proxy's the token received from the user to send to nova via
this
admin users creds,
# basically acting like the client via that proxy token.
nova_proxy_admin_user = admin
nova_proxy_admin_pass = ADMIN_PASS
nova_proxy_admin_tenant_name = service
taskmanager_manager = trove.taskmanager.manager.Manager
```

7. Configure the `trove` database:

```
mysql -u root -p
mysql> CREATE DATABASE trove;
mysql> GRANT ALL PRIVILEGES ON trove.* TO trove@'localhost' \
IDENTIFIED BY 'TROVE_DBPASS';
mysql> GRANT ALL PRIVILEGES ON trove.* TO trove@'%' \
IDENTIFIED BY 'TROVE_DBPASS';
```

8. Configure the Database service:

   1. Initialize the database:

      ```
      su -s /bin/sh -c "trove-manage db_sync" trove
      ```

   2. Create a new datastore for the MySQL database:

      ```
      su -s /bin/sh -c "trove-manage datastore_update mysql ''"
      trove
      ```

9. Create a new image for `trove` in the MySQL database. Edit the `trove-guestagent.conf` file and make the following changes:

```
rabbit_host = controller
rabbit_password = RABBIT_PASS
nova_proxy_admin_user = admin
nova_proxy_admin_pass = ADMIN_PASS
nova_proxy_admin_tenant_name = service
trove_auth_url = http://controller:35357/v2.0
```

10. Next, use the `trove-manage` command and execute the following commands to make use of the new image:

```
trove-manage --config-file /etc/trove/trove.conf
datastore_version_update \
mysql mysql-5.5 mysql glance_image_ID mysql-server-5.5 1
```

11. Register the newly created Database service in the list with the Image service:

```
keystone service-create --name trove --type database \
--description "OpenStack Database Service"
```

Also, set the endpoint:

```
keystone endpoint-create \
--service-id $(keystone service-list | awk '/ trove / {print $2}')
\
```

```
--publicurl http://controller:8779/v1.0/%\(tenant_id\)s \
--internalurl http://controller:8779/v1.0/%\(tenant_id\)s \
--adminurl http://controller:8779/v1.0/%\(tenant_id\)s \
--region regionOne
```

12. Restart the service for the settings to take effect:

```
service trove-api restart
service trove-taskmanager restart
service trove-conductor restart
```

# The Data Processing service

The OpenStack Data processing service is used by users for setting up clusters for data processing. Some of the examples are Hadoop and Spark. Users need to specify the configuration for the clusters, namely, version, topology, and nodes. With this information, the Data Processing service will deploy the cluster in the cloud. This cluster is scalable and users can add/remove nodes on demand.

## Installing the Data Processing service

We will now discuss the procedure to install the Data Processing service known as sahara on the controller node. The steps are as follows:

1. Install the package for the Data Processing service:

```
apt-get install python-pip
pip install sahara
```

2. Make the following changes to the /etc/sahara/sahara.conf configuration file:

   1. Go to the [database] section and set the parameter connection to point it to a database:

   ```
   connection = mysql://sahara:SAHARA_DBPASS@controller/sahara
   ```

   2. Next, in the [keystone_authtoken] section, set the auth_uri and identity_uri parameters as follows:

   ```
   auth_uri = http://controller:5000/v2.0
   identity_uri = http://controller:35357
   ```

3. We should have a keystone user with administrative rights. Use the same user to set the admin_user, admin_password, and admin_tenant_name parameters in the same file.

4. In the [DEFAULT] section, set the following:

```
use_neutron=true
```

3. We had installed the MySQL database in the previous section. We will make use of the same for storing job binaries belonging to Data Processing service. Make the following changes to the my.cnf file and restart the MySQL server:

```
[mysqld]
max_allowed_packet = 256M
```

4. Next, we create a database schema:

```
sahara-db-manage --config-file /etc/sahara/sahara.conf upgrade head
```

5. Let's add the Data Processing service to the Identity service list, so that other services can get to know about it:

```
keystone service-create --name sahara --type data_processing \
--description "Data processing service"
```

Also, set the API endpoint for sahara.

```
keystone endpoint-create \
--service-id $(keystone service-list | awk '/ sahara / {print $2}') \
--publicurl http://controller:8386/v1.1/%\(tenant_id\)s \
--internalurl http://controller:8386/v1.1/%\(tenant_id\)s \
--adminurl http://controller:8386/v1.1/%\(tenant_id\)s \
--region regionOne
```

6. Finally, we start the sahara service:

```
systemctl enable openstack-sahara-all
```

# OpenStack flashback

We have installed, configured, and set up all of the core and optional components of the OpenStack system. By now, we should have a complete setup of the OpenStack software on our Ubuntu Server. Let's discuss some tips and best practices for working with the Ubuntu Server.

# Best practices for Ubuntu Server

Here are some of the best practices that we as Ubuntu Server administrators can follow to keep the system safe and secure, and to avoid any issues that may occur due to users' negligence and/or forceful attempts to access restricted areas. This list is a good starting point, but not exhaustive:

- Be sure to enable only SSH-based logins.

- Provide users with limited access to files and software. Make sure that proper ownership is applied everywhere.

- Create a password policy and encourage users to change their passwords periodically. Also, check whether your server needs a setup to lockdown users after a certain number of failed login attempts.

- Allow only certain ports that are in use by your applications. Make use of the UFW features for this.

- If you intend to use your server as a mail server as well, then it is best to enable TLS on it.

- Allowing access to MySQL from localhost can enforce security to a great level.

- This goes without saying, but a reminder is always helpful. Make sure that no users have write access to the configuration files for the packages.

- Secure the shared memory.

- Scan open ports from time to time and shut them off if not used by any service.

- Use your best judgment when it comes to providing users with sudo access. Be absolutely sure the user cannot misuse the sudo powers.

- Make use of groups for handling access and security for a collection of users in a better manageable way.

- Secure the FTP access to your Ubuntu Server.

# Summary

In this chapter, we set up and configured the remaining components of the OpenStack system on our Ubuntu Server. Towards the end of this chapter, we saw some best practices for your Ubuntu Server. Hope this journey has been enjoyable and helped you with information for your work in the administration of systems.

# Index

## A

access control lists (ACL) 62
account ring
  creating 233, 234
Advanced Packaging Tool (APT) 9
application updates 26
apt-cache tool
  about 17
  package, searching with apt-cache search
    command 18, 19
apt-get package management tool
  about 9
  broken dependencies, checking for with
    apt-get check command 17
  cleaning, with apt-get clean command 14
  package, installing with apt-get install
    command 10-12
  package, purging with apt-get purge
    command 15
  package, upgrading with apt-get upgrade
    command 13, 14
  repository list, updating with
    apt-get update command 9
  unsuccessful installations, fixing with
    apt-get -f command 16
aptitude
  about 20
  command keys 21
authorized keys file 138
automatic updates
  about 25
  application updates 26
  kernel updates 26
  security updates 25
  unattended-upgrades package 26-28

## B

background processes
  & (ampersand) 126, 127
  about 126
  bg command 128, 129
  fg command 129
  jobs 126
  jobs -p 127, 128
  suspended state, with Ctrl + Z 128
bash profiles, shell optimization
  /etc/bash.bashrc file 145
  /etc/profile file 146
  variables in bash 146, 147
Berkeley Internet Name Daemon (BIND)
  about 46
  named 46
  resolver 46
  tools 46
binding 42, 43
Block Storage service
  about 217
  controller node, configuring 217
  controller node, installing 217
  storage node, configuring 220
  storage node, installing 220
bonding 44-46

## C

chmod command 149
chroot environment 47
ClusterSSH (cssh)
  about 106
  installing 106

**compute node, OpenStack networking**
  common components, configuring 210
  components, installing 209
  configuring 209, 212
  installation, finalizing 213
  installing 209
  ML2 plugin, configuring 211
  OVS service, configuring 212
  prerequisites, configuring 209
**Compute service**
  about 192
  compute hypervisor component,
      configuring 196, 197
  compute hypervisor component,
      installing 196-198
  compute node, configuring 196
  compute node, installing 196
  configuring 192
  Image service components,
      configuring 194, 195
  Image service components,
      installing 194, 195
  installation, finalizing 196-198
  installing 192
  prerequisites, configuring 192, 193
**container ring**
  creating 234, 235
**controller node, Block Storage service**
  components, configuring 219, 220
  components, installing 219, 220
  configuring 217
  installing 217
  prerequisites, configuring 217, 218
**controller node, NTP**
  service, configuring 180
  service, installing 180
**controller node, Object Storage service**
  components, configuring 224, 225
  components, installing 224, 225
  configuring 223
  installing 223
  prerequisites, configuring 223
**controller node, OpenStack networking**
  components, installing 200
  configuring 199

  configuring, on compute node 203
  installation, finalizing 203
  installing 199
  Modular Layer 2 plugin, configuring 202
  prerequisites, configuring 199
  server components, configuring 200, 201

**D**

**dashboard**
  about 215
  configuring 216
  installation, finalizing 217
  installing 216
  packages, installing 216
  prerequisites 216
**database**
  about 182
  installation, finalizing 183
  server, configuring 182
  server, installing 182
**Database service**
  about 248
  Database module, installing 249-251
  installing 248
  prerequisites 248
**Data Processing service**
  about 252
  installing 252, 253
**DHCP**
  about 35, 36
  configuring 38
  installing 36, 37
**directory information tree (DIT) 58**
**DNS**
  about 46
  hints file 50
  local host file 50
  primary server, setting up 49
  primary zone file 51, 52
  reverse zone file 51
  secondary server, setting up 49
  setting up 46-48
**dpkg**
  using, for package management 3-8
**Dynamic Host Configuration Protocol.** *See*
      **DHCP**

# E

**external networks**
about 214
creating 214
subnet, creating 214

# F

**file permissions**
about 148
changing, with chmod 149, 150
default permissions, setting with
umask 152
managing 148
ownership, modifying with chown
and chgrp 151
special file permissions 152, 153

# G

**graphical user interface (GUI) 156**

# I

**Identity service**
about 184
components, configuring 185
components, installing 185
configuring 184
installation, finalizing 185, 186
installation prerequisites 184
installing 184
prerequisites, configuring 186
roles, creating 186, 187
service entity and API endpoint,
creating 188
tenants, creating 186, 187
users, creating 186, 187
**Image service**
about 188
components, configuring 190-192
components, installing 190-192
configuring 189
installation, finalizing 192
installing 189
prerequisites, configuring 189, 190

**Infrastructure-as-a-Service (IaaS) 192**
**initial networks**
creating 213
external networks 214
router, creating for attaching external and
internal network 215
tenant network 214
**installation, JeOS**
about 165
ACPI handling 169
auto updates 169
bridge, enabling 166
final command 169
final steps 168
first boot 168
first login 168
IP address 166
partitions 167
user and password, setting 167
**installation, libvirt**
about 156
virt-clone 157
virt-install 156, 157

# J

**JeOS**
about 160
installing 165
**jobs, scheduling with cron**
about 139, 140
job schedule security 143
jobs, configuring with at utility 142
user cron jobs, scheduling 141
**Just Enough Operation System.** *See* **JeOS**

# K

**Kerberos**
about 64
client, setting up 72
database setup 69-71
installing 65-68
SSH logon 73-75
**Kernel-based Virtual Machine (KVM) 155**
**kernel updates 26**
**key distribution center (KDC) 64**

# L

**Layer 3 (L3) agent**
  configuring 206
**LDAP Data Interchange Format (LDIF) 58**
**LDAP integration, with Kerberos**
  about 75
  database setup 76, 77
  LDAP installation 75
**LDAP (Lightweight Directory Access Protocol) 57**
**libvirt**
  about 156
  installing 156
  virtual machine, managing 158

# M

**messaging server**
  about 183
  RabbitMQ message broker service, configuring 183
  RabbitMQ message broker service, installing 183
**mirror 24**
**Modular Layer 2 (ML2)**
  configuring 205, 206

# N

**Nagios**
  about 81
  external commands, enabling 99-101
  host, adding 87, 88
  hostgroups 90-92
  installing 81-86
  NRPE plugin 97-99
  plugin, writing 94-97
  services 91, 92
  setup alerts 92-94
  templates 88, 89
**nagios3 86**

**Nagios remote plugin executor.** *See* NRPE plugin
**network address translation (NAT) 214**
**networking**
  database 182
  messaging server 183
  NTP 180
  OpenStack networking 177
  OpenStack packages 181
**networking concepts**
  about 31
  DHCP client, for dynamic address 33
  IP addressing 32
  static IP address, assigning 34, 35
**network node, OpenStack networking**
  components, configuring 204, 205
  components, installing 204
  configuring 204
  DHCP agent, configuring 207
  installation, finalizing 209
  installing 204
  Layer 3 agent, configuring 206
  metadata agent, configuring 207, 208
  Modular Layer 2 plugin, configuring 205, 206
  OVS service, configuring 208
  prerequisites, configuring 204
**network sniffing, with tcpdump**
  about 39
  packets, capturing from eth0 39, 40
  packets of specific protocol, reading 42
  packets on specific port, reading 42
  saved packet, reading 41
  tcpdump results, saving in file 40
  TCP packets, reading between two hosts 42
  timestamp, making readable 41
**nodes, NTP**
  configuring 181
  service, configuring 181
  service, installing 181
**NRPE plugin 97**
**NTP (Network Time Protocol)**
  controller node, configuring 180

# O

**object ring**
creating  235
**Object Storage**
about  223, 233
account ring, creating  233, 234
configuration files for rings, copying  236
container ring, creating  234, 235
controller node, configuring  223
controller node, installing  223
object ring, creating  235
ring installation, finalizing  236, 237
rings, creating  233
storage node, configuring  226
storage node, installing  226
**OpenLDAP**
about  57
access control  62-64
database, populating  60
installing  57-59
logging  61
**OpenStack architecture**
about  171, 172
Block Storage  173
compute  173
dashboard  172
Database Service  173
Identity Service  173
Image Service  173
networking  173
Object Storage  173
orchestration  173
Telemetry  173
**OpenStack environment**
about  174
networking  176
Object Storage nodes  175
resource requirements  174
security  176
security, password  176
**OpenStack networking**
about  177, 198
compute node  179

compute node, installing  209
controller node  178
controller node, configuring  199
controller node, installing  199
network connectivity, verifying  180
network node  178, 179
network node, configuring  204
network node, installing  204
**OpenStack packages**
about  181
installation, finalizing  182
repository, enabling  181
**Orchestration module**
about  237
components, configuring  239
components, installing  239, 240
configuring  237
installation, finalizing  240
installing  237
prerequisites, configuring  237, 238

# P

**package management**
.deb packages  2
about  1
dependency  2
dpkg, using for  3-8
open source  2
package  2
repository  2
with aptitude  20-22
**packet sniffer  39**
**password authentication**
disabling  79
**passwordless SSH**
setting up  78
**physical network infrastructure (PNI)  198**
**primary zone file**
about  53, 54
components  53
**process management**
$$  110
$PPID  110

basics 109
exec command 112, 113
fork() 112
parent and child 110, 111
pidof 110
ps command 113-117
**process priorities**
about 125
nice command 126
renice command 125, 126
**ps command**
about 113
ps -C and pgrep 119
ps fx 118
pstree 118
**PTR records 55**
**Puppet**
about 101
client, setting up 105
installing 102-104
manifest, setting up 105
resource categories 102

# R

**repositories**
configuring 22-24
failed to get error, resolving 24
software, downloading from outside
repository 25
**repository mirror**
/etc/apt/mirror.list file, configuring 29, 30
creating 28
local mirror, using 30
mirror machine, setting up 29
**reverse zone file 54, 55**

# S

Secure Shell. *See* SSH
**security updates**
about 25
users, allowing to 79
users, denying to 79

**service entity and API endpoint**
creating 188
prerequisites, configuring 188
service entity, creating 188
**shell optimization**
about 144
bash profiles 144
**signaling processes**
about 122
kill -1 or SIGHUP 123
kill -9 or SIGKILL 123
kill -15 or SIGTERM 123
killall command 125
kill command 122
pkill 124
SIGCONT command 124
signals, listing 122
SIGSTOP command 124
**special file permissions**
SGID (set group ID) 152
SUID (set user ID) 152
**SSH 77**
**SSH server**
about 131
configuration 132
configuration file 133-136
default settings 132
installing 131, 132
passphrases, using 136, 138
**storage node, Block Storage service**
components, configuring 221, 222
components, installing 221, 222
configuring 220
installation, finalizing 223
installing 220
prerequisites, configuring 220, 221
**storage node, Object Storage service**
components, configuring 228-230
components, installing 228-230
configuring 226
installing 226
prerequisites, configuring 226, 228

# T

**tcpdump**
  network sniffing with  39
**Telemetry module**
  about  240
  Block Storage agent, adding  247
  components, configuring  242-244
  components, installing  242-244
  Compute agent, configuring  244-246
  Compute agent installation, finalizing  246
  Compute agent, installing  244
  controller node, configuring  240
  controller node, installing  240
  Image service, configuring  246
  installation, finalizing  244
  Object Storage, configuring  247, 248
  prerequisites, configuring  241
  prerequisites, configuring for
      Compute agent  245
**tenant network**
  about  214
  creating  214
  subnet, creating  215
**ticket-granting ticket (TGT)  64**
**top command  120, 121**

# U

**Ubuntu**
  package management  1
**Ubuntu Security Notices (USN)**
  reference  25
**Ubuntu Server**
  best practices  254
**unattended-upgrades package  26-28**
**user management**
  about  148
  users, adding  148
  users, removing  148
**users**
  allowing, to SSH  79
  denying, to SSH  79
  greeting, with banner  80

# V

**virtualization  155**
**virtual machine, libvirt**
  managing  158
  virsh  158
  virtual machine manager  158
  virtual machine viewer  159
**virtual network infrastructure (VNI)  198**
**virt-viewer  156**
**vmbuilder**
  about  160
  installing  163
  setup  161, 162
  users, adding to groups  162
  virtual machine, defining  163-165

# X

**xterm  106**

# Z

**zone transfer  49**

**Thank you for buying**
# Troubleshooting Ubuntu Server

## About Packt Publishing

Packt, pronounced 'packed', published its first book, *Mastering phpMyAdmin for Effective MySQL Management*, in April 2004, and subsequently continued to specialize in publishing highly focused books on specific technologies and solutions.

Our books and publications share the experiences of your fellow IT professionals in adapting and customizing today's systems, applications, and frameworks. Our solution-based books give you the knowledge and power to customize the software and technologies you're using to get the job done. Packt books are more specific and less general than the IT books you have seen in the past. Our unique business model allows us to bring you more focused information, giving you more of what you need to know, and less of what you don't.

Packt is a modern yet unique publishing company that focuses on producing quality, cutting-edge books for communities of developers, administrators, and newbies alike. For more information, please visit our website at www.packtpub.com.

## About Packt Open Source

In 2010, Packt launched two new brands, Packt Open Source and Packt Enterprise, in order to continue its focus on specialization. This book is part of the Packt Open Source brand, home to books published on software built around open source licenses, and offering information to anybody from advanced developers to budding web designers. The Open Source brand also runs Packt's Open Source Royalty Scheme, by which Packt gives a royalty to each open source project about whose software a book is sold.

## Writing for Packt

We welcome all inquiries from people who are interested in authoring. Book proposals should be sent to author@packtpub.com. If your book idea is still at an early stage and you would like to discuss it first before writing a formal book proposal, then please contact us; one of our commissioning editors will get in touch with you.

We're not just looking for published authors; if you have strong technical skills but no writing experience, our experienced editors can help you develop a writing career, or simply get some additional reward for your expertise.

## Instant Ubuntu

ISBN: 978-1-78328-087-2          Paperback: 54 pages

Your complete guide to making the switch to Ubuntu

1. Learn something new in an Instant!
   A short, fast, focused guide delivering
   immediate results.

2. Focuses on making new users feel comfortable
   switching to Ubuntu.

3. Discover the top applications and features.

4. Learn everything you need to know to install,
   configure, and get started with using the
   Ubuntu desktop.

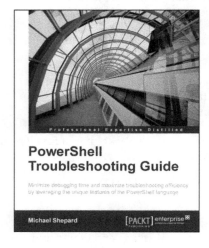

## PowerShell
## Troubleshooting Guide

ISBN: 978-1-78217-357-1          Paperback: 206 pages

Minimize debugging time and maximize
troubleshooting efficiency by leveraging the
unique features of the PowerShell language

1. Reduce troubleshooting surprises by
   understanding the PowerShell language.

2. Avoid parameter passing mistakes by using
   PowerShell's unique pipeline
   binding capabilities.

3. Answer questions such as what, how, and
   why in troubleshooting sessions by utilizing
   PowerShell's various write- cmdlets.

Please check **www.PacktPub.com** for information on our titles

## Troubleshooting vSphere Storage

ISBN: 978-1-78217-206-2          Paperback: 150 pages

Become a master at troubleshooting and solving common storage issues in your vSphere environment

1.  Identify key issues that affect vSphere storage visibility, performance, and capacity.

2.  Comprehend the storage metrics and statistics that are collected in vSphere.

3.  Get acquainted with the many vSphere features that can proactively protect your environment.

## vCenter Troubleshooting

ISBN: 978-1-78355-403-4          Paperback: 184 pages

Resolve some of the most commonly faced vCenter problems with the use of this troubleshooting guide

1.  Isolate common vCenter issues and use proven troubleshooting methods to resolve them.

2.  Understand how the different components of vCenter work together and what to do when things do not work the way they should.

3.  A step-by-step guide to dealing with some of the day to day challenges and issues associated with vCenter.

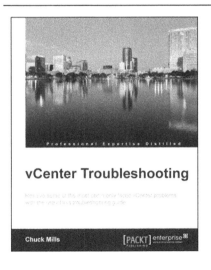

Please check **www.PacktPub.com** for information on our titles

www.ingramcontent.com/pod-product-compliance
Lightning Source LLC
Chambersburg PA
CBHW060523060326
40690CB00017B/3363